TOURISM ENTERPRISES AND THE
SUSTAINABILITY AGENDA ACROSS EUROPE

New Directions in Tourism Analysis

Series Editor: Dimitri Ioannides, E-TOUR, Mid Sweden University, Sweden

Although tourism is becoming increasingly popular as both a taught subject and an area for empirical investigation, the theoretical underpinnings of many approaches have tended to be eclectic and somewhat underdeveloped. However, recent developments indicate that the field of tourism studies is beginning to develop in a more theoretically informed manner, but this has not yet been matched by current publications.

The aim of this series is to fill this gap with high quality monographs or edited collections that seek to develop tourism analysis at both theoretical and substantive levels using approaches which are broadly derived from allied social science disciplines such as Sociology, Social Anthropology, Human and Social Geography, and Cultural Studies. As tourism studies covers a wide range of activities and sub fields, certain areas such as Hospitality Management and Business, which are already well provided for, would be excluded. The series will therefore fill a gap in the current overall pattern of publication.

Suggested themes to be covered by the series, either singly or in combination, include – consumption; cultural change; development; gender; globalisation; political economy; social theory; sustainability.

Also in the series

Emotion in Motion
Tourism, Affect and Transformation
Edited by David Picard and Mike Robinson
ISBN 978-1-4094-2133-7

Social Media in Travel, Tourism and Hospitality
Theory, Practice and Cases
Edited by Marianna Sigala, Evangelos Christou and Ulrike Gretzel
ISBN 978-1-4094-2091-0

Tourists, Signs and the City
The Semiotics of Culture in an Urban Landscape
Michelle M. Metro-Roland
ISBN 978-0-7546-7809-0

Stories of Practice: Tourism Policy and Planning
Edited by Dianne Dredge and John Jenkins
ISBN 978-0-7546-7982-0

Tourism Enterprises and the Sustainability Agenda across Europe

Edited by
DAVID LESLIE
Freelance Consultant and Researcher

ASHGATE

Published by
Ashgate Publishing Limited
Wey Court East
Union Road
Farnham
Surrey, GU9 7PT
England

Ashgate Publishing Company
Suite 420
101 Cherry Street
Burlington
VT 05401-4405
USA

www.ashgate.com

British Library Cataloguing in Publication Data
Tourism enterprises and the sustainability agenda across
 Europe. -- (New directions in tourism analysis)
 1. Sustainable tourism--European Union countries.
 2. Sustainable tourism--European Union countries--Case
 studies. 3. Environmental policy--European Union
 countries.
 I. Series II. Leslie, David, 1951-
 338.4'7914-dc23

Library of Congress Cataloging-in-Publication Data
Leslie, David, 1951-
Tourism enterprises and the sustainability agenda across Europe / by David Leslie.
 p. cm. -- (New directions in tourism analysis)
 Includes bibliographical references and index.
 ISBN 978-1-4094-2257-0 (hbk) -- ISBN 978-1-4094-2258-7 (ebk)
 1. Sustainable tourism--Europe. 2. Tourism--Environmental
aspects--Europe. 3. Europe--Environmental conditions. I. Title.
 G156.5.S87L47 2012
 338.4'7914--dc23

2011042508

ISBN 9781409422570 (hbk)
ISBN 9781409422587 (ebk)

Printed and bound in Great Britain by the
MPG Books Group, UK

Contents

List of Figures and Tables

Figures

Tables

List of Contributors

Alina Badulescu is Professor of Microeconomics and Economics of Tourism and Vice-Dean of the Faculty of Economics at the University of Oradea, Romania. She has a PhD in Economics and has written numerous journal articles and books. Her research interests include the economics of entrepreneurship, tourism policy and development.

Daniel Badulescu graduated from the Academy of Economic Studies in Bucharest and has a PhD in Economics. He is Reader in Business Economics and Business Financing at the University of Oradea, Romania. His current research interests include business economics and management, start-ups and business finance.

Paulina Bohdanowicz is a Sustainability Manager at Hilton Worldwide and holds the position of Visiting Fellow at the International Centre for Responsible Tourism at Leeds Metropolitan University, UK. Her areas of interest include Corporate Social Responsibility and environmental issues in the hotel, travel and tourism industry, with a focus on energy aspects, benchmarking and eco-certification.

Kenneth Button is a University Professor and Director at both the Center for Transportation Policy, Operations and Logistics and the Center for Aerospace Policy Research in the School of Public Policy, George Mason University, USA. He has published, or currently has in press, some 100 books, over 400 essays in academic journals and collected volumes, and has developed forecasting software. He is editor of the journals *Transportation Research Part D: Transport and the Environment* and *Journal of Air Transport Management*, and is on the editorial board of approximately a dozen other journals.

René van der Duim is Special Professor of Tourism and Sustainable Development at Wageningen University, the Netherlands. He completed his PhD at Wageningen University studying tourism from an actor-network perspective. His current research focus is the relationship between tourism and sustainable development and on the relation between tourism, conservation and development in Sub-Saharan Africa.

Jacqueline Holland is Senior Lecturer at Newcastle Business School at Northumbria University, UK. Her primary research interests are adventure tourism and responsible tourism and her doctoral research project focuses on the implementation of responsible tourism practices within the adventure tourism market, which draws upon her experiences working for some of the UK's largest adventure tour operators.

Richard Holland was awarded a PhD for his work at the Transport Operations Research Group at Newcastle University, UK. From there he joined Nexus, the Tyne and Wear Passenger Transport Executive, where he was involved in data analysis and policy formulation. He later joined consulting engineers WYG and now provides consultancy services in relation to intelligent public transport systems, including smart ticketing and real time passenger information.

Dimitri Ioannides is Professor of Human Geography at Mid-Sweden University. He is also Professor of Tourism Planning and Development at Missouri State University, USA where he has been working since 1993. He is author of several manuscripts on topics ranging from the economic geography of tourism to issues of sustainable development.

Jana Kučerová is Associate Professor at the Department of Tourism and Hospitality, Faculty of Economics, Matej Bel University in Banska Bystrica, Slovakia. She is involved in teaching and research activities in sustainable tourism development, regional tourism planning. She is a member of international professional associations – AIEST, ATLAS and EUROHODIP.

Sonja Sibila Lebe is Professor of Tourism at the University of Maribor, Slovenia. Additionally, she heads the scientific board of the Multidisciplinary Research Institute Maribor, which presents strategic documents to the Slovene Government and the National Tourism Organisation (for example, strategic papers on green tourism, rural area development, product strategies for cultural tourism or gastronomy development etc.). She is active as consultant to the tourism industry in Slovenia and is author of several essays, articles and book chapters on tourism in Slovenia.

David Leslie has just retired from his long-standing position as Reader in Tourism at Glasgow Caledonian University, UK, where he was instrumental in the development of Tourism Studies following on from the introduction of the tourism degree at Leeds Metropolitan University, UK. The recurrent theme in his scholarly activity and research has been tourism and the environment, which is manifest in a diverse range of his publications spanning two decades.

Ferry van de Mosselaer is Researcher at Wageningen University, the Netherlands. He completed his MSc in Leisure, Tourism and Environment at Wageningen University with a minor in International Development Studies. Furthermore, he is Co-director at Atelier on Tourism Development, a multidisciplinary platform for knowledge dissemination and solutions in sustainable tourism development.

Evangelia Petridou is a doctoral student at the Department of Political Science at Mid-Sweden University. Her research is funded by the EU project Social Entrepreneurship in Sparsely Populated Areas and focuses on political entrepreneurship as well as territorial cohesion, creativity and cultural industries in peripheral areas.

Jakomijn van Wijk is Assistant Professor of Sustainable Business at the Maastricht School of Management, the Netherlands. She completed her PhD at VU University Amsterdam and her MSc in political science of the environment at Radboud University Nijmegen, the Netherlands and Linköping University, Sweden. Her current research focus is the institutional innovations for sustainability in the tourism industry.

Piotr Zientara is currently lecturer in Human Resource Development at the Faculty of Economics of the University of Gdansk, Poland. His primary research interests focus on human resource management and Corporate Social Responsibility in the hospitality industry and tourism. He also takes an interest in industrial relations and regional development.

Saša Zupan graduated at the Faculty of Law, University of Ljubljana, Slovenia. Due to professional challenges (practicing corporate law; managing mergers, acquisitions and restructuring projects; being CEO in a hotel business) she has enhanced her knowledge of business administration (MBA) at Clemson University, South Carolina, USA. Currently she is involved in several tourism-related projects and preparing her PhD thesis at the University of Maribor, Slovenia.

Preface

The genesis of this book lies in a long-standing interest, study and research revolving around tourism and the environment for well over two decades. During this period we can trace increasing attention to tourism in the academic literature including texts designed to inform the study of tourism, books covering a range of management themes, diverse practices and different forms of tourism product and activity. In addition to this, there has been a remarkable expansion in journals devoted to tourism interests. In total, this represents a wealth of knowledge and practice covering all dimensions of this field of study and practice – a veritable cornucopia of publications. Within this body of work, the environment tends to be less considered comparative with other major dimensions of tourism such as economics, sociology and policy, planning and management. This is perhaps surprising given that earlier attention to tourism, it is argued, was often catalysed by the concern for the physical impacts of visitors on the environment whether this was in the context of the countryside or the development of tourist destinations. However, attention to the environmental impacts of tourism gained a substantial boost in the late 1980s, following the United Nations Environment Congress of 1987 in Stockholm and the appearance of the Brundtland Report. Further impetus arose as a result of the following Congress in 1992 – the "Earth Summit", which catalysed a range of tourism initiatives in both policy and practice arenas as well as encouraging much academic discussion and publications which aimed to capture such debate and in many ways laid the groundwork for subsequent study and myriad research projects. However, one area gained but limited attention – that of tourism supply and more specifically tourism enterprises and their role and impact on the environment. Yet, the very *raison d'être* for such attention lies within the Stockholm Congress primarily and the outcomes of the "Earth Summit" and encapsulated in the concept of sustainable development, now more often cited as 'sustainability'. Certainly there are texts which discuss tourism and sustainable development/sustainability, notably Hunter and Green (1995), Hall and Lew (1998), Mowforth and Munt (2003) and McCool and Moisey (2008) and other texts focusing on various terminologically defined tourism such as "ecotourism" (see Cater and Lowman, 1994; Buckley, 2004) or themes such as "responsible tourism" (Spenceley, 2010). Other texts which might be considered within this context tend to focus on maintaining tourism, as in "sustainable tourism". What we therefore find is a dearth of expositions in the context of sustainability on what is fundamental to tourism, namely tourism enterprises, in particular their impacts on the environment (taken in its widest sense) and the responses and actions of these enterprises to the policies and initiatives which have been catalysed by the international sustainability agenda.

The manifest lack of attention to this quintessential facet of tourism lead to the development of the publication *Tourism Enterprises and Sustainable Development: International Perspectives on Responses to the Sustainability Agenda* (Leslie, 2009), which aimed to provide an overview of what is happening in major tourist receiving regions of the world as regards progress towards the objectives of sustainable development. More specifically, it explores the application to and response of tourism enterprises to these objectives within the context of a country's attention to the quest for sustainable development in tourism policy and related initiatives in promoting tourism development. The pursuit of this objective required extensive searching to identify and investigate what research has and is being undertaken, which further affirmed the dearth of research in this field. In effect, a lack of comprehensive sources on tourism supply and even more so in terms of sustainability, environmental and related developments/initiatives. The text is *not* on or about 'sustainable tourism' *per se* (or ecotourism) which is more nostrum than panacea in terms of sustainability given the invariable failure to consider provision for touristic consumption and, all the more so, the travel element. The travel element is fundamental, which is a major reason why, as Porritt argued, '… the industry cannot begin to claim it's even remotely sustainable' (2005: 2), a view which is further supported in an incisive critique of tourism in terms of sustainable development from the United Nations Commission on Sustainable Development (UNCSD, 2005). This critique in part accounts for the inclusion of substantive contributions on travel/transport and tourist demand, areas that are often notable omissions in such contexts as this one.

This text seeks to present a comprehensive analysis of what is happening across Europe in regard to sustainability in the context of different elements of tourism supply, with the emphasis on small/medium enterprises. It provides a sound study into the principles and practices involved covering a cross section of categories of enterprise involved in tourism supply, in the process aiming to investigate and highlight initiatives introduced and developed in response to the sustainability agenda on the part of the European Union and, further, illustrate this in the context of different European countries. The text is thus complementary to *Tourism Enterprises and Sustainable Development* not only because of the central theme and narrower geographic scope and focus on Europe, but also given the attention to the key elements of "the tour" which brings into contention additional dimensions of the sustainability spectrum.

A key feature of this edited collection is that it differs from many such publications in that it is neither the product of a conference nor an ad hoc collection of chapters offered and related to a broad theme. It is based on bringing together authors who have been specifically invited to contribute chapters on defined areas within the overall context of tourism enterprises and the sustainability agenda. Each contribution is current and underpinned by research. In effect, they combine to provide a high quality, informative, comprehensive text of some originality, based on analyses of current issues and initiatives and, importantly, inform steps towards sustainability on the part of tourism enterprises across Europe.

References

Buckley, R. (ed.) (2004) *Environmental Impacts of Ecotourism.* Wallingford: CABI.

Cater, E. and Lowman, G. (1994) *Ecotourism: A Sustainable Option?* Chichester: Wiley.

Hall, C.M. and Lew, A.A. (eds) (1998) *Sustainable Tourism: A Geographical Perspective.* Harlow: Pearson.

Hunter, C. and Green, H. (1995) *Tourism and the Environment: A Sustainable Relationship?* London: Routledge.

McCool, S.F. and Moisey, R.N. (2008) *Tourism, Recreation and Sustainability: Linking Culture and the Environment.* 2nd ed. Oxon: CABI.

Mowforth, M. and Munt, I. (2003) *Tourism and Sustainability: Development and New Tourism in the Third World.* 2nd ed. Oxon: Routledge.

Spenceley, A. (2010) *Responsible Tourism: Critical Issues for Conservation and Development.* London: Earthscan.

UNCSD (2005) *Tourism and Sustainable Development: A Non-Governmental Organisation Perspective.* Background Paper 4, New York. UN: CSD NGO Steering Group, April.

Acknowledgements

This text would not have come to fruition without the support of Ashgate, in particular Katy Crossan (née Katy Low), who has been a veritable pillar of patience. However, the book itself would not have materialised without the commitment of those authors invited to contribute and in two instances, step in at the last minute. In addition to such commitment, a number of the authors also took on the task of reviewing other chapters and I am indeed indebted to everyone concerned. I would particularly like to thank Tony Harrison for his feedback, Marc Leslie for his support and help in the actual processing of constituent elements of this book and to Susan Leslie for her contributions to the review process. Indeed, she may now be one of the most informed and unheralded proponents of the significance of sustainability issues in the context of tourism.

In closing, I would particularly like to note that during the process of identifying potential contributors evidencing research in this field already, or with the necessary expertise to draw on or undertake current research in the geographic areas proposed, the theme of entrepreneurship and local resources was identified and Clara Stefania Petrillo of the Institute for Service Industry Research, National Research Council in Italy agreed to contribute to the chapter on this theme. I have known Clara since the early 1990s when she came over to Glasgow to participate in "The Environment Matters" conference which I was hosting. It is therefore with sadness that I say that Clara, after a period of illness, passed away in the autumn of 2010.

David Leslie,
Scotland, 2012

Introduction
Sustainability, the European Union and Tourism

David Leslie

Recognition of the impacts of economic development, predominantly associated with industrialisation, gathered momentum during the 1980s with the emphasis of attention on environmental impacts. This was heralded in the Brundtland Report, *Our Common Future*, which aimed '… to help define shared perceptions of long-term environmental issues and the appropriate efforts needed to deal successfully with the problems of protecting and enhancing the environment, a long-term agenda for action during the coming decades, and aspirational goals of the world community' (Brundtland, 1987: ix); and laid the foundation for the United Nation's International Congress of 1992 – the Earth Summit. A period which evidenced much discourse on sustainable development (SD) – a term which itself has generated thousands of words of debate mainly over its definition and meaning – a debate which serves little constructive purpose in itself when we should be attending to interpretation, application and progress (for example, see Pearce, 1994; Visser, 2009). Think not so much of the distant future but two generations hence, that is, grandchildren. In essence, and at the individual/home level, it is little more than good housekeeping – living within one's means and the resources of today and tomorrow in such a way as not to reduce the natural and social capital; which is equally applicable on a global scale. But fundamental to this is the principle of equity of access to resources and a "fair share" for all people across the globe, which is undoubtedly the main stumbling block, and manifest in the disparities between "north and south" – disparities that are often evident in the nexus between tourist demand and destination supply. Overall, sustainability or SD is well elucidated as a concept that '… weaves together normative ideas such as equity, participation, prudence, welfare and environmental concern' (Lafferty and Meadowcroft, 2000: 16, cited in Lightfoot and Burchell, 2004: 338). This leads us from the objectives of SD, involving equitable social progress, effective conservation, wise use of resources and economic development to shifts from discourse and rhetoric on industry in general to more focused, specific policies and actions (see Visser, 2009) which is so applicable to tourism given its dependence on a quality environment, the destinations' communities and their resources.

Tourism may well be a social phenomenon – how else might one describe the "maddening crowds" which troop regularly to the sun-kissed beaches, metropolises and myriad other types of destination when the opportunity arises, a movement of people recognisable at any international airport which is projected to reach 1.6 billion by 2020 (WTO, 2011)? If we exclude business-related trips, the figure is still over one billion people. In the destinations, in the areas visited, domestic tourists will swell these international visitors in number; a phenomenon that is not easily explained, let alone understood. This short-term migration, varying temporally and spatially across the globe, collectively accounts for a level of consumption beyond comprehension. This is conveyed in part in the reported statistics that tourism accounts for approximately 10 per cent of global domestic product (GDP) and eight per cent of worldwide employment (WTO, 2011). These statistics convey little about tourism and related activity and arguably serve more political purposes, used to advance vested interests in tourism. In effect, a manifestation of the Emperor's New Clothes in the 21st century – thus *inter alia* "tourism is good"; it generates millions of dollars in expenditure and supports millions of jobs. To be objective, and allowing for how the associated spending is enumerated, then so too do many other areas of consumer spending yet in comparison they gain little such attention. However, and allowing for traditional manufacturing industries, mineral extraction and processing, oil and agriculture, what other economic sectors are so agglomerated? Even more significantly how many sectors are of such economic significance (for example, oil, coal, steel – the latter two fundamental to the origins of the EU) as to go as unregulated as tourism? That tourism is this so called "industry" is more the result of the agendas of leading organisations, business and governmental, but tourism is not an industry, rather it is a compendium of diverse products and services provided by myriad enterprises of which the majority are by far small or micro-enterprises (see Chapter 7; Leslie, 2009). Collectively these enterprises are major consumers of resources (energy, water etc.) and waste producers which account for substantial pollution and the consumption of non-renewable resources (Leslie, 2007a).

It is in consideration of this that this book comes about, influenced as it is by the sustainability agenda, the three pillars of sustainability and how they are entwined and applicable to tourism enterprises. How has the sector and these enterprises responded to policy initiatives of such bodies as the United Nations Commission on Sustainable Development and their Environment Programme, the issues promulgated by the Intergovernmental Panel on Climate Change, and most pertinently to this context, EU initiatives? Further, on the one hand has the rise of green consumerism influenced the development and provision of tourism products and services whilst on the other hand, in what way(s) has supply – the enterprises themselves – responded to this greening not only of the political agenda but increasingly the business agenda? These questions are all germane to the sustainability of tourism enterprises and the European marketplace; a market which is considered within the EU as the third largest sector of the economy, accounting for 40 per cent of international arrivals (EC, 2010a) and involving some 1.8 million businesses, 9.7 million jobs (5.2 per cent of the workforce) and five per cent GDP. When linkages are included, the figures rise to 12 per cent of jobs and 10 per cent

GDP; furthermore approximately three quarters of tourist revenues (€233 billion) is attributable to EU residents (EC, 2010a). It is thus not surprising to identify that the EU's main objective for tourism is to increase demand and visitor spending. This is something of a turnabout given the scant attention tourism gained prior to the 1990s (Leslie, 2011). This was in no small way due to their orientation to industry and "big" business with comparatively little attention given to the preponderance of small enterprises. Indeed, tourism was not a competence at the time being first established through the Lisbon Treaty, which included promoting a community framework for European Tourism, and was subsequently clarified and affirmed in 2010 (EC, 2010a). This sea-change bears witness to the decline of major traditional and manufacturing industries across Europe, which catalysed a substantial increase in recognition of the diversity, contribution and impact of small- and medium-sized enterprises (SME) (see EC, 2007a), which are seen by the EU as: '… at the heart of the Lisbon Growth and Jobs strategy, notably since 2005 with the use of the partnership approach, which has achieved tangible results' (EC, 2008: 2) They account for by far the majority of enterprises, employment and evidence the highest growth rates in new starts, recognised in the promotion of entrepreneurship (see Chapter 7). As regards tourism enterprises, very few (approximately one per cent) are not SMEs; though the majority are actually micro-enterprises (i.e. employ less than 10 people. In contrast for most of the last century these enterprises are now increasingly subject to general EU policy instruments. In particular, there is a clear emphasis in EU policy on enterprises and the promotion of eco-efficiency – reducing ecological impacts and resource use towards more sustainable levels manifest, for example, in the EU's initiative the "Think Small First" principle (EC, 2008), which reinforces the value of SMEs within the EU and notably encourages increased energy efficiency and the implementation of environmental management systems (Leslie, 2011). This serves to affirm a facet of the Single European Act which, following on from Maastricht, requires European policy to be based not only on the precautionary approach to development potentially involving pollution but that preventative measures should be taken to stop or at least reduce possible pollution, environmental damage must be addressed and resolved and that ultimately the polluter should pay.

It is therefore important to establish a contextual framework and background to Europe and in regard to how the EU has responded to this international sustainability agenda and steps taken to progress this in the context of tourism. There is no doubt that the EU has been notably active in the environment field for decades which has been of benefit to tourism/tourists (Leslie, 2011). However, sustainability gained marked attention in the fifth Environmental Action Plan (EAP) entitled "Towards Sustainability", which was developed in tandem with the UNEP's Earth Summit and Agenda 21. Arguably this was the first major initiative on the part of the EU to gain recognition as a leader in environmental matters (Lightfoot and Burchell, 2004) and the objective of integrating the aims of sustainable development into its decision making across the whole spectrum of its activity.

This theme of progressing the objectives of SD has continued to grow in significance, heralded in the sixth EAP (2001-2010), which includes the objective: '… working with business and consumers to achieve greener forms of production and consumption and, in general, greening the market' (Connelly and Smith, 2003: 284). Further evidencing their leadership aspirations and attention to sustainable production and consumption was involvement at the Rio+10 Summit in Johannesburg (2002), and particularly following this the promotion and support for the task force set up by the Swedish Ministry of the Environment (the Marrakech Task Force) which was formed to address and promote 'Sustainable production and Consumption' (SPC). All of this is encompassed in "Europe 2020", including reducing the use of non-renewable resources and waste, wherein a key feature is the aim of promoting a sustainable and efficient, green and more competitive economy (Anon, 2010). Commitment to sustainable development though has apparently weakened since the earlier part of the century – contrary to the stance taken in the 5th and 6th EAPs (EEA, 2010). This is partly due to the tensions arising from the EU's quest for economic growth but what was and is still lacking '… are the attitude changes and the will to make the quantum leap to make the necessary progress to move towards sustainability' (Hughes, 1996: 30). In this, the expansion of the EU is also a factor such that today, Directives are increasingly presented as frameworks which are often complex and open to interpretation resulting in variances in application on the part of Member States (for example, see Sheate et al., 2004). Basically, the main problem for the EU, the inner tensions and conflicts which are inherent, is the wider context of SD, that is, beyond environmental policy (see Lightfoot and Burchell, 2004). Since the early years of the 20th century, the EU has been notably active in relation to tourism and the incorporation of sustainability encapsulated here in the EU's aim to '… promote sustainable development of tourism activities in Europe by defining and implementing an Agenda 21' (EC, 2003b: 4) and further evidencing this approach '… promoting sustainability in the tourism value chain and destinations' (EC, 2003c: 3; see EC, 2007b).

Today, tourism is very much on the EU's agenda, recognised far more so for its economic aspects and job creation potential than for any other consideration (see EC, 2008). Witness: 'Tourism is one of the biggest and fastest expanding sectors of the European economy. When considered together with its related activities, tourism can be seen to impact on almost every other sector, from transport to construction and from culture to agriculture' (Ianniello, 2008: 4). The EU thus aims to maximise tourism which is to be achieved through the following priorities.

1. Stimulate competitiveness in the European tourism sector;
2. Promote the development of sustainable, responsible and high-quality tourism;
3. Consolidate the image and profile of Europe as a collection of sustainable and high-quality destinations;
4. Maximise the potential of EU financial policies and instruments for developing tourism.

> These four priorities provide the skeleton for a new action framework for
> tourism which the Commission intends to implement in close cooperation
> with the Member States and the principal operators in the tourism industry.
> (EC, 2010a: 70)

Furthermore, the promotion of tourism is desirable not only because it is seen
as a contributor to economic growth but also due to the EU's view that it has a
role in the '… transformation towards a greener and more sustainable economy'
(EC, 2010b: 2). In part this is seen through the aim: 'To promote responsible and
ethical tourism and especially – social, environmental, cultural and economic
sustainability of tourism' (EC, 2010b: 2) As presented in the Madrid Declaration
on Tourism (EC, 2010b) this will involve promoting quality orientated tourism
(including the development of the *Qualité Tourisme* brand [a European Prize label])
and sustainable management indicators to promote destinations that demonstrate
the principles of sustainable tourism. There is also a proposal for a charter based
on criteria for sustainable and responsible tourism and the objective to improve the
integration of tourism in EU policies and initiatives (EC, 2010b). More explicitly,
the EU recently stated that:

> Other structural challenges must be fully integrated into tourism policy. Thus the
> supply of tourism services must in future take into account constraints linked to
> climate change, the scarcity of water resources, pressure on biodiversity and the
> risks to the cultural heritage posed by mass tourism. Tourism businesses need to
> reduce their use of drinking water where there is a risk of drought, and reduce
> their greenhouse gas emissions and environmental footprint. (EC, 2010a: 5)

A laudable objective indeed, which most succinctly brings together earlier
initiatives in both the environmental and tourism policy arenas and reinforces
the need for tourism enterprises to address their environmental performance (see
EC, 2000; Leslie, 2012). As Hunter and Green (1995) noted, this requires that
an enterprise contributes as much as possible to maintaining the quality of the
environment – the product – thus the quality of the resources, the community and
their social cultural capital and the equitable distribution of the associated benefits.
In total therefore not only are the providers of tourism products and services being
encouraged to take on responsibility for sustainability, but so too are consumers
and tourists. It is in cognisance of this that the chapter themes herein have been
defined. In the process of introducing these themes the opportunity is presented to
further highlight EU policy and objectives designed to advance progress towards
sustainability in the provision and delivery of tourism products and services. This
also serves to bring into contention what progress in tourism has there been over
the past 20 years and, given the raft of initiatives since the 1990s, in particular the
last 10 years, in Europe. On the premise that so much of tourism development is
market-led, our starting point and thus the first theme is that of tourist demand,
which is addressed in Chapter 1.

Consumers have been encouraged to "go green" for at least the last two decades and whilst there has been an increase in the demand for and the availability of greener products, produce and services this is not particularly evident despite EU policy and complementary initiatives, including educational initiatives (see OECD, 2002). As Welford et al. (1999) argued, there was little evidence of such demand in tourism during the 1990s. Indeed, it may be argued that "it is business as usual". Let us take an example of an activity not discussed elsewhere within these pages – that of skiing. According to Standeven et al. (1999: 250) in the European Alps alone it is estimated that there are 40,000 ski runs with 14,000 ski lifts that are capable of handling 1.5 million skiers an hour. The construction of new ski resorts create the greatest cause for concern due to infrastructure such as pylons, overhead cables, lifts and tows that need huge amounts of space and, ultimately, spoil the natural landscape (McCool et al., 2001: 79); as well as being substantial users of non-renewable energy supplies. Overall, the ski industry has incurred a plethora of negative impacts to the environment including deforestation and soil erosion (Standeven et al., 1999). Despite such negative impacts skiing continued to grow in popularity such that by mid-2000s the global ski market spend amounted to £39 billion (Mintel, 2006). Certainly there are tourists who do exhibit pro-environmental concerns, attitudes and behaviours. Studies often identify that such tourists are of comparatively higher educational attainment and above average income (see Lawton and Weaver, 2009). This evidently does not necessarily stop them from participating in skiing or visiting endangered places (see Chapter 1); albeit that this could influence demand for the introduction of Environmental Management Systems (Leidner, 2004; also Chapter 7). Secondly, those consumers who do not partake in such trips (though can afford them) due to their environmental attitudes will not be found in such studies! Such choices made on the basis of environmental attitudes and behaviour are most likely due to intrinsic influences as opposed to extrinsic push factors. For example, educational initiatives, which can influence particularly when in the context of the tourist's interests (see, for example, Tubb, 2003) but may have little influence in the wider context; as Sasidharan et al. argued '… environmental education of consumers and increasing environmental awareness does not stimulate environmentally responsible behaviour' (2002: 179). Thus effectively influencing tourists in ways of "responsible" environmental behaviour is not so simple yet it has been part of the EU's agenda for some time and increasingly so today.

        The importance of this was noted more generally in the early 2000s (EC, 2003a), reinforced in the conclusions to the EU's "Strategy for Integrating the Environment into Industry" which stated the need to: '… encourage changes in the behaviour of consumers' (EU, 2004: 12); and most recently in the promotion of '… responsible attitudes of European tourists as demand increases for responsible tourist products and services' (EC, 2010a: 3). An effort to promote responsible products and services on the part of the EU is manifest, for example in the establishment of the EU ecolabel scheme introduced in 1992. The definition of an eco-label merits attention; it is 'A mark, seal or written identification attached or affixed to products which provides consumers with information relating to the environmental characteristics of products and thus allows for comparison of environmental performance between products of the same type' (EC, 2011). This initiative well reflects Johnson and Turner's view that '... policy makers are increasingly seeking to use policy instruments that tap into market dynamics such as taxation, eco-labelling ...' (Johnson and Turner, 2003: 15); which is further illustrated in Chapter 7. However, the value of eco-labels has been questioned. Sasidharan et al. noted that '... no conclusive evidence exists to support their (the ecolabelling agencies) assertive claims that ecolabels improve the environment' (2002: 171) and further: '... potential tourists may not respond favourably to ecolabels ...' (2002: 172). This is not so much the case today as evident in the following chapters. Even so, consumers and thus tourists may be largely unaware of such labels and the ever increasing array and on examination it has been found that there are substantial variances between them and a lack of consistency and criteria (see www.ecolabelindex.com); not surprisingly there have been calls for clearer and more robust guidance on green claims for products (Defra, 2011).

Irrespective of the extent to which green consumerism has translated into the choices made by tourists there is little to support counter-arguments that the purveyors of tourism products and services needs to address sustainability. The tour commences with travel, thus our next theme is transportation. The significance of the transport element cannot be overstated as this is the Achilles heel of tourism in the context of sustainability. This is well illustrated in the estimate that tourism's contribution to climate change, suggested at five per cent in 2005, will increase by 160 per cent by 2035 (WTO cited in NHTV, 2010). This is an overall figure and the contribution of different forms of transport and holiday packages will vary (see Chapters 1 and 2). In respect of this NHTV undertook a study that aimed to benchmark the carbon footprint of Dutch holidaymakers which found that transport accounted for the largest share and that accommodation was also a major component. The "worst" holidays involved air travel (second to which was the car). Of special note is that whilst total emissions per head evidenced a decline over the period 2002-2008, the emissions for holidays have gone up partly due to an increase in holidays involving air travel; of the types of holidays, cruises had the highest average impact by far (then long haul based holidays). The impact of air travel has been well recognised. British Airways in 1994 acknowledged the fact that air travel has a role in climate change and their "One Destination" initiative '... seeks to ensure that our customers fly confident that, together, we are acting responsibly to take care of the world we live in' (BA, 2011: 2). They are also part of the Government CO_2 Carbon Offsetting Quality Assured Scheme designed to encourage everyone to reduce their CO_2 emissions (DECC, 2009) though awareness of such schemes is limited (see Chapter 1) despite promotion, for example, in the UK (Defra, 2005).

French (1994) noted that the EU is a major driving force in encouraging improvements to and development of airports, which is essential to reduce congestion due to capacity constraints causing planes to take up holding positions in the air and thus consuming additional fuel. Yet more development means more air travel (see Chapter 1). It is not just air travel but rather there is a need to develop a comprehensive policy based on integrating modes of transport and sustainability (see Chapters 2 and 3). However, the EU has certainly been slow in this regard. As Tolley and Turton argued, this failing of transport policy and environment lead them to describe the EU as '... a negative environmental force' (1995: 351). One year later, the EU commented that the 'Promotion of collective transport policy is a vital component of efforts to integrate environmental objectives into transport policy' (EC, 1996: 62). However, Haq (1997) argued that the creation of a Common Transport Policy appears to be almost as far away now, that is, 1997 as it was in the 1990s; to a large extent this was considered to be due to the manifest variances in approaches between Member States – a situation which has not been helped by the ongoing increase in the number of Member States. It is with consideration of such matters that our second theme, transportation, is introduced commencing with "Air Transport in Europe and the Environmental Challenges to the Tourist Market". Button, quite rightly, does not restrict his analysis to current dimensions of air travel and sustainability but also draws into context environmental politics and their potential impacts and the economic stability of the European airline sector. In the process he makes a key point that the airline sector is international and requires international co-ordination and policies, that is, world-wide not just EU, to have real effect and debates the introduction of an emissions tax and carbon trading. Beyond such steps there is also the potential of alternative fuels; a highly contentious area albeit Virgin Airlines partly fuelled a Boeing 747 flight to Singapore with biofuel in 2008 but we have heard little of such since. The use of alternative, that is, renewable fuels, has long been part of the climate change agenda and is manifest in two recent EU Directives, the European Renewable Energy Directive which aims for 10 per cent of transport fuels to come from renewable sources and then the Fuel Quality Directive that aims for a reduction by six per cent by 2020 in GHG emissions from petrol and diesel fuels. It is perhaps in the use of alternative transport to air flights – a shift from fast, that is, air, to slow travel, that is, ground based – that holds most potential of success. Encouraging tourists to take travel options (and holiday packages) other than by air has been encouraged for much of the past decade (OECD, 2002; Defra, 2005). This theme is addressed by Holland and Holland – "Non-Aviation-Based Tourism: A UK-based perspective" who examine alternatives to air travel, by way of discussing innovations by transport providers and travel operators in the provision of non-aviation based tourism products. Due attention is given to national and international policies on sustainability and climate change as they relate to travel and in the process different behavioural choice models used by the aviation industry and the individual consumer are reviewed.

Transportation is an integral part of tour operations and thus the next subject area to be addressed is that of tour operators and what they can and are doing in response to the sustainability agenda; in the process highlighting the greening of supply chain management. Scheyvens noted some 10 years ago that 'Tour companies will need more encouragement to implement socially and environmentally responsible initiatives' (2002: 231). This theme is taken up by van de Mosselaer et al. who through their discussion based on "Corporate Social Responsibility in the Tour Operating Industry: The Case of Dutch Outbound Tour Operators" (Chapter 3) demonstrate what progress can be made and actions taken; in the process identifying the importance of the role of tour operators and innovation in greening supply chains and tourism more generally and within this context the role of trade associations. The attention here to CSR is by no means chance as this is another facet of sustainability in business that the EU have been promoting since the turn of the century; furthermore that '... its wider application in SMEs including micro-businesses is of central importance given that they are the greatest contributors to the economy and employment' (EC, 2001: 8) and was just recently reinforced by the EU, in the process noting that CSR is essential in tourism sector (EC, 2010b). The focus on CSR thus is continued in our next theme – namely accommodation. Accommodation is a key element of any tour and accounts for the major proportion of tourism enterprises – as well as the more substantial part of tourist expenditure (excluding travel costs). Within this category there is a clear dichotomy – international and national hotel chains on the one hand and the plethora of small independent operations on the other. It is the former who are the major players in tourism, particularly in the political and policy arenas. They are also far more likely to be addressing the environmental performance of their operations and often not just through the introduction of environmental management systems but also CSR and thus, to varying degrees, the broader social, cultural and community aspects of sustainability. This is taken up by Bohdanowicz and Zientara in their chapter: "CSR-inspired Environmental Initiatives in Top Hotel Chains", which examines a number of CSR-inspired environmental initiatives carried out by international hotel chains. They demonstrate, through a range of selected pan-European international hotel companies, what can be achieved within CSR programmes to reduce their environmental footprint and to promote environmental sustainability.

To this point the contributions on progress in tourism towards sustainability have largely been concerned with the major players in the market. But what of the myriad small and micro-enterprises, particularly accommodation operations which dominate supply numerically? These operations are brought into contention in Chapters 6 and 7 and provide further value by way of their contexts, which are rarely present in mainstream tourism press namely, Slovakia and Slovenia. The EU for over a decade has been advocating that: 'Business must operate in a more eco-efficient way, in other words producing the same or more products with less input and less waste, and consumption patterns have to become more sustainable' (EC, 2001: 3). In effect the "ecological modernisation" of enterprises; the new name for environmental politics in the EU introduced in 2002 (Revell, 2003). The response to this ecological modernisation has been particularly impressive if the number of ecolabel schemes developed across Europe in the 1990s (Hamelle, 2001) is taken as a sign of progress. These schemes (eco-labels) have since increased; witness the Voluntary Initiatives for Sustainability in Tourism (VISIT), which aims to unite all eco-labels in Europe under one umbrella – the "Green Travel Market" (Mintel, 2005; see Chapter 7). The adoption of these schemes or rather the certified EMS they represent is seen by the EU as an important element of the environmental performance (EP) of operations. The EU also considers that they have the potential to influence the behaviour of guests through promoting perceived environmentally friendly behaviour (EC, 2000). Furthermore, engaging tourism enterprises in environmental improvements is viewed as vital by the EU (Hillary, 2004: 561). Vital it may be, but despite the raft of such initiatives, invariably promoted by national or regional tourist organisations, there was all too little evidence of progress in their take up in the early 2000s; as various studies attest (Leslie, 2005); a situation which appears to have changed little by the mid-2000s (Revell, 2004; Leidner, 2004). Apparently SMEs in general were largely uninterested in addressing their EP and introducing an EMS (Hillary, 2004). General reasons for this are neatly summed up by Hillary: the need for formalising and/or costs of verification; lack of time; expense, whilst further barriers were low awareness, limited understanding and attitude. Essentially the large majority of tourism enterprises were neither convinced of the need for an EMS nor that customers were interested (Hillary 2004). Since the mid-2000s there have been further developments, promotion of eco-labelling and also, as noted earlier, some increase in customer demand. What progress there has been is limited and this is well illustrated in "Environmental Management and Accommodation Facilities in Slovakia" by Kučerová (Chapter 6). However, how to achieve substantial progress in the adoption of EMSs is the focus of the study discussed by Lebe and Zupan in their chapter "From Eco-ignorance to Eco-certificates: environmental management in Slovene hotels".

As noted, tourism supply is dominated by small/micro enterprises – predominantly in hospitality as the EU argue tourism holds opportunity for growth and employment; as such it might be considered not only a rich field for entrepreneurs but also for attention to sustainability. This theme is the focus of Badulescu and Badulescu's chapter "Entrepreneurship and sustainability" who introduce, after initial exploration of the terms *entrepreneurship* and *entrepreneur*, specific issues in tourism entrepreneurship with the focus on sustainable entrepreneurship, which is subsequently illustrated through a range of examples prior to a more in-depth discourse on wine tourism. Following on from this, the scope of enquiry widens and provides an opportunity to consider Badulescu and Badulescu's discussion in the broader context of Zientara's discussion "Is Sustainable Tourism a Viable Development Option for Polish Rural Areas?". This chapter, taking tourism as just one among many possible development options, sets out to answer the question of whether sustainable tourism can indeed constitute a development option for Polish rural and remote areas, which are not only excessively reliant on inefficient agriculture, but are also lagging behind big cities in terms of all basic economic indicators and general life quality; a discourse which is also important for setting tourism development opportunities in the wider context of a region's economy. Finally, and rather completing the circle are Ioannides and Petridou in their discussion "Tourism Workers and the Equity Dimension of Sustainability". I say finally because the *raison d'être* for promoting tourism throughout Europe is to promote economic growth and jobs. Secondly, sustainability is also about equity and "fair shares". Is this manifest in employment in tourism? Evidently, as Ioannides and Petridou demonstrate, the answer is more in the negative than positive despite the generation of jobs. This is an area which gains all too little attention. In developing their theme the authors bring into debate policy-making events and initiatives relating to sustainability in tourism labour specifically within Europe; subsequently highlighting the inequities arising from the noticeable division of labour that characterises this sector.

In combination these themes aim to establish a comprehensive analysis of tourism, enterprise and sustainability across Europe that represent the main facets of a typical tour and bring into contention the opportunities that arise and the challenges that need to be addressed. There are no doubt other themes and aspects of sustainability that could have been addressed but constraints of space and producing a manageable tome limit the extent of scope and themes. However, we believe that within the following pages our aim of establishing substantive insights into what steps have been made by tourism enterprises across Europe towards sustainability are achieved and in so doing contribute to the debate and inform development.

References

Anon. (2010) Putting Europe back on track. *Social Agenda*, 21-22 April.

Bennett, L. (2006) Duty Free? *Resource*, 20 (July-August), 20-22.

British Airways (2011) Available at: http://www.britishairways.com/travel/csr-corporate-responsibility/public/en_gb [Accessed: 22 February 2011].

Brundtland, G. (1987) *Our Common Future: The World Commission on Environment and Development*. Oxford: Oxford University Press.

Chen, W. and Clarke, A. (2007) *International Hospitality Management: Concepts and Cases*. Amsterdam: Elsevier/Butterworth-Heinemann.

Connelly, J. and Smith, G. (2003) *Politics and the Environment: From Theory to Practice*. London: Routledge.

DECC (2009) *The UK Government's Quality Assurance Scheme for Carbon Offsetting*. Department of Energy and Climate Change. Available at: http://offsetting.decc.gov.uk/cms/about-the-quality-mark-4 [Accessed: 22 February 2011].

Defra (2005) *Green Holidaymaking*. Press Release Department of Environment, Food and Rural Affairs, 25 July.

Defra (2011) *New Guidance on Green Claims for Products*. London. Department of Environment, Food and Rural Affairs, February.

EC (1992) *The Future Development of the Common Transport Policy.* Brussels: Comm. of European Commission.

EC (2000) *Towards Quality Rural Tourism: Integrated Quality Management [IQM] of Rural Destinations.* Brussels: DG XXIII Tourism Directorate. Comm. of the European Communities.

EC (2001) *Promoting a European Framework for Corporate Social Responsibility.* Green paper. Directorate-General for Employment and Social Affairs Luxembourg EC, July.

EC (2003a) *Basic Orientations for the Sustainability of European Tourism.* COM (2003) 716 Enterprise Directorate-General, European Commission. Brussels, 21 November.

EC (2003b) *Using Natural and Cultural Heritage to Develop Sustainable Tourism.* Directorate-General Enterprise – Tourism Unit. Brussels. Comm. of the European Communities.

EC (2004) *The European Union 6th Environmental Action Programme: Towards a Thematic Strategy on the Sustainable Use of Natural Resources. "Pathways through Society"* – Working Group 2 – use of natural resources. Final Report COM (2003) 572 Brussels. Comm. of the European Communities, 15 October.

EC (2007a) *Small and Medium-sized Enterprises – Key for Delivering Growth and Jobs: A Mid-term Review of Modern SME Policy.* COM (2007) 592 Final Brussels. Comm. of the European Communities, 4 October.

EC (2007b) *An Agenda for a Sustainable and Competitive European Tourism* (COM (2007) 621 Final, Brussels. Comm. of the European Communities, 19 October.

EC (2008) *"Think Small First." A "Small Business Act" for Europe.* Brussels, COM (2008) 394 Final Brussels. Comm. of the European Communities, 25 June.

EC (2010a) *Europe, The World's No.1 Tourist Destination – A New Political Framework for Tourism in Europe.* Communication from the Commission to the European Parliament, the Council, the European Economic and Scial Committee and the Committee of the Regions. Brussels COM (2010) 352 final, 30 June.

EC (2010b) *Declaration of Madrid.* European Commission. Madrid, April.

EC (2011) Available at: http://ec.europa.eu/environment/ecolabel/about_ecolabel/ ecolabel_and_gpp_en.htm [Accessed: 16 February].

EEA (2010) *Butterflies or Business – Europe can have both.* Available at: http:// www.eea.europa.eu/pressroom/newreleases/butterflies-or-business-europe- can [Accessed: 9 December 2010].

French, T. (1994) Transport and European Airports: Capacities and airport congestion. *Travel and Tourism Analyst*, 5, 5-10.

Hamele, H. (2001) Ecolabels for tourism in Europe the European Ecolabel for Tourism? in Font, X. and Buckley, R.C. (eds) *Tourism Ecolabelling: Certification and Promotion of Sustainable Management.* Oxon: CABI, 175-84.

Haq, G. (1997) *Towards Sustainable Transport Planning.* Aldershot: Avebury.

Hillary, R. (2004) Environmental management systems and the smaller enterprise. *Cleaner Production*, 12, 561-69.

Hughes, P. (1996) *Sustainable Development: Agenda 21 and Earth Summit II* Research Paper 96/97, Science and Environment Section, House of Commons August.

Hunter, C. and Green, H. (1995) *Tourism and the Environment: A Sustainable Relationship?* London: Routledge.

Ianniello, F. (2008) *EU Tourism Policy*. Research*EU Focus. Number 1 September, 4-7.

Johnson, D. and Turner, C. (2003) *International Business: Themes and Issues in the Modern Global Economy*. London: Routledge.

Lawton, L.J. and Weaver, D.B. (2010) Normative and innovative resources management at birding festivals. *Tourism Management*, 31(4), 527-36.

Leidner, R. (2004) *The European Tourism industry – A Multi-sector with Dynamic Markets. Structures, Developments and Importance for Europe's Economy*. EC, Enterprise DG (Unit D.3) Publications.

Leslie, D. (1996) Consumer Policy, in R. Thomas (ed.) *The Hospitality Industry, Tourism and Europe: Perspectives on Policies*. London: Cassell, 182-99.

Leslie, D. (2005) Rural Tourism Businesses and Environmental Management Systems, in D. Hall, I. Kirkpatrick and M. Mitchell (eds) *Rural Tourism – Issues and Impacts*. Aspects of Tourism Series 26. Clevedon: Channel View, 228-49.

Leslie, D. (2007a) Scottish Rural Tourism Enterprises and the Sustainability of their Communities: A Local Agenda 21 Approach, in R. Thomas and M. Augustyn (eds) *Tourism in the New Europe, Perspectives on SME Policies and Practices*. Advances in Tourism Research Series. Oxford: Elsevier, 89-108.

Leslie, D. (2007b) The missing component in the 'greening' of tourism: The environmental performance of the self-catering accommodation sector. Special Issue on Self-catering Accommodation. *International Journal of Hospitality Management*, 26(2), 310-22.

Leslie, D. (ed.) (2009) *Tourism Enterprises, Environmental Performance and Sustainable Development: Perspectives on Progress from across the Globe*. Advances in Tourism Research Series. New York: Routledge.

Leslie, D. (2011) The European Union, Sustainable Tourism Policy and Rural Europe, in D.V.L. Macleod and S.A. Gillespie (eds) *Sustainable Tourism in Rural Europe: Approaches to Development*. London: Routledge, 43-60.

Leslie, D. (2012) Key Players in the Environmental Performance of Tourism Enterprises, in M.V. Reddy and K. Wilkes (eds) *Tourism, Climate Change and Sustainability*. London: Earthscan.

Lightfoot, S. and Burchell, J. (2004) Green Hope or Greenwash? The actions of the European Union at the World Summit on sustainable development. *Global Environmental Change*, 14, 337-44.

McCool, S.F. and Moisey, R.N. (eds) (2001) *Tourism, Recreation and Sustainability: Linking Culture and the Environment*. 2nd edn. Oxon: CABI.

Mintel (2005) *Sustainable Tourism in the Travel Industry*. Available at: http://
    academic.mintel.com/sinatra/oxygen_academic/search_results/show&&t
    ype=RCItem&sort=relevant&access=accessible&archive=hide&source=n
    on_snapshot&list=search_results/display/id=148248/display/id=148394#hit1
    [Accessed: 18 February 2010].

Mintel (2006) *Skiing Holidays*. Available at: http://academic.mintel.com/
    sinatra/oxygen_academic/search_results/show&/display/id=187832/display/
    id=203907?select_section=203908 March [Accessed: 15 January 2011].

NHTV (2010) *Travelling Large in 2008*. Centre for Sustainable Tourism and
    Transport, NHTV, Breda University of Applied Sciences, NRIT Research and
    NBTG-NIPO Research.

Oceana (2011) *Oceana's Stop Cruise Pollution*. Available at: http://na.oceana.org/
    en/our-work/stop-ocean-pollution/cruise-ship-pollution/overview [Accessed:
    16 February 2011].

OECD (2002) *Household Tourism Travel: Trends, Environmental Impacts and
    Policy Responses*. Environment Directorate, Paris: Organisation for Economic
    Co-operation and Development, April.

Pearce, D. (1993) *Blueprint 3: Measuring Sustainable Development*. London:
    Earthscan.

Revell, A. (2003) *The Ecological Modernisation of Small Firms in the UK*.
    Business Strategy and Environment Conference. Leicester, September.

Sasidharan, V., Sirakaya, E. and Kerstetter, D. (2002) Developing countries and
    tourism ecolabels. *Tourism Management*, 23, 161-74.

Scheyvens, R. (2002) *Tourism for Development: Empowering Communities*.
    Harlow: Prentice Hall.

Sheate, W.R., Byron, H.J. and Smith, S.P. (2004) Implementing the SEA
    Directive: Sectoral challenges and opportunities for the UK and EU. *European
    Environment*, 14, 73-93.

Standeven, J. and Knop, P.D. (1999) Sport tourism, Human Kinetics and Potential
    Climate Change Policies. *Journal of Sustainable Tourism*, 15(4), 351-68.

Tolley, R. and Turton, B. (1995) *Transport Systems, Policy and Planning: A
    Geographical Approach*. Harlow: Longman.

Tubb, N. (2003) An evaluation of the effectiveness of interpretation within
    Dartmoor National Park in reaching the goals of sustainable tourism
    development. *Journal of Sustainable Tourism*, 11(6).

Visser, W. (2009) *Landmarks for Sustainability: Events and Initiatives that have
    Changed our World*. Sheffield: Greenleaf.

Welford, R., Ytterhus, B. and Eiligh, J. (1999) Tourism and Sustainable
    Development: An analysis of policy and guidelines for managing provision
    and consumption. *Sustainable Development*, 7, 165-77.

WTO (2011) Available at: http://www.unwto.org.

Chapter 1
Tourism, Tourists and Sustainability

David Leslie

Introduction

An obvious but all too often missing dimension in studies of tourism and related impacts are the very people who catalyse tourism development – be it indirectly or directly – the consumers, the tourists. Unlike most other popular consumer products in the marketplace, produced and/or designed to meet actual or perceived needs of potential customers – the "tourism product" is ill-defined. Is it a destination – a package holiday – a trip created through self choice by one's own hand interfacing with the internet or just an activity undertaken somewhere else? What we can identify is that it is in the main a package – a potential complexity of services brought together for a trip away from home for a relatively short period of time. Therefore what tourism is not is an industry – there is no industrial process replicating production across the globe nor is there a singular product. Yet this small detail appears to be lost in many a discourse on tourism and sustainability (Leslie, 2009).

In effect, it is demand which leads – demand driven by consumers for the want of something different – to get away – to escape briefly the usual daily activity or even seasonal weather patterns. This is by no means a trend of the 20th and 21st centuries being manifest in earlier times – witness the Romans and their "Companon Littorals" – a way of escaping the city during oppressive summer months – to enjoy fresh air driven by coastal breezes; or later, for example, high society escaping the confines of capital cities to their country houses during the height of summer. Thus, in today's terms, tourism developments have taken place for well over two millennia but it is only relatively recently that concerns have arisen over such development in terms of impacts on their locational environment. In the 19th century our attention is drawn to 'new' seaside resorts – "turned inside out" but little as to other environmental impacts such as the loss of oyster beds off the north-west coast of Lancashire in the UK as the major resorts of Blackpool and Morecambe developed. Indeed, in today's view, these popular seaside resorts of England and the many other cold-water resorts which developed across northern Europe in the 19th century – were 'blots on the seascape' – not that dissimilar to the developing resorts along the northern Mediterranean coast of Spain in the 1960s and the Balearic Islands. To suggest that the development of these resorts was in some way resource based – as if the existent community sought to develop and market their environmental resources would be fallacious indeed. Invariably there were leading players, for example dominant landowners or railway entrepreneurs, who recognised the potential demand and developed these cold-water resorts of northern Europe. Their success in the 19th century and in many cases for much of the 20th century bears witness to the perceived desire of people to 'get away' for a short period. However, such retrospective critiques of the changing physical environments where such resorts developed have little to offer, but what is not so easy to dismiss is that in many cases they subsequently became major urban communities with socio-economic problems, which can be traced back to their primary development and the emergence of mass tourism.

However, with the growing affluence of the 1960s, and the comparative degree of stability across Europe during this period, questioning of the impacts of people, of industry and industrial processes started to gain substantive attention. The 'green' movement gathered momentum, notably in attention to agriculture and the use of pesticides. The United Nations Environment Programme gains momentum, heralded by the Stockholm Conference of 1972 through to the Brundtland Report and the concept of 'sustainable development'. More importantly to this context, commentators and organisations start to question the environmental impact of tourist and tourism developments during this period leading to the emergence of 'green tourism' and related terminology, for example, alternative, soft, hard; in effect, calling for the 'greening' of tourism. However, the initiatives in the 1970s and 1980s predominantly focused on the destinations and physical impacts – thereby conveniently ignoring consumption, that is, demand. It is demand itself which defines if a product is sustainable *but* it is by reference to the sustainability of its production and consumption which decides if it is/or is not a pattern of unsustainable consumption which in essence means can tourism be sustained on the basis of not reducing capital resources? Evidently not but, and as with so many other facets of westernised consumption, demand appears to be insatiable; constrained only by the availability of leisure time, disposable income and transportation.

Since the 1980s, it is argued that both tourists and tourism organisations and enterprises have become more aware of the potential impact of tourism activities on the environment (Andereck, 2009; see Bennett, 2006). This awareness lead to many initiatives from international organisations by the public sector (for example, the World Tourism Organisation [WTO]; United Nations Environment Programme [UNEP]) and private sectors (such as the World Tourism and Travel Council). Reference to UNEP brings into focus the Earth Summit of 1992. This gave impetus in attention to tourism, arising from Agenda 21, and in terms of local planning and community involvement, most specifically through Local Agenda 21 (Chapter 28; see Leslie and Hughes, 1997). However, what gained all too little attention was the Rio Declaration, a rarely cited outcome of the Earth Summit, which is a listing of principles to aid progress towards SD. One of these Principles is that unsustainable patterns of western consumption should be discouraged. The *key* point here is the explicit attention to consumption and thus implicitly consumers. Tourism is the most conspicuous form of consumption and one which is sustained on non-renewable resources. There is no sign of any decrease in demand, which itself is built on unsustainable consumption patterns of affluent societies (or the comparatively affluent within society) thus for tourism to be more in tune with sustainability – the product and indeed the tourist needs to develop in environmentally friendly ways. An agenda promulgated by the EU, which is committed to boost awareness of the necessity for such a shift in behaviour on the part of tourism enterprises and indeed tourists/consumers in the quest for sustainability. Witness the objective of promoting '… harmonious, balanced and sustainable development of economic activities' and 'A high level of protection and improvement of the quality of the environment' (Connelly and Smith, 2003: 261) and manifest in a raft of recent Directives and initiatives (see Leslie, 2010).

Thus, first this chapter briefly focuses on initiatives on the supply designed in response to this greening of tourism, which are extensive though their effects are undoubtedly less so. The aim is to provide a range of insights into such developments rather than any detailed discussion. For such commentary one need go no further than the other chapters herein. We then turn our attention to tourists and, in particular, the outcomes of surveys into their attitudes and behavioural patterns in relation to demand for 'greener' tourism products and services. Following on from this we bring into discussion consumers – the tourists precursors.

Greening Supply

Media coverage on a weekly basis on climate change has shifted the focus away from sustainable development to predominantly polluting emissions; in other words green house gases (GHG) (Leslie, 2009a). Rightly or wrongly, travel – transportation – gains much attention for being a major contributor to such emissions. Furthermore, the use of transport be it by air, road or rail is increasing in demand: 'Forecasts by the IEA (2006) indicate that 20 per cent of the growth in energy demand between now and 2030 is due to increasing demand for transportation worldwide' (Becken and Hay, 2007: 697) Thus it is to transportation that our attention briefly turns first before highlighting responses by tour operators and subsequently accommodation operations.

The main transport element for the majority of international tourist arrivals is the air flight, which is the primary mode of transport for tourists travelling any distance across Europe is air travel (see Chapter 2). In spite of GHG, air travel is itself incompatible with the principles of sustainable development, that is, use of non-renewable resources; for example, a trip to Fiji from London can generate approximately 4.5 tonnes of CO_2, which equals the total annual energy use in the average home in the UK (Bennett, 2006). These emissions and other pollutants arising from flying have been recognised for some time, though addressing and responding to such problems is comparatively recent. The manufacturers of airplanes seek to build 'cleaner, greener' aircraft and airlines have and continue to seek to reduce fuel consumption. Organisations such as Green Aviation support this progress and suggest that carbon free flights will be in operation by 2028 (Green Aviation, 2011). The likelihood of such an achievement is doubtful and appears to be dependent on carbon offsetting schemes and the potential of bio-fuel. There are over forty carbon offsetting schemes available to tourists (Baobab, 2011); tourists could purchase "carbon credits" through programmes such as CO_2 Balance and Target Neutral and Climate; the revenues gained funding environment projects (Dunn, 2006) but to what extent such revenue is actually committed to sustainability related projects is a matter of concern (see Kirkup, 2008). Even so, their potential success is further constrained by awareness and interest; as Defra's (2009) survey found, the majority of people surveyed had no knowledge of such schemes or had never heard of it at all, and less than three per cent of those surveyed said that they had personally paid into a carbon offsetting scheme; also a reason found for not supporting a carbon tax are perceptions that it will make no difference (Brouwer et al., 2008). Despite the benefits voiced by champions of carbon offsetting schemes, Mintel's (2008) study suggests that such schemes at best will account for but a small reduction in emissions. This study also stated that even then assessing their effectiveness is problematic, as such these schemes are seen as little more than a facade in terms of carbon emission reducing behaviour for political and commercial agendas. A view which is supported by the little attention given in the travel/holiday press to CO_2 emissions (Johns and Leslie, 2008). An alternative is to increase charges for airport duty and introduce green taxes. In effect, a tax on users when what could be more effective in influencing choice of transportation is to introduce a reward system for non-users thus creating a reverse green tax (Hanlon, 2006; Darling, 2008). More basically: 'Emissions could be reduced the old-fashioned way by flying less, turning off the air-conditioning or buying a more fuel-efficient car. But that would probably require some sacrifice and perhaps even a change in lifestyle. Instead, carbon-offset programs allow individuals to skip the sacrifice and simply pay for the right to pollute' (DePalma, 2006: 1).

The potential for alternative fuels such as liquid bio-fuel is limited at best whilst its production raises many issues (for example, see Grewock, 2010). A more realistic target, for example, is that of the Sustainable Aviation Group, (includes major airlines such as British Airways and Virgin Atlantic), which aims to reduce the CO_2 emissions of new aircraft by 50 per cent per kilometre by 2020 (WTO, 2006). Airlines also seek to promote tourists' awareness of their impacts; for example Flybe have introduced passenger information on the impact of their journeys in terms of carbon emissions (Flybe, 2011) whilst First Choice (UK and Ireland) has introduced an in-flight video on its flights to the Gambia with Air 2000, to raise awareness of the needs of the people of the Gambia (TOI, 2005). How much of this is greenwashing is debatable; perhaps little more than good PR implying that the Company is more responsible in its actions/operations than its competitors?

There are many other initiatives and indeed alternatives, for example as well captured in the concept of 'slow travel' (Dickinson and Lumsden, 2010; see

Holland and Holland, Chapter 10). Promoting alternative travel (to air) appears a positive step towards progress but how effective is it? To encourage longer journey times and perceptions that such are to be enjoyed is directly opposite to the pattern of demand over the last century which is 'to get there quicker'. Miller et al.'s (2007) research also holds a note of caution in that they found that whilst tourists may indicate a willingness to change from plane to train they noted the following caveats: when considered practical and lower fares; an outcome which is similar to that of Defra's (2009) study, which found that a third of the persons surveyed rejected the idea of reducing their air travel. This brings into question demand and within that context how many people in the market actually have a choice in terms of what is available/desirable to them in the marketplace. The options are limited both intrinsically, given established behavioural patterns, and extrinsically, in many instances, because of time, cost and geographic accessibility – in other words they may have little real choice. Many people select their holiday destination on the basis of the product offering – the packages – of tour operators (TOs). Thus, what actions have they been taking? This is well illustrated by the Tour Operators Initiative for Sustainable Tourism Development (TOI), established in 2000, with the aim of promoting sustainable tourism development and to encourage tour operators to make a corporate commitment to sustainable development (Tepelus, 2005). But to what real effect? Certainly there has been the introduction of various awards promoting destinations/packages considered to meet best practice in specific fields. Whilst these products undoubtedly are attractive they are few, invariably expensive and usually, from a European based perspective, involve a long-haul air flight. Another major initiative is the establishment of the Travel Foundation, a partnership including major international companies such as MyTravel, Thomson, Thomas Cook and First Choice, which promotes sustainable tourism initiatives. But are tourists interested or even aware of this and if so, do/would they consider it is more tokenism than anything more substantive (see responsibletravel.com).

At a national level, for example, there is the UK Federation of Tour Operators, which launched its Supplier Sustainability Code in 2006 (ITP, 2006). This might be considered unnecessary given the earlier introduction of guidance and so forth by the TOI on how to develop sustainability supply chains. However, this serves well to illustrate the unnecessary proliferation of more 'localised' initiatives, as if every organisation/enterprise grouping must put their own spin on what is otherwise generic guidance. Whilst such international and national organisations are not to be decried for trying it does rather raise the question over the effectiveness of not only current and recent initiatives but also those of longer standing, such as the Manilla Declaration or the agreement of the International Union of Overseas Tour Operators of the early 1970s, both of which basically addressed many similar issues and aimed to promote better practices, more in tune with what today we term sustainability. A perception which is further affirmed by Mosselaer et al. (see Chapter 4). However, whilst TOs collectively provide a diverse range of products/packages – some of which may be termed eco-friendly in one way or another, they evidently are in many cases promoting a 'greener' marketing message the value of which is supported by Mintel's (2007) study, which found that consumers are more likely to buy from organisations which are socially responsible (see also Choat, 2004). Indeed, 80 per cent of respondents indicated that they would be more likely to purchase a holiday from operators with a sustainable tourism policy. For example, Studiosus, a German tour operator specialising in educational holidays, aims to reduce energy use by three per cent per customer through such measures as reducing the time coaches spend idling, using more rail and non-stop flights (TOI, 2005 and Chapter 3). But does the prospective purchaser ask? To what degree the potential tourist is interested in such aspects or indeed aware of such is open to conjecture particularly when there are indications that potential customers think they may be rather superficial (Choat, 2004). Do they notice such messages and if they do what is their understanding given that their interpretation of concepts such as sustainable tourism or responsible tourism is probably limited (Miller et al., 2010).

Even so, there are on the market various brands of eco-tour, nature tours and so forth, promoted with green messages, but the reality of such, as noted above, is that these products are comparatively expensive and the evidence suggests demand is very limited. They do not provide the economy of scale and thus profit that the major operators seek and are therefore far more likely to be supplied by small, well focused operators working in niche markets. Operators who also recognise that such opportunities should be offered as a package thereby providing choice and opportunity for those potential tourists (the majority) who would not seek out the necessary information to make up a trip themselves (Mintel, 2005). But their future may be limited, given the view that the role of the environmentally concerned tour operator could be declining and the responsibility shifting to the individual travellers and airlines instead given '… the rise of 'free, independent travellers' due to the availability of cheap, internet-booked flights' (TOI, 2011b). Certainly, some will do this but how successful they will be is a mute point. Further, whilst research suggests that tourists will seek out information on environmentally sustainable practices for their holidays (Bergin-Seers and Mair, 2009) what is not well established is to what effect? Apart from any other considerations is it because they perceive that enterprises which are 'ecolabelled' are better in some way(s)? Alternatively they may wish to maintain their general environmental behaviours when they go away, thus 'green tourists', or perhaps these are Mintel's (2007) green travellers, who are seen as a very small minority, albeit expanding, accounting for approximately one per cent of the market. However, their green travellers include participants in eco-tourism. It is a major assumption to consider all tourists purchasing eco-tourism trips are 'green' and second, that ecotourism itself when compared with other tourism packages is always more environmentally friendly. Further to seeking to create more environmentally friendly holiday packages and alternative travel options and promote behaviours more in tune with the destination locality and peoples, TOs can, as with any enterprise, introduce environmental management systems and best practices into their operations and adopt Corporate Social Responsibility (CSR) (see Chapters 4 and 5).

Accommodation enterprises are probably the one element of the supply which in many cases across Europe demonstrates some consideration for and the adoption of environmental management practices (see Chapters 5, 6, 7; Leslie, 2009); for example, the increasingly common practice of encouraging guests to re-use towels rather than change them daily. Many hotels and international hotel companies have bought into environmental management systems (see Chapter 5), often accredited under one eco-label scheme or another (see Chapters 1, 6, 7), predominantly with regard to energy, water and waste management (see eHow, 2011); areas which are notable for financial savings (see Leslie, 2009). These eco-labels, and other practices/initiatives seen as eco-friendly are often used in promotion and for public relations (PR), as it is seen as a way of promoting a positive corporate image. Indeed, some tourism enterprises may merely view 'green initiatives' as favourable PR (see Valor, 2008) and/or because it may be seen to hold a competitive advantage. In contrast some '… firms prefer not using the environment as a major selling point to avoid development of any "negative" corporate associations or dissatisfaction' (Crane, 2000: 277, see also Hudson and Miller, 2005).

Today, whilst more enterprises are involved in green accreditation schemes, yet again we find it is the comparatively larger companies which also perform better compared with other categories of supply, in promoting environmental matters to their customers (Wijk and Persoon, 2006). But such promotion is not without pitfalls; for example, Mintel (2007e), found that many people (64 per cent in their survey) believed that such companies were trying to "green wash" customers, which has generated many complaints over the truthfulness of green messages (Leslie, 2009a). However, as Gustin and Weaver's (1996) study found, there is a correlation between pro-environmental consumers and the market for 'green' hotels – albeit they acknowledged that the strength of correlation is not known – demand has arguably increased; witness Marriott's introduction of 'green rooms' which are let at an added premium and were increased in number due to demand, whilst the Saunders Hotel Group has gained conference business which they attributed to their environmental programme promoted through green messages and eco-label accreditation. In the former case, this could be due to customers seeking a more 'fashionable product', even so there is evident support for a higher price for accredited 'green hotels' – albeit small (for example, one to three per cent, see Dalton et al., 2008), whilst the latter arguably bears witness to the rise of CSR activity and environmental policies in general business organisations.

Goodwin and Francis (2003) identified that eight per cent of consumers are influenced by promoting a green image, which is not an insignificant market segment. This market can be further refined through establishing past environmentally friendly behaviour of tourists at destinations and then using such knowledge to target more accurately environmentally friendly tourists (Dolnicar and Leisch, 2007). In contrast, the majority of tourism enterprises evidence little responsiveness to the purported trend in 'green consumerism' demand; encapsulated here as follows '… 90% of tourists would not adjust their holiday arrangements for environmental issues and guests are not interested' (Leslie, 2001: 144, Leslie, 2012).

The point of these eco-labels is to provide information on environmental aspects of the so accredited products and services thus enabling consumers to select products on the basis of comparative environmental performance indicators, for example, energy saving, thus environmentally friendly in some way or other. Across Europe, this is most recognisable through the EU eco-label certification programme (see www.eco-label.com/default.htm), which now includes over 240 labels and notably the EU's Eco-Flower (see Chapter 7). If we add to the Eco-Flower those other eco-labels for which tourism and travel enterprises can seek accreditation that are to be found within the Member States as well as more widely, the evident proliferation not only raises concern over their credibility but also leads to consumer confusion and even competition for support between these multiple labels (Valor, 2008; Bowen and Clarke, 2009). Furthermore, as Thogerson et al. (2010) argue, there is limited evidence as to whether tourists are aware and interested in such labels and if they really influence choice of product or service. There is some suggestion that at best this is limited, particularly as it appears from research by Dalton et al. (2008) that tour operators make little effort to promote environmentally friendly accommodation on the grounds that tourists are not really that interested! To explore this theme, our focus now shifts to tourists and more particularly to question tourist demand for greener products and services.

Tourists

The foregoing discussion suggests (albeit more implicit than explicit) that there are tourists who are concerned about their destination environment, about the impact of tourism development and of the enterprises involved in supply. Surveys predominantly continually attest to this and suggest that such concern and the possibility of related action has increased but perhaps not in terms of any substantive increase in actual demand. As Millman (1989) opined over 20 years ago the number of 'green aware' tourists willing to spend more on a holiday, for example, to help local communities, is increasing, which is further supported by Wight (1994), who also found, and more recently Bennett (2006), that tourists indicate a *willingness* to pay more for what they perceive as environmentally considerate tourism packages. Mintel's (2005) survey found that approximately 50 per cent of participants would be *prepared* to pay more for their holiday if this benefited the local community; a similar proportion indicated they would pay extra if the revenue contributed towards conservation initiatives in the destination locality (see also Goodwin and Francis, 2003) whilst 65 per cent indicated that when choosing a holiday company it should have a reputation for environmental best practices. Putting aside other considerations for a moment one cannot escape the question of just how do the prospective purchasers of a holiday package actually know if local communities are to benefit as a result of their purchase? That is, if they have given thought to such an aspect in the first place – which is highly doubtful – why would they? However, few commentators would argue that the number of tourists willing to support local employment, local communities and conservation/preservation measures has increased over the last twenty years. But even so, as noted above, it is a very small market of tourists who put into practice what they say they are willing to do. Surveys and research studies consistently find that the majority of tourists indicate they are willing to pay higher prices for environmental best practice. But are they going to do so and if so, how much?

According to Mintel (2005) one in five people suggested an extra 10 per cent on air ticket costs to cover environmental impacts and two in five people suggested five per cent extra as a contribution to conservation. The reality of such increases being readily accepted is highly questionable given, for example, the furore in the UK over the proposed increase in 2010 of Advance Passenger Duty and the continuing success of low cost carriers such as EasyJet and RyanAir. Further countering the likelihood of support for actual price increases, for example in relation to air travel due to GHG emissions, is that some tourists consider travel has a lesser environmental impact than holiday activities and that long haul flights cause only a little more harm to the environment than short haul ones (Miller et al., 2007). Thus, they are unlikely to be willing to pay a substantive additional premium for long haul travel comparative with short haul trips or, in general, support a price increase in the first instance. This is further supported by Defra's (2009) survey which found that 55 per cent of respondents considered that they were not responsible for the air pollution generated by air travel. Secondly, Miller et al.'s (2010) study found limited understanding of the issues involved, believing rather that small, everyday changes have a greater impact than changes to their tourism practices (Miller et al., 2007). As regards paying extra for conservation measures, the supporting evidence is limited and then often only in specific cases where conservation is a key element of, and underpinning to, the holiday package (see Ballantyre et al., 2010). In those instances where such a measure is general (i.e. non-trip/tour specific) for the majority of tourists the very opposite is evident. Witness the outcry over the imposition of a tourism tax for such measures in the Balearic Islands. According to reports, tourist demand dropped by 20 per cent (Brown, 2003) and the tax was subsequently dropped. Furthermore, one of the most successful tourist contributory conservation based initiatives in Europe, the Tourism and Conservation Partnership in the UK's Lake District National Park, does not benefit from all visitors. The scheme involves a nominal voluntary contribution (originally approximately one Euro), for example to a guest's account in participating accommodation operations. However, despite the very small sum involved, and especially so when compared with the total bill, the number of visitors who agree to donate is well below the total visitor numbers involved (Leslie, 2001). A situation which has changed little over the years and reflects Dalton et al.'s (2008) findings that the majority of tourists would not be willing to pay more for green tourism initiatives, irrespective of their income; and further, Edgell reported a study that found that 75 per cent of American travellers "… feel that their visits do not damage the environment" (2006: 7). Conversely, wherein tourists might have paid then, as Cater and Lowman argue, they "… may rationalise that we have paid and they have taken our money, so we are entitled to enjoy our holidays as we wish" (1994: 32).

Even so, there are undoubtedly 'green tourists' albeit of varying shades of green, who hold values more aligned with sustainability and who also seek to continue their environmentally friendly ways whilst being a tourist (see Bergin-Seers and Mair, 2009). This is well exemplified on the one hand by those tourists who opt for what they perceive to be more environmentally friendly behaviours, such as slow travel, selecting ecolabelled accommodation and so forth. They may also opt for packages which come labelled as ecotourism. But how truly eco-friendly many such packages are is a matter of some debate (see Pleumarom, 2009). Furthermore, participants in such tours may be just seeking to impress their affluent friends (see Mowforth and Munt, 2003). However, as noted, there are tourists who do continue their 'green consumer' practices away from home. For example, a TOI study found that 18 per cent of tourists surveyed said that they switched off air-conditioning to save energy and take a shower instead of a bath to save water. German tourists in particular appear to be more environmentally concerned about 'green initiatives' (TOI, 2005). Fairweather et al. (2005) have labelled such tourists as 'biocentric segments' due to their high pro-environmental attitudes and interest in ecolabels. But, as noted, they constitute at best a very small market (see Leslie, 2009a). As for the majority there is all too little evidence to demonstrate that their willingness to support and indeed contribute through additional payments for sustainability initiatives translates into practice. More recently, surveys have found that few participants would change their holiday plans based on ethical and environmental issues (Mintel 2007e). Add to this the increase in number of those flying due to the availability of low cost airlines and it can be seen that financial and logistical factors are more important and evidence little change over the last four decades (see Leslie, 2009a). Furthermore, they may well see no point in altering their behaviour to reduce their environmental impact or contribute to environmental schemes if no one else does (Miller et al., 2007). Alternatively, tourists may see environmental concerns as something that could infringe on their holiday and make it less enjoyable (Miller et al., 2007), which further supports the view that tourists are likely to conform to their usual environmental behaviour while on holiday. As Mintel's (2011) study found, once on holiday, one in five holidaymakers admit to not considering the environment and that their green habits are forgotten once they are away from home.

To varying degrees, such findings are evident in other research (for example, see Valor, 2008) and, as noted above, the caveat in many of the findings is 'willingness' not 'does'. In effect, tourists say one thing and act differently, as if 'tourists' are 'other people' or indeed 'another self'. Overall the reality is more a matter of tourists saying what they like to think is the 'right' answer, which also makes them feel good (see Swarbrooke and Horner, 2007). For example, 71 per cent of respondents in Mintel's (2007) survey indicated that visitors should not damage the environment; a not surprising outcome, which leads to two observations. First, the data implies that some 30 per cent may think it is acceptable for damage to occur as a result of the presence of tourists; an interpretation with which few commentators would likely agree. Second, by reference to the term 'visitors', respondents are more likely thinking of 'other' people thus in a sense an abstraction. This reflects Miller et al.'s point that '... on the whole, participants do not think about the environment when making leisure and tourism choices' (2007: 8) and that tourism is concerned mainly with fulfilling tourists' needs and not seen as an environmental behaviour, which also helps explain why surveys invariably find the majority of those surveyed indicate support for positive action.

Consumers

For there to be tourists – the embodiment of consumption – we first need consumers. Therefore it is the values, attitudes and behaviours of consumers which underpin whether or not there is demand for what most simply we can term the greening of tourism products and services. Thus first we should establish whether consumers themselves are aware of the issues of sustainability. The attention given to climate change throughout the media over the last few years leads to the premise that people know about climate change, and issues of sustainability, through its representation and the discourse that surrounds it. Thus the media play an important role in influencing the views on climate change which is not aided by the finding that newspaper coverage of climate issues contains conflicting messages which vary from tabloid to broadsheet and with the political stance of the publication (see Futerra 2006; Johns and Leslie, 2008; Holmes et al., 2008). However, it remains unclear how this information is noticed, interpreted and used by consumers when making choices; in particular what influence, if any, it has on consumer choice when, for example, it comes to choosing the mode of transport for touristic activities. Further to such media comment there has also been a remarkable increase in advertising containing green messages. For example, it has been reported that nearly £17 million was spent between September 2006 and August 2007 on advertising containing the words 'CO_2', 'carbon', 'environmental', 'emissions', or 'recycle' (Bowen and Clarke, 2008). As Valor (2008) argued, no matter what is advertised or promoted in an attempt to raise awareness, many consumers who articulate that they try to behave responsibly, suffer "cognitive ambivalence", that is, the effort, in this instance, required to find the information in order to act more responsibly in tourism, is deemed too much. Indeed, Miller et al. (2010) opine that the climate change debate is being misunderstood, many may know of the damage being done but do not understand why they have any part of it – the 'bystander effect'. Thus whilst consumers may be becoming more aware of environmental issues that surround their holiday and chosen destination there is little evidence that this is changing their touristic behaviour. Many people are now so accustomed to this lifestyle (or aspire to such lifestyles) they would be unwilling to relinquish this perceived standard of living in order to reduce their carbon footprint (Johns and Leslie, 2008). This is reinforced in the view that tourism demand is based on 'irrational factors' (Kamp, 2003: 1) – associated with fashion trends, relaxation and escapism; people just do not want to think about the effects that their trip has caused to the environment. Certainly awareness may be increasing and there are consumers who express they are prepared to adapt; more likely the older generation than those persons under 25 years of age whilst families are less likely given they place more significance on safety and concern for their children (Mintel, 2007e). But indicators of 'willingness' all too often do not translate into responsive action, described as cognitive dissonance theory (Festinger, 1957) whereby individuals do not always behave in accordance with their professed aspirations; for example consumers may show interest in green holidays but this is not reflected in demand (Manaktola and Jauhari, 2007).

Even so, over the last two decades public awareness of sustainability issues has grown. This is particularly evident in the last decade as a result of media coverage of global warming/climate change which partly accounts for an increase in the number of 'green consumers' (of varing shades). Basically, green consumers are people who in essence practice the three Rs – reduce, reuse, recycle and more comprehensively, show concern for others, purchase, for example, Fairtrade goods, contribute to charities and the local community etc. Support for an increase in green consumerism is not hard to find. Witness a survey of 22,000 US shoppers, which found: '... consumers are focused more and more on the social and environmental impact of their consumer packaged goods purchases. [This has led] to a viable and growing US market for sustainable products and packaging ...' (Info, 2008: 3). In contrast, a survey of small business found that the majority considered that customers will not pay higher prices for environmentally friendly goods or services and indeed the number saying yes had declined since 2007, which may partly be accounted for by the economic recession (Greenbiz, 2009). Such perceptions are supported by research into people's preferences in food choice buying behaviour (Defra, 2011). This study found that consumers consistently say they prefer fresh, seasonal and sustainable foods, for example fish – 70 per cent said sustainable fish is important but only 30 per cent said they buy it.

Evidently, the true extent of the green consumer market is largely unknown and will certainly vary between countries (Wagner, 2003, OECD, 2011). If, for example, estimates of the market were to be based on belief in the need for change due to climate change then it would be small given that '... 9% of UK population believe in climate change and that it will have a significant impact upon them personally' (Downing and Ballantyne, 2007: 4) and only a proportion of this 9 per cent will actually take action and even fewer will translate such action into their tourist activities. As a Travel Group Index (2008) report suggested, only two per cent of the population of the UK, USA and France are eco-adapters (willing to put their environmental beliefs into practice), and over half of the eco-adapters in the UK flew in the last year. A finding that is further supported by Barr et al.'s

(2010) study, which found that a person's general environmental behaviours are unlikely to stop them taking short- or long-haul flights. This reinforces Holmes et al.'s (2008) finding that environmental awareness and concern tend to revolve around the home at best and rarely translate into actions in leisure based behaviour outside of the home environment, which is further supported by the unwillingness on the part of consumers to change to less energy consuming modes of transport. Even so, as Simmons and Widmar (1990) argued, there is a relationship between environmental concern and ecologically responsible behaviour, for example recycling. People in general do not wish to harm the environment but it is habit and convenience which has and continues to dominate environmental concerns (NCC, 2003). Studies have also shown that environmental concerns and actions are more concentrated within specific population groups (Davidson et al., 2008; NCC, 2003, Brouwer et al., 2008) and evidence strong links with education (see Schwartz and Miller, 1991; Newell and Green, 1997). This is reinforced by Crouch et al. (2008) who note that if an individual is brought up from an early age with environmental concerns, the chances of them demonstrating pro-environmental behaviour on holiday is considerably higher. Further, Davidson et al. (2008) found that people who are more educated and of a higher social class engage more with environmental concerns. Lower earners are also just as willing to participate in green initiatives (NCC, 2003). Willing they may be, but when allegedly 'environmentally friendly packages' such as ecotours to Kenya are available, can they afford them? As they go onto to note, people with low incomes are often excluded from participating in such behaviour as the green option is seen as the expensive option (NCC, 2003). Thus they may purchase a package holiday to Benidorm which, it can be argued, is more in tune with sustainability concerns that an ecotourism package to Costa Rica. By default the less affluent in society are comparatively more environmentally friendly in their behaviours compared with persons who are comparatively affluent.

The price of the product invariably is a key determinant of choice and all the more so in difficult economic situations, for example, recession, unemployment, which will further reduce possible other considerations to be taken into account such as eco-labels (see Keynote, 2008). In such situations, it is arguable that as and when economic conditions improve consumers so affected may start looking for ethical and 'green' services; in much the same way as membership of green organisations, such as the World Wide Fund for Nature or Greenpeace, rises in prolonged periods of 'good times'. However, as Thogerson et al. (2010) note, it is only a small minority who are prepared to adapt to change and try new ideas, some consumers will do so to follow trends and fashions, perhaps 'to do something different' whilst at the same time reflecting social issues (Belk et al., 2003); even to enhance their social standing amongst their peers (Swarbrooke and Horner, 2007). This, particularly in choice of an especially attractive (thus expensive) holiday, that economists would term a 'positional good', well portrays 'symbolic consumption' (Bowen and Clarke, 2009). However, for the majority of consumers the reality is that if they feel that as an individual they cannot make a difference then they are far less likely to purchase responsibly (Valor, 2008) and even then seek assurance that their own actions will be matched by others (Downing, 2007). In effect, this is the 'I will if you will' syndrome' (see SCRT, 2006). On such a basis then few consumers are going to change their desire for tourism given the global scale of demand.

Conclusion

The foregoing discussion, though somewhat dependent on the stance taken, suggests little progress is being made in influencing demand for more sustainable tourism products and services and so too the environmental behaviour of tourists. This is perhaps surprising given the initiatives of the late 1980s and particularly since "Rio 92", the attention then given to consumption and consumers, for example Chapter 4 of Agenda 21 – Changing Consumption Patterns, and the principles enshrined in the Rio Declaration itself. As Hauff (2007) argued, it can be said that two decades on there has been little improvement as the same issues and concerns are still being raised. Even so, the discussion does evidence signs of some progress (as the following further chapters all attest). Over the intervening decades, destinations have been encouraged to address tourism's impact on the environment and suppliers of tourism products and services to address their environment behaviour and introduce environmentally friendly management practices. Testament to this is also manifest in a host of eco-labels. But, we need to develop a much better knowledge of the how, why and when consumers select to use such products and services, which as Bergin-Seer and Mair (2009) argue is a complex matter which tourism suppliers need to understand in order to be able to identify with and how they relate to the travel and holiday choices and the decisions made and actions taken. Furthermore, there is a real need to understand how buying-behaviour may change in times of recession and prosperity. How does this affect green consumers and how do various depths of 'greenness' reflect differences in consumers in terms of their awareness, knowledge and attitudes towards the environment in general; as well as other priorities in life such as making a living, housing, health, family commitments and so forth.

As Mokower (2009) argued, the recession this time is having a positive impact on consumerism, albeit by default, as consumers seek to save on costs and reduce expenditure though altruism may also partly account for this. But, significantly and not surprisingly, Mokower found at the same time on the business side interest in environmentally friendly behaviours comes behind jobs, protecting workers and improving the quality of products and price. In effect being a good employer ranks higher than being environmentally responsible. In terms of sustainability these are all-important factors, but, it might be argued, the short term economic imperatives, for example, profit and jobs, underpinning the promotion of tourism are less easily justified when such are possibly at a cost to the longer term social and environmental aspects. The problem is that tourism products and services, like many other consumer goods, are a short-term purchase, indeed more and more reflective of the instant gratification culture that is growing within western societies. Consumers may well be interested in sustainability issues and show concern but this is more evident around the home environment than in the pursuit of pleasure. As Britton argued, the consumers, the prospective tourists: '… are purchasing the intangible qualities of restoration, status, life-style signifier, release from the constraints of everyday life, or conveniently packaged novelty' (Britton, 1991 cited in Hall, 1994). Yes, they may be '… expressing concern over environmental problems …, but unwilling to make difficult or inconvenient lifestyle changes that cumulatively could ameliorate these problems' (Lawton and Weaver, 2009: 2). Rather they adopt '… the "have a good time" ideology and the "tomorrow we shall be gone again" attitude set the tone. Responsibility is rejected, egoism rules. And when entire groups of people behave this way the result is bewildering' (Krippendorf, 1987: 33). A view that recently is perhaps most manifest in 'clubbing resorts' such as Faliraki in Greece. In many ways the manifestations which bear witness to capitalism's most conspicuous form of consumption – tourism. Demand for tourism is the market, which comprises consumers and, in effect, the tourist is also the embodiment of consumption which leads us to recognise that tourists are an integral part of the package – in effect – a seasonal crop for destinations to harvest.

As this century has progressed so too has the attention to consumerism, which is being brought more into focus as the clamour to address the reported impacts of climate warming increases and hence the emphasis on energy production and consumption and ways to reduce this through international protocols such as the Kyoto Agreement. In combination with other policy initiatives, this has catalysed national and international policies, and initiatives designed to promote the three Rs – reduce, reuse, recycle. In this process the consumer is becoming the centre of attention. They are being encouraged, through varied means, to adjust their behaviour and adopt more environmentally friendly practices; to 'go green', an approach which evidences signs of success in some areas of consumer behaviour but hardly in tourism. More generally though this has lead to a shift towards the polluter pays principle; an approach manifest in the proposed introduction of CO_2 caps and carbon trading for airline operators. This would have the effect of raising costs and hence airfares which, coupled with fuel taxes, is seen by the EU as part of an effective solution to the problem (Mintel 2006). The potential impact on demand of putting such a "green" tax on tourist flights would not just be restricted to the EU but across the world. Also, the impact on prices will increase disparities between the "haves" and "have nots" in society and between communities across the globe. Challenges would arise from stakeholders based on the potential competitive disparities amongst and between other stakeholders, which undoubtedly will limit, at the least, the real impact of such initiatives. Aligned with such approaches is the drive towards sustainable production and consumption, heralded at the 'Rio + 10' World Congress in Johannesburg in 2002, which subsequently gained impetus through the involvement of and promotion by the EU. This approach seeks to address the start of the process rather than 'end of pipe' adjustments, which, like the polluter pays principle, have their place but evidently are of limited impact. For example, the fact that people recycle more waste today across the EU than in 2000 could be just a function of local government action and not due to a change in attitude, an activity that has arisen as a result of extrinsic actions and would probably decline if the supporting infrastructure is not present. In contrast, what lies at the heart of sustainable production and consumption is the 'what of' and way in which we consume thus to achieve sustainable production and consumption requires behavioural change (Jackson, 2005). But, as Jackson so cogently argues, behaviour is not easily changed. It is influenced by society and institutions and as much by 'others' as through personal choice therefore to achieve real progress in sustainability requires incentives and supporting frameworks; knowledge of options and access to such and exemplars in all facets to demonstrate how change can be achieved. However, as the foregoing discussion exemplifies, consumers/tourists are not simply rationale in their choice nor is individuality the key to their behaviour and choices as these are also influenced by social context, personal relationships and so forth. Indeed, what we see others doing is more influential than information campaigns. Thus, whilst global demand continues to increase, until environmental behaviour and related decision-making becomes primarily influenced by intrinsic values and attitudes (in other words personal) then a substantial increase in demand for more sustainable tourism products and services, which address and respond effectively to the issues encompassed under the umbrella of sustainability, is unlikely to be achieved. In the meantime perhaps the real conundrum to be addressed is *why do* people *want* to take a holiday in the first place?

References

Andereck, K.L. (2009) Tourists' perceptions of environmentally responsible innovations at tourism businesses. *Journal of Sustainable Tourism*, 17(4), 489-99.

Ballantyne, R., Packer, J. and Falk J. (2010) Visitors' learning for environmental sustainability: Testing short- and long-term impacts of wildlife tourism experiences using structural equation modeling. *Tourism Management*, 32, 1243-52.

Barr, S., Shaw, G., Coles, T. and Prillwitz, J. (2010) 'A holiday is a holiday': Practising sustainability, home and away. *Journal of Transport Geography*, 18, 474-82.

Bauer, T.G. (2001) *Tourism in the Antarctic: Opportunities, Constraints, and Future Prospects*. Binghamton: The Hawthorn Hospitality Press.

Becken, S. and Hay, J. (2007) *Tourism and Climate Change: Risks and Opportunities*. Clevedon: Channel View Publications.

Belk, R.W., Ger, G. and Askegaard, S. (2003) The fire of desire: A multisided inquiry into consumer passion. *Journal of Consumer Research*, 30(3), 326.

Bennett, L. (2006) *Duty Free?*, Resource, July-August, 20-22.

Bergin-Seers, S. and Mair, J. (2009) Emerging Green Tourists in Australia: Their Behaviours and Attitudes. *Tourism Hospitality and Research*, 9(2), 109-19.

Bowen, D. and Clarke, J. (2009*) Contemporary Tourist Behaviour: Yourself and Others as Tourists*. Wallingford: CABI.

Brouwer, R., Brander, L. and van Beukering, P. (2008) "A convenient truth": Air travel and passengers' willingness to pay to offset their CO_2 emissions. *Climatic Change*, 90, 299-313.

Brown, T. (2003) Holiday Isles scrap 'ecotax'. *The Daily Telegraph*, 14 July, 12.

Choat, I. (2004) Package firms urged to be responsible. *The Guardian*, 13 March, 16.

Connelly, J. and Smith, G. (2003) *Politics and the Environment: From Theory to Practice*. London: Routledge.

Crane, A. (2000) Facing the backlash: Green marketing and strategic reorientation in the 1990s. *Journal of Strategic Marketing*, 8, 277.

Crouch, G., Dolnicar, S. and Long, P. (2008) Environment-friendly Tourists: What Do We Really Know About Them? *Journal of Sustainable Tourism*, 16(2), 197-210.

Dalton, G.J., Lockington, D.A., and Baldock, T.E. (2008) A survey of tourist attitudes to renewable energy supply in Australian hotel accommodation. *Renewable Energy*, 33(10), 2174-85.

Davidson, S., Martin, C. and Treanor, S. (2008) *Scottish Environmental Attitudes and Behaviours Survey 2008*. Available at: http://www.ipsos-mori. com [Accessed: 21 February 2011].

Defra (2009) *Survey of Public Attitudes and Behaviours towards the Environment*. Available at: http://www.defra.gov.uk [Accessed: 19 February 2011].

Defra (2011) Department of Environment, Food, Rural Affairs. Available at: http://defra.gov.uk/statistics/foodfarm/food/ [Accessed: 11 April 2011].

DePalma, A. (2006) Gas guzzlers find price of forgiveness. *New York Times*. Available at: http://www.nytimes.com/2006/04/22/nyregion/22guilt.html [Accessed: 16 March 2008].

DESA (1999) *Commission on Sustainable Development: The Global Importance of Tourism*. Department of Economic and Social Affairs. Available at: http://www.un.org/esa/sustdev/csd/wttc.pdf [Accessed: 22 February 2011].

Dickinson, J. and Lumsdon, L. (2010) *Slow Travel and Tourism*. London: Earthscan.

Downing, P. (2007) *Political Commentary – Public: Government Should Intervene on Climate Change ... Just Don't Tax Us*. Available at: http://www. ipsos-mori.com [Accessed: 21 February 2011].

Downing, P. and Ballantyne, J. (2007) Tipping Point or Turning Point? –Social marketing and climate change. London: MORI.

EHow (2011) *Which Hotel Chains have Green Initiatives*? Available at: http://www.ehow.com/list_6939843_hotel-chains-green-initiatives_html [Accessed: 8 February 2011].

Flybe (2011) Available at: http://www.flybe.com/corporate/sustainability/eco_labelling_scheme.htm [Accessed: 20 February 2011].

Fairweather, J.R., Maslin, C. and Simmons, D.G. (2005) Environmental values and response to ecolabels among international visitors to New Zealand. *Journal of Sustainable Tourism*, 13(1), 82-98.

Futerra (2008) The Greenwash Guide [online] Available at: www.futerra.co.uk/revolution/leading_thinking [Accessed: 20 February 2011].

Goodwin, H. and Francis, J. (2003) Ethical and responsible tourism – consumer trends in the U.K. *Journal of Vacation Marketing*, 9(3), 271-84.

Green Aviation (2011) Available at: http://www.greenaviation.com/about [Accessed: 9 February 2011].

Greenbiz (2009) *Most Small Biz Owners say Customers Won't Pay More for Green*. Available at: http://www.greenbiz.com/news [Accessed: 21 June 2010].

Grewock, L, (2010) *Biofuels: Creating or Solving Global Problems*. Available at: http://responsibletravelnews/blogspot.com/2010/06/biofuels-creating-or-solving-global-problems [Accessed: 12 March 2011].

Gustin, M.E. and Weaver, P.A. (1996) Are hotels prepared for the environmental consumer? *Hospitality Research Journal*, 20(2), 1-14.

Hall, C.M. (1994) *Tourism and Politics: Policy, Power and Place*. Chichester: Wiley.

Hauff. J. (2007) *European Sustainable Development Network*. Available at: http://www.sd-network.eu/pdf/doc_berlin/ESB07_Plenary_Hauff.pdf [Accessed: 10 February 2011].

Hudson, S. and Miller, C.A. (2005) The responsible marketing of tourism: The case of Canadian Mountain Holidays. *Tourism Management*, 26(2), 133-42.

Infor. (2008) *Performance Management Strategies: Creating Social and Financial Value by Going Green*. Alpharetta, Georgia. Info, February.

Jackson, T. (2005) *Motivating Sustainable Consumption – A Review of Evidence on Consumer Behaviour and Behavioural Change*. Centre for Environmental Strategy. Guildford: University of Surrey.

Keynote (2008) *Green and Ethical Consumer Market Assessment* Available at: https://www.keynote.co.uk/market-intelligence/view/product/2179/green-and-ethical-consumer/chapter/1/executive_summary?highlight=Green%20consumers%20and%20tourism [Accessed: 22 February 2011].

Keynote (2008) *Green and Ethical Consumer Market Assessment*. Available at: https://www.keynote.co.uk/market-intelligence/view/product/2179/green-and-ethical-consumer/chapter/7/transport-and-holiday-travel [Accessed: 18 February 2011].

Krippendorf, J. (1987) *The Holidaymakers*. Oxford: Heinemann.

Lawton, L.J. and Weaver, D.B. (20 2010) Normative and innovative resources management at birding festivals. *Tourism Management*, 31 (4), 527-36.

Leslie, D. (2001) Serviced Accommodation, environmental performance and benchmarks. *Journal of Quality Assurance in Hospitality & Tourism*, 2(3), 127-47.

Leslie, D. (2009a) Introduction, in D. Leslie, (ed.) *Tourism Enterprises and Sustainable Development: International Perspectives on Responses to the Sustainability Agenda*. London: Routledge, 1-16.

Leslie, D. (2010) The European Union, sustainable tourism policy and rural Europe, in D.V.L. Macleod and S.A. Gillespie (eds) *Sustainable Tourism in Rural Europe: Approaches to Development*, 43-60.

Leslie, D. (2012) Key players in the environmental performance of tourism enterprises, in M.V. Reddy and K. Wilkes. (eds) *Tourism, Climate Change and Sustainability*. London: Earthscan.

Leslie, D. and Hughes, G. (1997) Agenda 21, local authorities and tourism in the UK, *International Journal of Managing Leisure*, 2(3), 143-54.

Lim, N., (1996) To Take a Stand: The greening of tourism. *BusinessWorld*, 4.

Marshall, G. (2007) *Carbon Detox: Your Step-by-Step Guide to getting Real about Climate Change*. London: GAIA.

Miller, G., Rathouse, K., Scarles, C., Holmes, K. and Tribe, J. (2007*) Public Understanding of Sustainable Leisure and Tourism: A Report to the Department for Environment, Food and Rural Affairs*. Guildford: University of Surrey.

Miller, G., Holmes, K., Rathouse, K., Scarles, C. and Tribe, J. (2010) Public understanding of sustainable tourism. *Annals of Tourism Research*, 37(3), 627-45.

Millman, R. (1989) Pleasure seeking vs the greening of World tourism. *Tourism Management*, 10(4), 275-78.

Mintel (2005) *Sustainable Tourism in the Travel Industry*. Available at: http://academic.mintel.com/sinatra/oxygen_academic/search_results/show&&type=RCItem&sort=relevant&access=accessible&archive=hide&source=non_snapshot&list=search_results/display/id=148248/display/id=148394#hit1 [Accessed: 18 February 2011].

Mintel (2007) *Holiday Lifestyles – Responsible Tourism – UK* – January. Available at: http://academic.mintel.com/sinatra/oxygen_academic/search_results/show&/display/id=221204/display/id=256088#hit1 [Accessed: 2 February 2011]

Mintel (2011) *Travellers Green Habits are Forgotten Once They are on Holiday*. Available at: http://academic.mintel.com/sinatra/oxygen_academic/search_results/show&/display/id=221204/display/id=532326 [Accessed: 17 February 2011].

Mokower, J. (2009) *Green Consumers and the Recession: Is it Really Different this Time?* Available at: Greenbiz.com [Accessed: 9 November 2009].

Mowforth, M. and Munt, I. (2009) *Tourism and Sustainability: Development, Globalization and new Tourism in the Third World*, 3rd edn. London: Routledge.

Munt, I. (1994) Eco-tourism or ego-tourism? *Race & Class*, 36(1), 49-60.

Newell, S.J. and Green, C.L. (1997), "Racial differences in consumer environmental concern", *The Journal of Consumer Affairs*, 31(1), 53-69.

NCC (2003) *Green Choice is Still Middle Class Affair*. Available at: http://www.ipsos-moiri.com [Accessed: 21 February 2011].

OECD (2011) *Greening Household Behaviour: The Role of the Public Policy*. Paris: Organization for Economic and Cultural Development.

Pleumarom, A. (2009) Asian Tourism; Green and Responsible, in D. Leslie (ed.) *Tourism Enterprises and Sustainable Development: International Perspectives on Responses to the Sustainability Agenda.* London: Routledge, 36-54.

Schwartz, J. and Miller, T. (1991) The earth's best friends. *American Demographics,* 13, February, 26-33.

SCRT (2006) *I will if you will: Towards Sustainable Consumption.* Sustainable Consumer Round Table. London, May.

Simmons, D. and Widmar, R. (1990). Motivations and barriers to recycling: Toward a strategy for public education. *The Journal of Environmental Education,* 22, 13-18.

Swarbrooke, J. and Horner, S. (2007) *Consumer Behaviour in Tourism.* 2nd ed. Oxford: Butterworth-Heinemann.

Tepelus, C.M. (2005) Aiming for Sustainability in the Tour Operating Business. *Journal of Cleaner Production,* 13, 99-107.

Thogerson et al. (2010) Consumer Responses to Ecolabels. *The European Journal of Marketing,* 44(11/12), 1787-810.

TOI (2011) *Tour Operator Initiative.* Available at: http://www.toinitiative.org [Accessed: 18 February 2011].

Valor, C. (2008) Can Consumers Buy Responsibly? Analysis and Solutions for Market Failures. *Journal of Consumer Policy,* 31(3), 315-26.

Wagner, A. (2003*) Understanding Green Consumer Behaviour: A Qualitative Cognitive Approach.* London: Routledge.

Wight, P. (1994) Environmentally Responsible Marketing of Tourism, in E. Cater and G. Lowman (eds) *Ecotourism: A Sustainable Option.* Chichester: Wiley, 39-56.

Chapter 2

Air Transport in Europe and the Environmental Challenges to the Tourist Market

Kenneth Button

Introduction

Tourism is a major sector, supporting the economy of numerous developing economies and providing large numbers of jobs and incomes in more established recreational markets. Tourism is also diverse, and this diversity is growing as boredom with traditional destinations and activities sets in among established travellers, as new markets are developed by countries and regions seeking additional incomes, and as transportation has become cheaper and its networks have become more extensive.

The transportation challenges in the past have often been ones of moving large numbers of people on a seasonal basis to a limited number of destinations. The ability to travel anywhere on the globe at short notice and throughout the year has changed the magnitude and some of the dimensions of the problem. Security of transportation supply, in the strictest sense of embracing reliability, safety and security, is now, however, much more assured despite the persistent threat of terrorism in the early 21st century. The objective data also points to the discomforts of tourism having been considerably reduced as travel times have fallen, transport itself has become much more comfortable, and modern information systems have allowed easy arrangements of trips. Romantic pictures of large Imperial Airways, multi-winged aircraft flying the British elite to exotic places in Africa and Asian seldom mention the widespread use of airsickness bags or long delays to cure the malaise of a failed aircraft. Their impact was also really trivial; British Imperial Airways only carried about 40,000 passengers in total in the inter-war period. The overall cost of tourism to the consumer has also fallen considerably, and this is in part due to more efficient transportation and the better management of its provision.

While the customers' situation has improved considerably, even if they sometimes ignore the benchmarks of the past, the wider adverse implications of air transportation are now often perceived to be in terms of negative environmental impacts, not only locally but in terms of emissions of climate change gases such as CO_2. There are also concerns about the capacity of the

European air transportation infrastructure, the airports and the air traffic control system, to handle growing numbers of tourists efficiently. The success of the industry has led to increasing amounts of congestion, especially at the major, nodal airports in the network and important tourist links in air corridors.

These challenges all fit within the general notion of ensuring sustainability. The oft-cited, but apparently seldom read, Brundtland Report (World Commission on Environment and Development, 1987) that underlies the modern notion of sustainable development embraces the need for sustainable economies and political structures as a necessary condition for a sustainable environment. The concepts of "sustainable tourism" or "sustainable transport", although convenient political billboards, and perhaps even practically necessary, run against the entire grain of the idea of sustainability. There is nothing wrong, for example, in expanding the use of resources, including environmental resources, for tourism provided there are at least comparable reductions in other sectors, say agriculture, home heating, manufacturing, or whatever.[1] The objective is to leave future generations with a resource base comparable to the one we have inherited, but there are many possible paths to achieve this.

The idea of sustainable development is thus a holistic one and, one that should strictly not be treated within the confines of any sector or activity. What this entails in policy terms has been widely debated, but political and environmental stability does logically seem to embrace acceptable levels of economic wellbeing. There is also the underlying challenge that there are often trade-offs between economic, political and environmental sustainability. In some cases these are positive; for example political stability can lead to more efficient use of economic resources. In other circumstances there may be conflicts; for example, increasing food production may lead to soil erosion and water contamination. Consequently our discussions seeks to cover more than just the narrow confines of the immediate environmental impacts of air transport based tourism in Europe, although by necessity the boundaries still remain quite narrow within the larger issues of sustainable development. In particular, there is a focus on the environmental policies that are being introduced in Europe and their possible impacts on tourism, but we do not confine ourselves to this and do offer some thoughts on the economic stability of the European airline sector.

---

1   In the context of air transport, for example, a combination of policies, that includes aggressive levels of technological and operations efficiency improvements, use of biofuels along with moderate levels of carbon pricing and short-haul demand shifts effects, Sgouridis et al. (2011) project a 140 per cent increase in capacity in 2024 over 2004 with emissions rising by 20 per cent. Airline profitability is only reduced by 10 per cent . The issue then is whether there could be cuts in carbon use elsewhere in the system to more than compensate for the benefits that come from this sort of policy scenario regarding aviation.

European Air Transport Markets

Air transportation is a major carrier of tourists both within Europe and to and from Europe.[2] The internal airline market went through a series of regulatory reforms beginning in the late 1980s, most notably the three packages of measures that led to removal of virtually all economic restrictions on providing air services within the European Union and a number of other countries such as Norway and Switzerland.

The overall impact within Europe has been for fares to have fallen dramatically, in particular on the most popular routes, as low cost carriers have entered the market and injected a much higher degree of competition than under the previous, highly restrictive regulatory regimes. As important, the choice of routes has increased as these low cost airlines in particular offer increasing numbers of services to secondary and regional airports. The major airports in Europe, including many that handle large tourist flows, have suffered from on-going problems of congestion for many years (Button and Reynolds-Feighan, 1999). Many of the most congested facilities, in terms of deviations in arrival times from the schedule, are the large hub airports such as Frankfurt, Heathrow and Schiphol Airport, Amsterdam. While a large share of their traffic involves business travellers, they nevertheless in absolute terms, carry a significant number of tourists, especially from other continents.

While the airline market within Europe, and to a lesser extent for movements to and from Europe has been liberalised, the associated infrastructure is still subject to significant amounts of regulation. The air navigation service providers are still largely state undertakings, with some notable exceptions such as NATS in the United Kingdom, and there are major differences in their performance (Button, 2011). Efforts are underway, led by EUROCONTROL to initially harmonise and then integrate the numerous systems that exist in Europe but this is a long-term program; the Single European Sky Initiative. In the meantime, the network of control centers is only as efficient as its weakest systems. Not only does this impose delays on tourists, but it also has adverse environmental consequences with planes taking longer routings than is efficient and, often having to spend extended periods circling airports waiting to land or on the ground waiting to take-off.

 ## Environmental Impacts of Air Transport

Tourism constitutes between 15 and 20 per cent of all miles traveled by passengers in Europe of which 61 per cent are domestic, 29 per cent inside the EU, four per cent to European countries outside the EU and six per cent to other continents.

---

2   Forsyth (2006) provides an account of the various economic impacts of air transport on economic development.

Research on the environmental impacts of tourism, however, mainly focuses on the impacts at the tourism destinations but with much less done on the impacts associated with transport to the destinations.[3]

Air transportation has long been looked at as environmentally intrusive; airports are noisy places, chemicals like deicing fluid contaminate local water systems, and large land takes for terminals and runways can adversely affect local flora and fauna. As with most forms of transport, it is often not the absolute amount of environmental intrusions associated with air transport that is the issue but rather the diversity of effects. Added to this, individuals like ready access to airports and thus seek to locate relatively close to them; but then complain about things such as noise. There is also a secondary dimension to many environmental debates involving tourism. Air transport is a facilitator for the development of the tourist industry that itself is not environmentally benign. This aspect of the debate is not addressed here; it is more a matter of how the strict, final tourist activities are managed, but it is obviously true that the growth in long distance tourism and its implications for local ecosystems, is a direct result of reliable and relatively cheap air travel.

Figure 2.1 provides a rough guide to the nature of some of the more important forms of environmental damage associated with air travel. It offers a stylistic impression of the geographical spread of the impacts of various emissions and the duration of these impacts.

More recently, the focus has switched to matters of climate changing gas and other emissions by aircraft. Despite emission reductions from more fuel-efficient and less polluting turbofan and turboprop engines, the rapid growth of air travel has contributed to an increase EU, greenhouse gas emissions from aviation of 87 per cent between 1990 and 2006. Emissions of passenger aircraft per passenger kilometer vary according to variables such as the size of the aircraft, the number of passengers on board, and the altitude and distance of the journey. The sorts of representative figures that are often cited are that average passenger aircraft emissions per passenger kilometer in CO_2 equivalents are 259 grams for domestic short distances of less than 463 km, 178 grams for domestic long distance greater than 463 km emissions; and 114 grams for long haul flights. The Intergovernmental Panel on Climate Change has estimated that aviation is responsible for about 3.5 per cent of anthropogenic climate change, a figure that includes both CO_2 and non-CO_2 induced effects.

While surface modes of transportation has, in particular, been the subject of various efforts to reduce CO_2 emissions, air transportation has largely been outside of the debate, in part because much of air travel is international requiring international coordinated policies and emissions relative to road transport are quite small. There

---

3   Some exceptions to this includes Peeters and Schouten (2006) that looks at a case study of the environmental footprint of the tourist movements to Amsterdam, and a larger geographical study whereby Peeters et al. (2007) looks at the environmental impacts of European tourists traveling from their places of residence to their destinations.

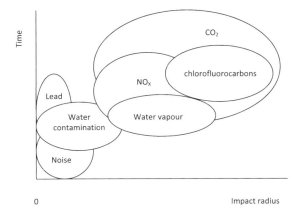

Figure 2.1   A stylised impression of the duration and geographical impacts of air transport on the environment

have also been debates about the effects of high level releases of CO_2 that have led to some caution in thinking about appropriate policies (Forster et al. 2006). The situation has been changing more recently with the lead being taken by the European Union, and in particular the idea of integrating aviation within the wider Union's Emissions Trading Scheme. Most of the studies of the potential impacts of trading have looked at systems that initially allocate a large number of free carbon permits based on previous airline activities with the ability to buy further permits from either a specific aviation pool or from other sectors, but tightens the number of free permits over time. They have focused on air transport in general and not specifically to tourist related services.

Noise around airports, mainly from aircraft taking off and landing but also from land traffic entering and exiting the facilities has traditionally been a major environmental concern for residents. The noise nuisance is normally estimated using hedonic price indices. They consider trade-offs between the noise level and the values of local property. Nelson (2004) examining 20 hedonic studies covering 33 estimates of 23 airports in Canada and the United States estimated the percentage depreciation in property values per decibel increase in airport noise; the noise discount. The weighted-mean noise discount across the studies is 0.58 per cent per decibel with country and model specifications having some effect on the measured noise discount; the cumulative noise discount in the United States is about 0.5 to 0.6 per cent per decibel at noise exposure levels of 75 dB or less, while in Canada it is 0.8 to 0.9 per cent per decibel. These are findings in line with the literature review conducted by Gillen (2003) who found that aviation noise seems to reduce the prices of similar houses by about 0.45 to 0.9 per cent for each decibel. These are all very much in line with the recent, case specific work done in Europe.

Putting these various environmental impacts into a simple metric is challenging, although there are some estimates expressed in money terms. Schipper (2004), for example, estimates of environmental costs associated with 36 European airline markets, focusing on noise, air pollution and accident risk using data on aircraft emissions, exposure-response parameters and economic valuation of environmental goods. The 'medium value' cost estimate is €0.0201 per passenger-km, suggesting that environmental costs represent only 2.5 per cent of the internal cost of aviation as measured by the average ticket price. Noise costs represent 75 per cent of the total environmental cost. The study also suggests that there are environmental economies of scale in air transport and that, in terms of noise nuisance for example, older Chapter 2 aircraft are about a factor four more environmentally costly than Chapter 3 aircraft.

Apportioning the appropriate share of these costs to tourism traffic, however, poses some problems. Many planes, particularly scheduled services, carry both tourists and business travellers, and in addition often move significant amounts of belly-hold cargo, particularly on longer routes. There are also inherent technical problems when it comes to mitigating the environmental impacts of aviation; for example by rerouting aircraft movements away from noise sensitive areas some local environmental concerns can be reduced, but this normally requires a larger fuel burn with consequentially adverse effects for the global climate. Nevertheless, the broad pattern that emerges is generally true for all air transportation with some contextual variation.

Trends in Air Transport Based Tourism in Europe

Prior to 2000 the vast bulk of European air transport based tourism involved charter operations within the context of inclusive tours ("package holidays"). The market liberalisation that accompanied the three Packages in the 1990s led to the need for the charter operations to confront not only traditional flag carriers now operating in a more open environment, but also to meet the challenges of the emergent low cost airlines (Lobbenberg, 1995). These latter, "no-frills" scheduled carriers with their focus on low fares produced major challenges not only to full service providers but also to the charter operators. A comparison of charter and "no-frills" airlines' operating costs indicated initially that while the differential in costs had been significantly reduced, the advantage still lay with charter airlines (Williams, 2001). The greater flexibility offered to the traveller by scheduled carriers, and notably low cost airlines, has, however, gradually and steadily impacted adversely on many short haul charter services.

Low cost carriers, often serving secondary airports, have been particularly important in the development of short stay vacation and longer stays. In the former case flights, in particular from the United Kingdom and Ireland to continental Europe have fostered increases in weekend, urban vacations for the young. At the other extreme, low cost services have been instrumental in the growth of second homes that have become accessible because of lower fares and often the proximity to smaller airports.

The pattern of airline deregulation also affected the costs of flying to different destinations. The gradual freeing-up of markets within Europe for scheduled services, both initially thorough the enactment of more liberal bilateral arranged between some pairs of countries and then through the introduction of the three Packages of reform from 1987, tend to favour shorter haul, intra-European tourism. Externally, the United States had began to try to deregulate international air transport pursing a policy of Open Skies from 1979, and in earnest from 1992 with the signing of an agreement between the United States and the Netherlands, but more especially 1996 when agreement was reached with Germany. These intercontinental agreements allowed for capacity increases and fare flexibility but also code sharing and the development of seamless services by combinations of carriers. They also led to the spread of Open Skies policies to across many other markets, including many that have been developed as long-haul tourist destinations.

Increasing numbers of travellers also began opting to put together their own holiday packages using the Internet and the more extensive range of scheduled services that were becoming available. To combat that, travel agents developed dynamic packaging that enables consumers to build their own package of flights, accommodation, and a hire car instead of a pre-defined package. Dynamic packages differ from traditional package holidays in that pricing is always based on current availability, escorted group tours are rarely included, and trip-specific add-ons such as airport parking and show tickets are often available. Frequently, the air, hotel, and car rates are available only as part of a package or only from a specific seller.

The advent of low cost airlines has broadened the range of potential tourists using air travel, but the pattern of those using this mode can be complex. The type of leisure travellers using low cost air transport, and the duration and destination of their trips, vary according to a range of socio-demographic factors (Raya-Vilchez and Martínez-Garcia, 2011), such as nationality and personal characteristics including, age, gender and marital status.

The Challenges of Policy Making

The majority of our discussions are related to economic and environmental sustainability, but some brief, introductory comments on some of the background policy challenge is perhaps justified. While a lot of tourism is domestic in nature, and this is especially so in larger countries and those with more temperate climates in the summer and snow in the winter, there is considerable international tourism. This makes policy formulation particularly difficult because of the diversity of the parties involved and the sovereignty of nation states. But even within many countries, regional differences in the importance of tourism to the local economy can make it difficult to formulate coordinated policies.

In terms of aviation policy, many international actions have to be in agreement with the UN's International Civil Aviation Organisation that was set up under the 1944 Chicago Convention. This, for example, defines the basis upon which air traffic rights can be negotiated between countries and parameters within which agreements may be made. It was not initially intended to deal with explicitly environmental matters, but rather to develop common frameworks, including such things as safety and technical matters, to allow for a freer flow of international air transport services. The latter set out to remove such things as the explicit manipulation of markets by a country to favour its air transport industry. This has subsequently presented challenges because it set out what amounts to basic accounting principles that have traditionally limited the use of such things as congestion charging at airports.

Since democratic government is basically steered, not by consensus but by some form of median voter system that is generally overlaid with coalition politics of one kind or another, internal policies to take the environment into account are often difficult to develop, especially if the costs are immediate and local with the benefits accruing over a much broader range and a longer time frame. At the more local level, there is ample evidence that air transportation facilitates economic development at suitable locations, although it is certainly not a panacea for all local economic ills.[4] This often makes it difficult for national policy makers who are confronted with what appear in the arguments of regional political interests as solid traditional economic grounds for investing in local air transport infrastructure, although many of the environmental implications, such as NO_x and CO_2 emissions, have much wider geographical implications.

Market Sustainability

While traditional, schedule and charter style airlines provide considerable input to the tourist market, the role of low cost carriers has clearly grown, and in many cases become the primary means of reaching tourist destinations. But the market for low costs airline services is not a stable one. While some scheduled European carriers such as Sabena have left the market, and other continually modify their networks and services in a way that affect the tourist industry, low cost carriers tend to come and go on a fairly steady basis.

Table 2.1 provides some details of European low cost airlines that were forced from the market between 2003 and 2005. The low cost airlines that are now defunct were diverse, and ranged from a number that hardly began operations

---

4   There is also often a tendency to exaggerate the effects by ignoring the opportunity costs of taking scarce resources from elsewhere to develop air transport facilities, including those associated with tourism (Green, 2007)

Table 2.1   European low cost carriers which have ceased to exist

Aeris	BuzzAway	Hellas Jet
Agent	Dream Air	Hop
Air Bosnia	Duo Airways	Jet Magic
Air Andalucia	Europe DutchBird	Jetgreen
Air Scotland	EastJet	JetsSky
Air Catalunya	EU Jet	JetX
Europe Air Exel	Europe Exel Aviation Group	Low Fare Jet
Air Freedom	Fairline Austria	MyAir
Europe Air	Flyglobespan	Maersk Air
Air Littoral	Fly Eco	Now
Air Luxor	Fly West	Silesian Air
Air Madrid	Flying Finn	Skynet Airlines
Air Polonia	Free Airways	Spirit of Balkan
Air Wales	Fresh Aer	Swedline Express
Airlib Express	Germania Express	V Bird
BasiqAir	GetJet Poland	VolareWeb
BerlinJet	Go Fly	White Eagle
Bexx Air	Goodjet	Windjet

Note: Most of these airlines operated for a period and then went into bankruptcy. Some such as Go Fly and BuzzAway merged with successful low cost airlines. In a few cases, the airline was registered but never offered actual services.

to others that were relatively successful but merged or were taken over;, for example, Go and Buzz. One could draw up a similar list for the United States, and many other countries. The simple situation is that with this level of attrition, the first-movers, Ryanair and EasyJet, now between them account for about 90 per cent of the scheduled low-cost market in Europe. There are, in other words, successful low cost companies, but that is not the same thing as successful and sustainable business model; successes seem to be those that entered the market first, indicating that replication of the business models is far from simple. From a tourism perspective, this pattern of behavior does not engender a high degree of certainty in terms of the ability to move individuals to their destinations.

Examining in detail just why the low cost airline business model is not very successful, despite the oft seen image of success conveyed in the media, is really beyond our scope. It is clear that in many cases, however, those entering the market do not have either sufficient experience or resources to develop a successful airline, particularly in a sector notorious for wild fluctuations in both short-term seasonal demand and over the longer business cycle. There are also issues involving the fixed cost nature of offering a schedule in a highly competitive market that for technical, economic reasons makes it extremely difficult to recover full costs.

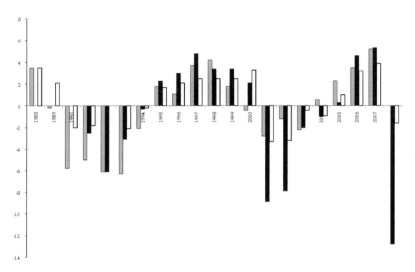

Figure 2.2   Airline operating margins: Global, European, and United States

Note: (i) A lack of a bar indicates a missing observation and not a zero operating margin, (ii) Memberships of the various reporting bodies vary over time and thus the reported margins reflect the associated carriers at the time of reporting.

Source: Boeing Commercial Airplane, Association of European Airlines, and Air Transport Association of America, International Air Transport Association.

To date the airlines, by being innovative on both the cost and revenue sides of their accounts, have managed collectively to expand services and meet the needs of a growing tourism market. For example, on the revenue side and in the context of traditional airlines, over the years the growth of airline alliances has made long distance tourism in particular more attractive as costs have been reduced and "seamless services" initiated. Frequent flier programs and yield management have resulted in more stable flows of revenue to airlines and the ability to better manage the mix of business and leisure passengers on aircraft. This has contained some of the instability in the sector, although clearly far from eliminated it.

From a sustainable development perspective, and in the context of air transport serving tourist markets, the challenge is to ensure that the sector remains viable in terms of offering capacity at fares tourists are willing to pay. While the carriers have continued to offer services, this has often been in the face of continued restructuring and loss making. As seen in Figure 2.2, since the 1980s the average annual operating margins in all major markets has been about zero (compared, for example, with about 5.5 per cent in the United States economy as a whole over the same time span) meaning investment costs have not been recovered; a fact highlighted by regular bankruptcies and financial restructuring in the industry. The upshot of this is that airlines have inevitably resisted any additional financial burden, including any associated with internalising environmental costs.

Balancing the Economic Benefits of Air Travel against the Environmental Costs of Air Travel

The issue of making air travellers, including tourists, more fully aware of their environmental costs has moved in recent years to matters of climate change gas emissions, and in particular CO_2. The introduction of more stringent environmental policy has taken time, in part because coalitions of interests have only gradually emerged to push it through. The integration of aviation into exiting emission trading schemes poses complex challenges for both environmental economics and the political sensitivities of countries. The implementation of a global environmental approach thus seems highly unlikely in the near future. Within Europe, however, there has been policy shifts at the individual country level, with other elements at the European Union level.

There has been substantial interest in the potential implications of these types of action, and to preempt our conclusions, the general finding is that the impacts of such things as carbon trading on airline costs, including those used for European tourism, are unlikely to be large, especially when compared with other costs that are affecting the sector. To give a flavour of this work, and the sorts of analytics approaches that have been used, a few studies are highlighted.

Beginning with national policies, the United Kingdom has an Air Passenger Duty (APD) that is aimed largely at reducing carbon emissions. The level and structure of charges has changed with time, but the Treasury forecast that a 2007 rise would cut carbon dioxide emissions by about 0.3 million tonnes a year by 2010-2011, and all climate change gas emissions by the equivalent of 0.75 million tonnes of carbon dioxide a year. Mayor and Tol (2007) by modeling domestic and international tourist numbers and flows estimated the impact of the pre- and post-2007 structure on tourism They looked at abolishing the APD, keeping the 2001 duty levels, the 2007 levels, and the "Green Miles" proposal. Although sensitive to the assumptions made, for example regarding the cross-elasticities of demand for different destinations, they found that the doubling of the Air Passenger Duty in 2007 had the perverse effect of increasing carbon dioxide emissions, albeit only slightly, because it reduced the relative price difference between near and far holidays. Tourists arriving into the country would also fall slightly and those travelling from the United Kingdom would fall with regard near countries. Tourists leaving the UK for countries further a field would increase.

In January 2008, charges were introduced at selected German airports aimed at reducing local emissions of nitrogen oxide and hydrocarbon by fostering the use of environmentally friendly engine technology. Because it is revenue-neutral, general landing fees need to be decreased by the amount of the emission charge.) Case studies have been conducted for selected German airports. Scheelhaase, (2010), for instance, finds the effects on airline's vary according to the engines employed and the aircraft population of airports. Airlines using NO_x and HC friendly engines, for example, have landing fee expenditures but becauses there are also local emission charges in Sweden and Switzerland, and at selected airports in United Kingdom, the implications for their competitive position is not serious. It can be debated, therefore, whether charges of €1.6 to €5.5 per unit of emission in Germany is high enough to trigger significant environmental benefits.

The larger, phased extension of carbon trading to air transport within the European Union from 2012 and affecting about 4,000 carriers, initially involves allocating an allowance to air transportation equivalent to 97 per cent the average historic aviation emissions for 2004 to 2006, an allowance of 212,892,052 tonnes, with the annual allowances from 2013 being reduced 208,502,525 tonnes. The airlines are allocated a free allowance amounting to 82 per cent of the total based on their historic carriage of freight and passengers, and can buy another 15 per cent through auctions. The remaining three per cent is to act as a reserve to be allocated to new entrance and particularly fast developing markets. Airlines can also buy additional carbon allowances in the open carbon trading market, although the air transport allowance cannot be used for other purposes.

The European Union carbon trading scheme is often seen as posing a threat to the air transport sector, although a number of empirical studies suggest that the impacts may be far less than some have projected. Morgan Stanley, for example estimate it will increase the average costs of tickets by the largest carriers in Europe by between €0.86 (Iberia) and €2.70 (BA) depending on network features and fleet composition, with the impact being less on the low cost carriers.[5] In a similar vein, Vespermann and Wald (2011) estimate the airline industry's costs of joining the European emissions trading scheme would average about €3 billion annually, but this number would vary according to prevailing business conditions. In the early years, with technology relatively inflexible, the overall carbon permit costs would be about 1.25 per cent of industry costs. The ecologic effect of the system assumes that higher costs will lead to lower demands for air transportation and technology changes resulting in a one per cent reduction compared to the do-nothing-case.

Scheelhaase and Grimme (2007), in a study prior to details of the Union's scheme being finalised, looked at implications of three carbon trading possibilities on the operating costs and demand for low cost, full service, holiday and regional airlines taking Ryanair, Lufthansa, Condor and Air Dolomiti. They found that implementing the European Commission's plans would produce relatively moderate

---

5   In all these types of calculation, much depends on the assumptions made about such things as the ability to pass on the cost in ticket prices – *de facto* the slopes of airlines' demand curves, the auction price for airline specific allowances, the spot price in the market for non-aviation specific carbon, and the reactionary changes in fleets and operations that the airline will adopted (Vespermann and Wald, 2011).

financial impacts on airlines subject to the system-wide European Trading Scheme. Even under unfavourable conditions, cost increases for Lufthansa would be lower than one per cent of its traffic revenues coming under the system, and Ryanair's costs would increase by up to three per cent. This is a minor effect considering that Lufthansa's jet fuel costs increased by €800 million between 2004 and 2005; the cost of carbon trading would add at most €101 million to costs in 2012.

More recently, Anger and Kohler (2010) reviewed various impact assessments of emissions trading schemes for airlines published between 2005 and 2009. It analyses the methods used and finds that the models used are often over-simplified, omitting important variables or that the reliability and robustness of the modelling results are reduced by linking models that are based on different assumptions. The paper also summarises the possible environmental (CO_2 emissions) and economic (air fares, demand for airline services, supply of airline services, competitiveness, GDP, carbon price) impacts in the studies reviewed for the year 2020. Overall, the effects are found to be small: for example, CO_2 emissions are expected to decline by a maximum of 3.8 per cent and the maximum impact on GDP in the EU was found to be -0.002 per cent.

Conclusions

Air transportation is important to the economic viability of large parts of the European tourist industry, but it is also has significant adverse effects on the environment that are seldom noticed by those flying, or perhaps more accurately there is little to make fliers take account of this damage in their decision-making. Over the years, the air transport industry has reduced its larger environmental footprint with aircraft becoming quieter and more fuel efficient, and air traffic control maneuvering traffic away from noise sensitive areas. The growth in air travel, including that for leisure purposes or visiting family and friends, however, has in some cases, as with CO_2 emissions, tended to over ride the reduced environmental implications of individual tourists and resulted in greater amounts of aggregate environmental damage.

The general concern with climate change gas emissions in particular, has gradually led to the adoption of policies to limit the environmental impacts of transport, and air transport is now coming under increased scrutiny. The evidence available suggests that in the short term at least, the initiatives of the European Union and national authorities will not push up the cost of air travel for tourists by a large sum. However the devil, as in many cases, may lie in the detail. While policies such as the carbon trading now being introduced in Europe may have only a relatively small effect on costs, most airlines have very low profit margins, if any at all. The analysis to date, therefore, may be missing the crucial point that it is the impact of higher costs on margins that are important and not simply costs. The airline industry in Europe, although not all individual carriers, has proven itself very robust in the past in meeting a range of challenges, and is probably inventive enough and flexible enough to handle the internalisation of carbon costs, but this may well have implications for the pattern of tourism and the way the airlines serve the tourist market. In the past, however, it has been very difficult to predict what the reaction of the industry will be to institutional change, and this pattern seems unlikely to be different for the introduction of matters such as carbon trading.

References

Anger A. and Kohler, J. (2010) Including aviation emissions in the EU ETS: Much ado about nothing? A review. *Transport Policy*, 17, 38-46.

Button, K.J. (2004) *Wings across Europe: Towards an Efficient European Air Transport System.* Ashgate: Aldershot.

Button, K.J. (2011) Comparative inefficiency of various air navigation systems, in H-M. Niemeier, H. Wolf, D. Gillen, P. Forsyth and K. Hüschelrath (eds), *Liberalizing Air Transport*. Farnham: Ashgate.

Button, K.J. and Reynolds-Feighan, A.J. (1999) An assessment of the capacity and congestion levels at European airports. *Journal of Air Transport Management*, 5, 113-34.

Forster, M. de F.P., Shine, K.P. and Stuber, N. (2006) It is premature to include non-CO_2 effects of aviation in emission trading schemes. *Atmospheric Environment*, 40, 1117-21.

Forsyth, P. (2006) Mutin Kunz Memorial Lecture: Tourism benefits and aviation policy. *Journal of Air Transport Management*, 12, 3-13.

Gillen, D. (2003) The economics of noise, in K.J. Button and D. Hensher (eds) *Handbook of Transport and the Environment*. Oxford: Pergamon.

Green, R.K. (2007) Airports and economic development. *Real Estate Economics*, 35, 91-112.

Lobbenberg, A. (1995) Strategic responses of charter airlines to Single Market integration. *Journal of Air Transport Management*, 2(2), 67-80.

Mayor, K. and Tol, R.S.J. (2007) The impact of the UK aviation tax on carbon dioxide emissions and visitor numbers. *Transportation Policy*, 14, 507-13.

Nelson, J.P. (2004) Meta-analysis of airport noise and hedonic property values: Problems and prospects. *Journal of Transport Economics and Policy*, 38, 1-28.

Peeters, P. and Schouten, F. (2006) Reducing the ecological footprint of inbound tourism and transport to Amsterdam. *Journal of Sustainable Tourism*, 14, 157-71.

Peeters, P., Szimba, E. and Duijnisveld, M. (2007) Major environmental impacts of European tourism transport. *Journal of Transport Geography*, 15, 83-93.

Raya-Vilchez, J.M. and Martínez-Garcia, E. (2011) Nationality and low cost trip duration: A microeconometric analysis. *Journal of Air Transport Management*, 17, 168-74.

Rey, B., Rafael, L., Myro, R.L. and Asun Galera, A. (2011) Effect of low-cost airlines on tourism in Spain: A dynamic panel data model. *Journal of Air Transport Management*, 17, 163-7.

Sainz-González, R., Núnez-Sánchez, R. and Pablo Coto-Millán, P. (2011) The impact of airport fees on fares for the leisure air travel market: the case of Spain. *Journal of Air Transport Management*, 17, 158-62.

Scheelhaase, D.J. and Grimme, W.G. (2007) Emissions trading for international aviation – an estimation of the economic impact on selected European airlines. *Journal of Air Transport Management*, 13, 253-63.

Scheelhaase, J.D. (2010) Local emission charges – A new economic instrument at German airports. *Journal of Air Transport Management*, 16, 94-9.

Schipper, Y. (2004) Environmental costs in European aviation. *Transport Policy*, 11, 141-54.

Sgouridis, S., Bonnefoy, P.A. and Hansman, R.J. (2010) Air transportation in a carbon constrained world: Long-term dynamics of policies and strategies for mitigating the carbon footprint of commercial aviation. *Transportation Research Part A: Policy and Practice* (10 May 2010).

Vespermann, J. and Wald, A. (2010) Much Ado about Nothing? – An analysis of economic impacts and ecologic effects of the EU-emission trading scheme in the aviation industry. *Transportation Research A: Policy and Practice*.

Williams, G. (2001) Will Europe's charter carriers be replaced by "no-frills" scheduled airlines? *Journal of Air Transport Management*, 7, 277-86.

World Commission on Environment and Development (1987) *Our Common Future*. Oxford: Oxford University Press.

Chapter 3

Non-Aviation-based Tourism: A UK-based Perspective

Jacqueline Holland and Richard Holland

Introduction

Transport is a key component within tourism, providing access to and within destinations. A significant proportion of the demand for travel is satisfied by air passenger transport. As the demand for tourism continues to grow, with the UNWTO expecting over 1.6 billion international arrivals by 2020 (UNWTO, 2010), so too will air travel. However, aircraft create carbon dioxide emissions and it is widely accepted that this is counter to the requirements of sustainability. Yet air travel is economically important; for example in the UK it accounted for 75 per cent of arrivals and 81 per cent of those travelling abroad in 2008 (DfT, 2009). The growth in tourist visits over the past 20 years has come primarily from air travel, with travel by air more than doubling for overseas residents to the UK and nearly trebling for UK residents' visits abroad. In comparison, visits to and from the UK by sea and the Channel Tunnel (since it was fully open) have remained fairly stable (DfT, 2009).

There are few policy frameworks that apply specifically to the tourism sector (Dickinson and Lumsdon, 2010: 29) although some policies do address land based travel and the reduction of airline emissions. In 2000, the IPCC (2000) detailed the impact of aircraft pollution on the global atmosphere. The report's key findings included the following:

- Aircraft released more than 600 million tonnes of CO_2 into the atmosphere in 1990.
- Aircraft currently cause about 3.5 per cent of global warming from all human activities.
- Aircraft greenhouse emissions will continue to rise and could contribute up to 15 per cent of global warming from all human activities within 50 years.

Most significantly, they concluded that improvements in aircraft and engine technology and in air traffic management will not offset the projected growth in aircraft emissions. Reducing the growth in aircraft greenhouse gas emissions will therefore require alternatives to air travel to be found in order to slow the growth in air travel overall. If the trends for airline growth continue, then by 2030 the carbon emissions from the airline industry will exceed the UK's total carbon allocation

Table 3.1   Carbon dioxide emissions by transport mode: United Kingdom, 1990-2008 (Million tonnes of carbon dioxide)

	1990	1999	2008
Railways	1.8	1.9	2.2
Buses and coaches	4.3	5.0	5.4
Tubes and trams	0.5	0.6	-
Taxis operation	1.5	2.1	2.5
Freight transport by road	16.1	17.4	16.6
Transport via pipeline	0.1	0.1	0.1
Water transport	16.9	16.5	19.8
Air transport	20.1	33.4	42.6
Total	61.2	77.0	89.2
Household use of private vehicles	59.4	63.8	63.5
Total emissions all sectors	**626.6**	**597.5**	**604.9**

(Tyndall Centre, 2006). It is for this reason that the reduction of emissions is important for the travel and tourism sector and alternatives to air travel with lower emissions must be explored (see Table 3.1).

The Kyoto Protocol of 1997, an international agreement linked to the United Nations Framework Convention on Climate Change (UNFCCC, 2010), sets binding targets for 37 industrialised countries and the European community for reducing greenhouse gas (GHG) emissions. These targets amount to an average total reduction of five per cent against 1990 levels over the five-year period 2008-2012. The United Nations Climate Change Conferences in December 2007 and 2009 (UNCCC, 2010) that led to the Copenhagen Accord (UNCCC, 2010) further strengthened the resolution for a global reduction in GHG emissions. The UNWTO (2010) recommended a "modal shift" from car to mass transit modes, in the process identifying short and long term solutions for reducing carbon emissions, including market mechanisms such as global emission trading schemes and innovative methods of transformation towards the Green Economy. In 2008 the UK introduced the Climate Change Act (Committee on Climate Change, 2010) which sets the target of an 80 per cent reduction in emissions by 2050 as compared to 1990 levels. This will ultimately have an impact on the operations of travel and tourism companies as it aims to include both aviation and shipping emissions in its assessment as currently water based transport and aviation are omitted from the international regulations such as Kyoto Protocol.

Land based transport has also been the focus of research and policy provision. A substantial body of EU-sponsored research has been carried out to identify and resolve technical, legal, institutional barriers and other barriers to interoperability of land transport. This research contributed to an EU white paper entitled 'European Transport Policy for 2010: Time to Decide' (EC, 2001) which proposed 60 or so measures to develop a transport system capable of shifting the balance between modes of transport, revitalising the railways, promoting transport by sea and inland waterway and controlling the growth in air transport. The White Paper supported the sustainable development strategy adopted by the European Council in Gothenburg in 2001 and proposed the development of the trans-European transport networks. The Trans-European Network of Transport (TEN-T) is complemented by Trans-European Energy Network (TEN-E or TEN-Energy) and the Trans-European telecommunications network (eTEN). The policy objective of the TEN-T was the establishment of a single, multimodal network covering both traditional ground-based structures and equipment (including intelligent transport systems) to enable safe and efficient traffic. It is believed that such a network would promote mobility of people and goods within the European Union. Only latterly has there been an increased focus on reducing carbon emissions.

In relation to local transport in particular, the Department for Transport's white paper 'Creating Growth, Cutting Carbon: Making Sustainable Local Transport Happen' (2011) acknowledged that transport had a role to play in helping to create economic growth and to tackle climate change by cutting carbon emissions.

Therefore, it is the aim of this chapter to examine alternatives to air travel, by way of discussing innovations by transport providers and travel operators in the provision of non-aviation based tourism products. It will begin by examining national and international policies on sustainability and climate change as they relate to travel, in the process reviewing the different behavioural choice models used by the aviation industry and the individual consumer. We will then discuss a range of examples of how the travel and transport organisations are responding to the challenge of sustainability and examine how they are seeking to adapt and create travel alternatives and holidays that reduce the reliance on the traditional aviation and car based holidays.

Behavioural Context for Changes in Transport Mode Choice

The aim here is to explore the theoretical and practical considerations of mode choice behaviour. Concepts from the science of travel demand forecasting and consumer choice theory are brought into focus, prior to discussing how barriers to the adoption of new transport modes might be overcome.

The demand for passenger air travel through UK airports is split into separate markets reflecting "… the likelihood of different trends, strength of driving forces, and availability of data" (DfT, 2007: 13). The UK Air Passenger Demand Model is an aggregate model, which forecasts demand for air passenger transport using key variables such as measures of economic activity (for example, consumer spending, GDP, or international trade), air fares, and exchange rates (Civil Aviation Authority, 2008). For example, the demand for leisure trips is expected to be driven by income or consumer spending, and, to some extent, is affected by air fares (DfT, 2007). In comparison travel for business purposes is expected to be driven more by factors such as international trade and may not be significantly affected by air fares at the aggregate, national level. Similarly, the strength of the causal factors varies between global regions, reflecting different stages in economic development. Demand is therefore based on:

- the global region the passenger is travelling to or from (for example, North America);
- whether the passenger is a UK or overseas resident;
- the passenger's journey purpose (leisure or business);
- whether the passenger is on an international scheduled, international charter, or domestic flight; and
- whether the passenger is making an international to international connection at a UK airport (as part of a journey between two other nations) (DfT, 2007: 13).

Transport models are typically validated by analysing the implied 'elasticities of demand' (DfT, 2007). It is important to note that these elasticities are outputs from the model and not inputs. Table 3.2 summarises the central estimates for the long run price elasticities for air travel in the UK. As would be expected intuitively, household income is a strong driver of demand for air travel for leisure purposes within the UK. Household income is less correlated to the demand for travel by chartered airline – in effect confirming the notion that people have a desire to "get away from it" during holiday periods.

Consumer Choice Theory

In contrast to the aggregate approach to demand forecasting embodied in the air passenger demand model above, an alternative approach to forecasting demand is to use consumer choice theory. This theory attempts to explain why consumers make the decisions about purchasing goods and services that they do, given that the market sets the price of a good. A choice theory is a collection of procedures that defines the following elements (Ben-Akiva and Lerman, 1985):

- the decision maker;
- the alternatives available;
- the attributes of those alternatives; and
- the decision rules and constraints.

Therefore the four elements of the consumer choice model are:

- the consumer's income;
- the price of the goods to be purchased;
- the consumer's tastes;
- and the assumption that consumers act selfishly to get the best outcome for themselves.

Table 3.2   Elasticities of travel demand from the UK National Air Travel Demand model

Sector	Share of demand	Elasticity with respect to income	Elasticity with respect to fare
UK business	8	1.5	-
UK leisure	29	1.4	-1.0
UK charter	16	0.4	-0.4
Foreign business	6	0.6	-
Foreign leisure	11	0.7	-0.2
International to international interliners	11	0.7	-0.3
Domestic	17	2.1	-0.3
Overall	**100**	**1.3**	**-0.5**

Source: DfT, 2009.

It is assumed that consumers are perfectly informed of the cost of the goods to be purchased. The prices of goods and the consumer's income together define the budget constraint of the consumer. Consumer tastes are included in the model through three assumptions. The first assumption is that consumers seek to maximise the utility, the satisfaction that the consumption of the goods provides and transport incurs a dis-utility and thus travellers seek to minimise the dis-utility incurred. The consumer thus seeks to maximise utility through the selection not just of mode and route, but also of destination.

It should be noted that in discussing alternatives to air travel, the act of travelling may actually generate positive utility, for example, the pleasure of travelling on a preserved railway or a cruise. The second assumption made is that consumers prefer more rather than less. Where the goods under consideration are not beneficial to the consumer, such as air pollution, the good is redefined so that the assumption is satisfied, for example by considering clean air rather than polluted air. The third and final assumption is that the consumer chooses a consumption bundle such that utility, in this case the holiday experience, is maximised. The micro-economic theory of consumer choice forms one theoretical basis from which it is possible to assess how it might be possible to influence travel behaviour. Note though, that there is no universally agreed model of behavioural change.

Influencing Travel Behaviour

Regardless of the theoretical framework applied, conclusive evidence from a variety of diverse disciplinary sources shows that influencing attitudes rarely leads directly to behaviour change. The DfT (2006) recognised that there exists a gap between attitude (towards climate change) and individual behaviour.

In considering how to bridge this gap, it was concluded that there is a need to understand behaviour change from a number of different perspectives (anthropological, socio-psychological and economic) and at a number of different levels in society.

In terms of the interventions necessary to influence travel behaviour, Defra (CCC, 2009) has conducted research into climate change communications and has identified four Es of behavioural change principles that need to be followed within a social marketing strategy aimed at promoting more sustainable behaviours. These can be usefully applied to behavioural change strategies employed in a transport context:

- Enabling – for example, making it easier by removing barriers and providing alternatives and opportunities for choice.
- Engaging – this involves the target audience from the outset by building a relationship with the target passengers over time.
- Encouraging – this refers to the use of information, education, incentives, penalties and the law to encourage, and where necessary, enforce behaviour change.
- Exemplifying – this means setting an example and ensuring consistency. For widespread behavioural change to occur, environmental organisations, councils, transport providers and governments must provide consistent information and demonstrate compliance with their own advice.
- Catalyst – this is required if the package of policies is still not enough to stimulate sufficient behavioural change. For instance, evidence shows that airline usage is self-sustaining because attitudes that are consistent with a modal choice are reinforced by the mode chosen.

In summary promoting changes in the way people travel for leisure purposes is more complex than simply expecting such a shift to take place in response to price signals. Leadership by example is a key resultant of the techniques for promoting behavioural change listed above. The destination of holidays taken by people in the public eye is thus more than just a personal decision – it is such opinion formers that others look for leadership.

The Contemporary Non-Aviation Tourist Market

This section considers some of the most viable alternatives on offer to the consumer and the potential developments that may take place. Two concepts need to be introduced here. First there is the potential for another mode to substitute for the line haul (long distance) part of a tourism journey, and the second is for the mode itself to be considered part of the holiday experience.

Rail-Based Trips

The choice between rail and air transport is often one of cost, convenience and travel time although not all trips are accessible by rail, for example Spain to Morocco, UK to Ireland. The use of trains as a transport mode can be a motivating factor in itself, whereby the train provides access to the destination but is also the destination itself, for example the Orient Express, and heritage railways such as North Yorkshire Moors Railway.

Rail is considered less harmful for the environment once operating as CO_2 emissions for trains are two-ten times lower CO_2 than road transport or air travel (Mintel, 2008). Rail provides an acceptable alternative to flying for domestic travel, but less acceptable for long distance routes.

The Committee on Climate Change (CCC, 2010) suggests:

- On journeys of less than 400km conventional rail will usually be faster than air for point-to-point journeys.
- On journeys below 800km high-speed rail has the potential to enable significant modal shift.
- However, above 800km the air option is likely to be faster in terms of overall door-to-door journey time and as a result the rail option would need to have other advantages (for example, significantly lower prices) to be competitive.

High-Speed Rail

Rail is able to compete with air transport for journeys of 500km and more if the speed of the train is of the order of 300km/h or greater – this is known as High Speed Rail (HSR). Air travel now includes significant excess time for security checks and baggage deposit and reclaim to which rail passengers are not subjected.

The expansion of high-speed infrastructure across Europe is part of the planned Trans-European Network for Transport (TEN-T) described above. Whilst in mainland Europe the network is now well developed with further extensions likely, passengers from the UK outside London face considerable time and cost to get to the high-speed railhead at St Pancras International. High speed rail can therefore be considered a (limited) substitute for air travel for non-UK holiday destinations.

Eurostar – Ski Train

One example where HSR can contribute to an attractive holiday offer is for journeys to the French Alps from London. Leaving London generally on a Friday night, the Eurostar train takes approximately 7.5 hours to access Bourg St Maurice. Skiers then have all day Saturday and Sunday to ski, returning by train overnight arriving in London on a Monday morning. Research conducted on behalf of Eurostar by Paul Watkiss Associates (Eurostar, 2010) claims that Eurostar emits a tenth of the CO_2 of flying to the same core destinations as evidenced in Table 3.3. Eurostar

Table 3.3   Carbon emissions comparison chart

6.6kg CO_2 per passenger: Return travel by Eurostar from St Pancras International to Paris Gare du Nord.
102.8kg CO_2 per passenger: Return flight from London Luton to Paris Charles de Gaulle.
8.2kg CO_2 per passenger: Return travel by Eurostar from St Pancras International to Brussels-Midi/Zuid.
140.6kg CO_2 per passenger: Return flight from London Heathrow to Brussels.
14kg CO_2 per passenger: Return travel by Eurostar from St Pancras International to Bourg-St-Maurice.
147.8kg CO_2 per passenger: Return flight from London Stansted to Geneva.
13kg CO_2 per passenger: Return travel by Eurostar from St Pancras International to Avignon.
197.2kg CO_2 per passenger: Return flight from London Heathrow to Marseilles.
5.8kg CO_2 per passenger: Return travel by Eurostar from St Pancras International to Disneyland® Resort Paris.
102.8kg CO_2 per passenger: Return flight from London Luton to Paris Charles de Gaulle.

Source: Eurostar (2010).

have also committed to reduce their carbon emissions by 35 per cent, to offset their carbon emissions and to commit to a 10 point plan to reduce other impacts on the environment (Eurostar, 2010).

Great Rail Journeys – Conventional and Heritage Rail

Great Rail Journeys (GRJ) is the UK market leader for escorted rail holidays and has expanded the number of tours on offer in the last four years. The Great Rail Journeys group now has several sub brands: Great Rail Journeys (GRJ), RailSelect, Treyn Holidays and The Rail Discovery Company, and currently it offers over 200 routes in 40 countries (Great Rail Journeys, 2010). The packages include the rail travel, accommodation, excursions and city tours and are escorted by a tour manager. The majority of trips are European, departing from London on the Eurostar although the return segment for longer journeys is often by air and long haul trips include return flights. More recent product developments include cruising, with the rail component to access the start of the cruise.

The company has been operating for 25 years and since 2005 has seen sales grow from 19,000 to 34,000 passengers annually. In the past year rail trips to Europe grew by 30 per cent to reach 25,000 (Great Rail Journeys, 2010). Treyn offers European escorted tours at a lower price point. Prices are lower than the GRJ as they include more basic accommodation, fewer excursions and fewer inclusive meals where as the Rail Select brand offers unescorted, tailor-made holidays for independent travellers. GRJ has also recently launched a programme of holidays by rail aimed at single travellers.

Conventional or heritage rail therefore provides an alternative to air travel through the mode being considered as part of the holiday experience.

Future of Rail

The development of High-Speed Rail (HSR) links would improve the accessibility of many European destinations, although these would not necessarily make all destinations equally attractive as tourism destinations. Although the HSR is relatively well-developed in Europe, there is only one high-speed line in the UK, linking the Channel Tunnel Rail Link (CTRL) with London. The alignment of the proposed second line (HS2) is currently the subject of political debate within the UK and is unlikely to be operational for some 15-20 years, although it should be noted that it is intended that this line will operate at the current upper limit of speed achievable on rail which is 400kph.

Road Transport

Road transport is the most popular form of transport for leisure travel, and of this the private motor car dominates. The ease of access, mobility and luggage capacity enable car drivers to travel freely and as car occupancy increases the price per person carried declines. Increased prosperity has led to an increase in the number of private cars owned. The proportion of car-owning households has risen from 14 per cent of households in 1951, to over 50 per cent in 1969, and to 75 per cent by 2009 (DfT, 2010), although the rate of increase has declined over recent years. This convenience has led to a heavy reliance on the car as a form of tourist transportation. Confidence and availability have led to rapid growth in independent international travel especially within Europe where border crossing are swift. For the UK, the crossing of the Channel or North Sea means an additional cost, but this can be circumvented by the hiring of cars abroad.

Although private and hire cars are considered to be less sustainable, they do however provide a key role in travel and tourism products. The debate as to whether car usage should be encouraged tends to focus only on the environmental impacts, which although key to the sustainability agenda, does overshadow the other positive impacts. Sustainability is providing socio-economic benefits to all stakeholders that are fairly distributed, including stable employment and income-earning opportunities and social services to host communities, and contributing to poverty alleviation. Tourists using private car have the potential to distribute wealth throughout destinations that may not have been visited. ; for example, The Cyprus Sustainable Tourism initiative is a Cyprus charity affiliated to the Travel Foundation have designed a series of self-drive village routes, encouraging tourists to discover the 'real Cyprus' by driving to villages that are less visited and have interesting attractions such as small museums. Members of the CSTI include Sunvil, TUI, Thomas Cook, village communities, village producers and crafts people, various environmental organisations and the Cyprus Tourism Organisation.

Although the Village Routes Initiative can be criticised as it encourages road transport, the benefits of encouraging tourists to visit less well know destinations and thus provide economic benefits to lesser known locations is considered to outweigh the environmental costs.

Caravans and Motors Homes

In the UK, camping and caravanning holidays regularly account for 20 per cent of domestic bed nights and generate a national income measured in billions (Mintel, 2009). Provisions within the parks have been changing for many years, aiming to attract the repeat visitors and new market segments. Parks aiming at the family market contain aqua parks, amusements and alternative activities. However, camping and caravanning tourism has been in a state of decline as it has been perceived a low status holiday, and other more desirable forms of tourism were affordable. Mintel's prediction for the next five years is that the overall market will grow to 12.59 million holidaymakers by 2014 (Mintel, 2009)

Coach

Coach travel is often essential form of transport within most EU countries, providing transport for domestic and international travel. Carbon emissions per passenger per Km are lower than by car; for example, driving 100 miles by car produces 18.34kg CO_2, whereas by coach only 4.67kg CO_2 (National Express, 2010) making it a more eco efficient offering than air travel (Gossling et al., 2005).

Coach travel can be divided into three categories: long distance, coach tours and hire coaches. Coach travel has the benefit of moving large numbers of passengers using a single transport product thus reducing the carbon emissions per person. Coach as a mode is differentiated from the use of "coach like" vehicles as buses, by the requirement (in the UK) for local buses to stop at least once every 15 miles (in order to qualify as a local bus and therefore enable the operator to claim Bus Service Operators Grant, previously Fuel Duty Rebate). Coach travel also tends (but does not have to be) pre-booked with ticket purchased off-vehicle. Coaches carry a minimum of 17 people and standing is not permitted.

Long Distance Intercity Coach Trips

Long distance coach trips are often cheaper than either air or rail alternatives. Companies such as National Express, City Link, Greyhound and Megabus provide frequent express intercity coach travel. This is particularly important as it provides access to/from destinations that have lost their rail connections and opportunities for passengers who do not have access to cars. National Express, for example, serves over 1,000 destinations including airports and holiday parks. They provide good value for money as they are cheaper than rail alternatives. However, long distance coach travel does have several problems, particularly with perceived comfort compared with rail (not just in terms of seat quality, but also in the ability to do work or pursue leisure interests, and in catering and sanitary facilities) and potential journey time unreliability through road traffic congestion.

Package Coach Trips

The benefits of coach packages are considerable as they are time and cost efficient for passengers. The alternative to the coach would be private vehicle as the routes would not be time efficient or sometimes even accessible by public transport. Routes are designed to visit many locations over relatively short periods of time. This high level of mobility enables route construction to incorporate the 'honey pot' attractions as well as less visited attractions that would be unachievable utilising public transport. The benefits for passengers include reduced risk for overseas destinations, less daunting for older passengers and ease of access. Primarily the markets for coach travel are older age groups, single passengers and the youth market due to their cost. According to Mintel (2009) there has been a small growth in the UK market for coach tours, but a decrease in overseas coach trips. The lack of growth makes is hard for operators to increase their product range.

The coach market is not without issues. The heavy reliance on the older age customer is concerning for operators as the next generation of older passengers may not be as likely to take part in such provision. The singles market that is a key segment for the coach sector are now being targeted by overseas packages with specialist singles holiday and reduced single supplements, which means that competition with air-based packages is greater, in particular for short breaks as coach travel is time intensive.

Clearly the opportunity for the coach market is to diversify their product and seek new markets to sustain their income. Recent developments include themed breaks, 'Hop on and Hop off' buses which are designed for independent travellers and allow passengers to alight and then recommence the journey when they want (for example, Haggis Adventures, Busabout Europe and Shamrocker).

Cycling

Cycling holidays are an expanding niche market and have been growing by an estimated five per cent per annum in recent years, driven by a buoyant overseas segment, whilst domestic cycling trips have remained stable (Mintel, 2009). An estimated 500,000 dedicated cycling holidays were taken in 2008; 100,000 overseas and 400,000 domestic (Mintel, 2009) The market is divided into leisure cycling, which usually is based on routes either guided or self guided, off road (mountain biking) and cyclo-sportives, which are competitive events. The degree of cycling within a holiday is variable, from excursionists, where cycles are used for day trips, to long distance routes for serious cyclists.

In Europe, organised self-led tours account for 44 per cent of the organised cycling holiday market (Mintel, 2009) whereas packaged leisure cycle holidays are escorted tours provided by an operator who prearrange accommodation and provide itineraries accounts for 56 per cent of the organised cycling holiday market in Europe (Mintel, 2009). The tour manager/escort will provide guidance for the route and is seen as a source of local knowledge, which is particularly important when cycling in remote regions or long haul destinations. Cycling is seen as the most desirable mode of transport after walking due to the low carbon emissions, but package cycling holidays may not be as 'environmentally friendly' as first considered. Cycling destinations are becoming more remote, with operators such as Exodus, Saddle Skedaddle, and CTC Cycling Holidays offering cycling holiday in destinations such as Morocco, Cuba, Tanzania and India where clearly air transport is necessary to access the tour. With the exception of self guided tours, operators will provide backup assistance vans that carry additional bikes, the passenger luggage and room for passengers if necessary.

While the main operators in the adventure field offer international cycling holidays, there has been a growth in interest in domestic cycling holiday. Traditionally the domain of the self packaging cyclist, the growth of prearranged domestic packages has grown by over 20 per cent (Mintel, 2009). In addition to the larger operators, such as Headwater and Exodus (both owned by TUI), Explore and Inntravel, the market is often serviced by small suppliers focusing on local destinations such as the Lake District, Hadrian's Wall and Dumfries and Galloway. Sustrans (Sustainable Transport) have developed a national network of cycle routes which provides access to 10,000 miles of signed cycle ways, for example, the Bath to Bristol trail, which has more than one million visits each year (Sustrans, 2010).

Walking

Walking is seen as the UK's favourite pastime, and an integral component within holidays, as it tends to be a fundamental part of most holidays from sightseeing and shopping to walking as the main pursuit of the holiday. Walking holidays, where the main purpose is to walk most days between accommodations points, is usually examined within the context of activity based holidays. Walking holidays may be independent or guided, with providers of guided tours including Explore, The Adventure Company, Ramblers Worldwide Holidays and Exodus. Adventure walking tours provide a tour manager and a set route, with baggage often being carried by supporting vehicles or animals. With no carbon emissions,

Table 3.4   UK international sea passenger movements by overseas country, 1950-2009 (000)

	1950	1959	1969	1979	1989	1999	2009
Ro-ro passengers on short sea routes							
Belgium	394	-	2,304	4,421	3,444	1,592	566
Denmark	83	-	142	413	292	188	99
France	1,666	-	4,408	11,112	19,246	22,454	16,002
Germany	-	-	101	261	178	222	1
Irish Republic	1,273	1,503	1,868	2,342	2,715	4,343	2,930
Netherlands	367	-	944	2,044	2,365	1,939	1,685
Norway	61	-	138	97	144	208	1
Spain	-	-	132	60	119	346	340
Sweden	62	-	148	308	263	87	3
Others	37	-	19	16	10	3	-
All short sea routes	3,942	6,141	10,204	21,074	28,776	31,381	21,626
Passenger on long sea journeys	587	609	345	40	31	26	55
Passengers on cruises beginning or ending at UK ports	-	-	-	175	129	445	1,347
All international passengers	**4,529**	**6,750**	**10,549**	**21,289**	**28,936**	**31,852**	**23,028**

Source: Transport Statistics Great Britain, 2010.

walking is clearly the most desirable form of transport although to access most destinations, some form of alternative transport is necessary, for example train, private car or coach.

Rural walking tours, through more remote regions are beneficial to the local communities as they provide a source of income and employment. Destinations that are seasonal may be able to extend their operating season by offering walking routes, for example, walking in Northern Greece around Metsovo, provides the traditional ski destination with summer visitors.

Ferries

Ferry services are long-established methods for crossing the bodies of water around the UK. However, the ferry industry is in decline and many sailings having ceased (see Table 3.4).

Ferry services still operate to mainland Europe but as a result of competition from the Channel Tunnel and low cost carriers, a number of changes have been made to add value to the ferry services. These include investment in new fleets, pooling services and the introduction of more crossings on shorter routes. Further developments include the provision of leisure services, retailing and entertainment to attract more customers and the operation of packages similar to cruises.

Many destinations in Europe are accessible by ferries and they provide a key transport for local communities. For example, many of the Greek Islands are still only accessible by ferry. The larger islands are now building airports but visiting the small islands still needs to be undertaken by ferry. Public ferries in Greece are still time consuming and problematic due to local weather conditions which make travel plans difficult to arrange, for example the Meltemi winds can often reduce sailing departures and high winds make trips uncomfortable.

Cruising (within Europe)

This section focuses on the European cruise markets, rather than the global cruises that are now being scrutinised for their environmental impacts. According to Climate Care (Responsible Travel, 2010), a cruise liner such as Queen Mary 2 emits 0.43kg of CO_2 per passenger mile, compared with 0.257kg for a long-haul flight (even allowing for the further damage of emissions being produced in the upper atmosphere). The cruise industry has seen phenomenal growth over the last decade, with a growth of over 50 per cent in volume over the last five years (Mintel, 2009).

One of the key growth areas is the short cruise market. The number of cruise passengers leaving from UK ports has increased by 23 per cent in the last year (Mintel, 2009). "More than 4.8 million passengers embarked on their cruises from a European port, a 3.2 per cent increase over 2008, with over 75 per cent of these being European nationals" (European Cruise Council, 2010 p. 1). Destinations from the UK include Amsterdam, Rotterdam, the Baltic, Zeebrugge, Bilbao and various parts along Scotland's west coast. Longer trips include routes through the Mediterranean and North Africa.

British cruises have grown considerably, surpassed only by the German and Italian markets. Over 4.9 million European residents booked cruises, a 12.1 per cent increase over 2008, representing nearly 29 per cent of all cruise passengers worldwide (European Cruise Council, 2010). The growth in this market is attributed to a number of reasons, in particular the desire for consumers to see many sites, without the need to change accommodation. The traditional formal cruise is being replaced by informal dining and optional on-board activities, where the emphasis has been changed from the destinations to the ships themselves such that today's cruise liner's now include cinemas, theatres, a range of dining experiences, lectures, spas, gyms and family shows. For example, MSC Mediterranean cruises offer activities such as dance classes, cookery lessons, spa facilities and shows, while children are catered for with kids clubs and gaming facilities. This has attracted newer markets to the cruises, which hitherto were seen as old fashioned and expensive. New segments include the younger demographic, family market, and even weddings.

Taster cruises are offered by operators to encourage new customers to try holidays by water without expending their annual leave. The ease of use, for example using pounds sterling on board enables consumers to budget their trip. At a time when the exchange rate is reducing spending power in Europe, the use of sterling may be seen as a safer environment for holiday spending. The all inclusive prices ensure that families can maintain their budgets and short haul trips are seen as cost effective for many larger groups although any additional excursions are charged separately, so often the overall cost can increase considerably.

Despite the obvious economic benefits of cruises to destinations given that each passenger visit at a European port generates an average total passenger expenditure of approximately €98 (European Cruise Council, 2010) their operation is not without criticism, particularly for the effects that it can have on destinations and eco systems. Large numbers of passengers disembark and spend limited amounts of time at destinations, thus reducing the economic benefits for the destinations and the increased pressure on limited resources while in situ. For example large number of tourists arriving when a cruise ship docks, can lead to problems of "... inadequate infrastructure because of the sudden increased passenger flows" (McCarthy, 2003 cited in Gibson and Bentley, 2007).

There are opportunities for short haul cruise operators to improve their environmental credentials by considering how they operate. For example, carbon emissions can be reduced by considering tide, current and weather conditions closely and minimising the fuel used. Locally purchased food provides income for host communities or encouraging passengers to eat in the disembarkation points. Some operators are using alternative vessels for transport, for example, caïques in Greece, sailing boats in Scotland and gullets in Turkey where the motors are used as secondary sources of power and wind as the main source.

Conclusion

As growth for travel and tourism products continues to grow, so too does the need for transport and tourism operators to meet the changing demands of the consumer and the global need to be more sustainable. Although consumer behaviour is demonstrating concern for the environment and some changes in purchasing behaviour are evident, there is little evidence to support the belief that consumers will abandon air travel industry for more environmentally benign transportation methods. In this 'cash rich, time poor' society, the maximisation of the holiday period is still critical to the consumers demand. Recent interest in non-aviation based holidays is certainly growing; but there is an emerging pattern of trip making which is 'mixed mode' tourism. The growth of activity based holidays, such as cycling and walking, is evident but this growth appears to be in medium and long haul destinations, where the air component is necessary. Clearly, it will be difficult to reshape the demand for air travel. However, the following principles could be adopted.

Enabling

- Enabling consumers to make informed choices. The consumer choice process for purchasing non aviation products needs to provide consumers with the information they require to make these decisions; for example, the carbon emissions for the transport methods, in particular the alternatives to air. National Express and Eurostar both enable passenger to see carbon emission savings on the websites.
- Enabling the consumer to switch transportation modes. At present, it is difficult to find alternatives to the air component of package holidays. Few tour operators will offer rail alternatives to be arranged as part of their packages.
- Enabling holidaymakers wishing to "build" their own holidays. The complexities involved in negotiating the international rail travel network means that consumers are unwilling to take risks in purchasing overland journeys. Websites, such as seat61.com, can provide information and ticket booking links for land based alternatives.
- While in the destination, consumers need to be encouraged to utilise public transport where convenient thus the provision of information by Destination Management Organisations and tour operators needs to be clear, accessible and useable.

Engaging

- Consumers need to change their attitudes by adopting and adapting more sustainable behaviour, for example to see the journey as part of the holiday, rather than a means to an end. Companies such as Great Rail Journeys encourage their passengers to enjoy the transport, in this case the train, both as the route to the destination and the destination itself.
- To increase public engagement with the alternatives to air and car, consumers need to be encouraged to change their behaviour within the destinations. To use public transport and to disperse tourism in the surrounding areas outside resorts.

Encouraging

- International and national policy making will be pivotal in the reduction of air based tourism. Government involvement is essential to promote changes in modal choice. They can encourage these consumer changes as the taxation and overall cost of holidays will increase. Fuel prices rises are being passed on to consumers and certainly, this may influence overall demand.
- Providing information is essential but it will not promote behavioural change alone as awareness is not the same as action. Incentives, penalties and legislation are likely to be used to promote behavioural changes, such as the use of restrictive policies. For example, limiting airport capacities, reducing access to destinations by private car, and investment in public transport systems.
- Pressure groups such as Friends of the Earth, the Travel Foundation and Greenpeace will become critical in the dissemination of information and provision of alternatives for consumers.

Exemplifying

- For consumer behavioural change to take place, the message needs to be consistent. For example environmental organisations, councils, governments must all demonstrate commitment to the changes. Setting a 'good example' will be key to raising awareness and convincing those consumers who are reluctant to change.

Catalysing

- An interventionist approach becomes necessary if the package of policies is insufficient to stimulate sufficient behavioural change. Any intervention strategy will need to establish new patterns of behaviour and attitudes, for example, compulsory offsetting of carbon emissions with the overall cost of air-inclusive packages.

In conclusion the air component of package holidays is still crucial to the tourism industry and it is unlikely, in the short term, to be replaced by land based alternatives. High Speed Rail may play some role, particularly in city breaks, but requires continued investment in the necessary infrastructure to support this. The greatest contribution to promoting alternatives to air travel for tourism probably lies in changing the expectations of the consumer – a change in which all stakeholders in the tourism system will need to play an active role.

References

Ben-Akiva, M. and Lerman, S. (1985) *Discrete Choice Analysis*. Cambridge, MA: MIT Press.

Civil Aviation Authority (2008) Recent trends in growth of UK air passenger demand. Available at: http://www.caa.co.uk/docs/589/erg_recent_trends_final_v2.pdf [Accessed: 12 December 2010].

Committee on Climate Change (2009) Technical Appendix to Chapter 6 & 7. Available at: http://www.theccc.org.uk/pdfs/Technical%20Appendix%20social%20research%20background%206&7%20final%20version%20.pdf [Accessed: 21 September 2010].

Committee on Climate Change (2010) Aviation Report. Available at: http://downloads.theccc.org.uk/Aviation%20Report%2009/21667B%20CCC%20Chapter%203.pdf [Accessed: 14 December 2010].

Committee on Climate Change (2010) Climate Change Act. Available at: http://www.theccc.org.uk/about-the-ccc/climate-change-act [Accessed: 12 December 2010].

Department for Transport (2006) A review of public attitudes to climate change and transport: Summary report. Available at: http://www.dft.gov.uk/pgr/sustainable/areviewofpublicattitudestocl5731?page=1#a1000 [Accessed: 10 October 2010].

Department for Transport (2007) UK Air Passenger Demand and CO2 Forecasts. Available at: http://webarchive.nationalarchives.gov.uk/+/http:/www.dft.gov.uk/pgr/aviation/atf/ukairdemandandco2forecasts/airpassdemandfullreport.pdf [Accessed: 10 October 2010].

Department for Transport (2009) Transport Trends 2009. Available at: http://www.dft.gov.uk/pgr/statistics/datatablespublications/trends/current/section6pa.pdf [Accessed: 10 December 2010].

Department for Transport (2009) UK Air Passenger Demand and CO2 Forecasts Available at: http://webarchive.nationalarchives.gov.uk/+/http:/www.dft.gov.uk/pgr/aviation/atf/co2forecasts09/co2forecasts09.pdf [Accessed: 10 September 2010].

Department for Transport (2011) Cm 7996 'Creating Growth, Cutting Carbon: Making Sustainable Local Transport Happen' 19 January.

Dickinson, J. and Lumsdon, L. (2010) *Slow Travel and Tourism*. London: Earthscan.

European Commission (2001) 'European transport policy for 2010: Time to decide' Available at: http://ec.europa.eu/transport/strategies/2001_white_paper_en.htm [Accessed: 17 December 2010].

European Cruise Council (2010) The Cruise Industry. Available at: http://www.irn-research.com/files/4513/0224/9897/ECC-Report-20107-LR.pdf [Accessed: 10 December 2010].

Eurostar (2010) Tread Lightly. Available at:http://www.eurostar.com/pdf/treadlightly/reports/treadlightlyreport_uk_uk.pdf [Accessed: 17 December 2010].

Gibson, P. and Bentley, M. (2007) A Study of Impacts – Cruise Tourism and the South West of England. *Journal of Travel & Tourism Marketing*, 20(3), 63-77.

Gossling, S., Peeters, P., Ceron, J.P., Dubois, G., Patterson, T. and Richardson, R.B. (2005) The eco-efficiency of tourism. *Ecological Economics*, 43(2-3), 199-211.

Great Rail Journeys. Available at: http://www.greatrail.com/ [Accessed: 20 December 2010].

Intergovernmental Panel Climate Change (IPCC) (2000) *Aviation and the Global Atmosphere.*

Mintel (2008) *Rail Travel – Europe*. London: Mintel.

Mintel (2009) *Bus and Coach Travel – Europe*. London: Mintel.

Mintel (2009) *Camping and Caravanning – Europe.* London: Mintel.

Mintel (2009) *Cycling Holidays – UK – July 2009*. London: Mintel.

National Express (2010) National Express Carbon Calculator. Available at: http://www.nationalexpress.com/coach/OurService/CarbonEmissionsCalculator.cfm [Accessed: 17 December 2010].

Responsible Travel (2010) 'Are Cruise Liners a Viable Alternative to Flying'. Available at: http://www.responsibletravel.com/copy/are-cruise-liners-a-viable-alternative-to-flying [Accessed: 14 October 2010].

Sunvil (2010) The Cyprus Sustainable Tourism Initiative (CSTI). Available at: http://www.sunvil.co.uk/sunvil/home/images/pdfs/Cyprus/brochure_cyprus_csti_wine.pdf [Accessed: 10 October 2010].

Sustrans (2010) National Cycle Network. Available at: http://www.sustrans.org.uk/what-we-do/national-cycle-network [Accessed: 12 December 2010].

Tyndall Centre for Climate Change Research (2006) Living Within a Carbon Budget. Available at: http://www.foe.co.uk/resource/reports/living_carbon_budget.pdf [Accessed: 10 December 2010].

United Nations Framework Convention on Climate Change (UNFCCC) (2010) Report of the Conference of the Parties on its fifteenth session, held in Copenhagen 7-19 December 2009.

UNWTO (2010) Towards a Low carbon Travel and Tourism Sector. Available at: http://www.unwto.org/sdt/mission/en/mission.php?op=1 [Accessed: 20 December 2010].

United Nations Framework Convention on Climate Change (UNFCCC) (2010) Available at: http://unfccc.int/resource/docs/convkp/kpeng.pdf [Accessed: 21 December 2010].

Chapter 4

Corporate Social Responsibility in the Tour Operating Industry: The Case of Dutch Outbound Tour Operators

Ferry van de Mosselaer, René van der Duim and Jakomijn van Wijk

Introduction

Corporate Social Responsibility (CSR) has become a leading concept in contemporary management and business literature (Egri and Ralston, 2008; Zadek, 2004). Numerous industries and firms, both in emerging and mature economies, have put CSR theory into practice by adopting responsible policies and practices like housekeeping measures, implementation of Codes of Conduct and certification schemes, development of green products or services and the formation of strategic partnerships with stakeholders like NGOs and local communities. This development towards CSR is also noticeable in the tourism sector, considered as one of the world's largest industries. Social and environmental issues are increasingly taken into account within tourism firms' daily operations, along their supply chain and in holiday destinations where they operate. Although the pros and cons of tourism development have been subject to debate ever since the 1970s (see for example Turner and Ash, 1975), only under the influence of broader post-Rio 1992 discussions on sustainable development, have they become part of the business agenda of tourism enterprises.

While CSR activities have been extensively studied in the hospitality industry (for example, Bohdanowicz and Zientara, 2008; Henderson, 2007; Holcomb, Upchurch and Okumus, 2007) and the airline industry (for example, Cowper-Smith and de Grosbois, 2011; Lynes and Andrachuk, 2008), understanding of CSR in the tour operating industry is limited (Dodds and Kuehnel, 2010). Addressing this knowledge gap is essential, as tour operators have a central position in the tourism supply chain and thus play a key role in directing tourism flows and coordinating supply chains, especially in the mainstream holiday market (Budeanu, 2009; Van Wijk and Persoon, 2006). Accordingly, this chapter draws on an intensive case study of Dutch outbound tour operations to examine how tour operators engage in CSR. Over a period of more than two decades, Dutch tour operators have increasingly adopted distinct management tools to enhance their CSR performance. Our case study presents a brief historical outline of this transformation process, identifies the main management tools in use and draws conclusions on the prospects of CSR in outbound tour operations.

As such, this chapter makes two important contributions to the discussion on the role of tour operators in "steps towards sustainability". First, our study contributes to the academic literature on CSR in the tour operations industry. Although the importance of tour operators in enhancing sustainability in tourism supply chains is widely recognised, few studies to date have systematically examined the generative mechanisms behind tour operators' engagement in CSR. Our study reveals the pivotal role trade associations play in this transformation process, thereby addressing Tyler and Dinan's (2001) call for more research on business-interest organisations in tourism. Second, the present work nuances the dominant view of tour operators as defensive players (for example, Mowforth and Munt, 2009). By showing how Dutch frontrunner firms act in concert with their trade association and sustainable tourism proponents to develop and apply new management tools that address sustainability issues, this study illustrates the innovative role tour operators may play in transforming the tourism sector.

The remainder of this chapter comprises four parts. Firstly, we introduce the concept of CSR in the tourism industry. Then, we discuss the scope of CSR in the tour operations industry. Thirdly, we present the case study of CSR in Dutch outbound tour operations. Finally, we draw conclusions.

CSR in Tourism

Scholarly and managerial attention for CSR has rapidly evolved in the tourism business community as a consequence of increasing concerns over the negative impacts of tourism on the natural and socio-cultural environment. The International Standards Organization (ISO, 2007, as cited in Dodds and Kuehnel, 2010: 222) defines social responsibility as:

> The responsibility of an organization for the impacts of its decisions and activities on society and the environment, through transparent and ethical behaviour that contributes to sustainable development, health and the welfare of society; takes into account the expectations of stakeholders; is in compliance with applicable law and consistent with international norms of behaviour; and is integrated throughout the organization and practiced in its relationships.

Based on an extensive literature review into CSR definitions, Dahlsrud (2008) concludes that consistently five dimensions are used in defining the concept of CSR; the environmental, social, economic, stakeholder and voluntariness dimension. The *environmental dimension* points at the relation between business and the natural environment. Examples in the tourism setting include the relation between airlines and emissions (Gössling and Peeters, 2007; Mak and Chan, 2006; Lynes and Andrachuk, 2008); cruise lines and waste disposal (Johnson, 2002);

hotels and natural resource management (Bohdanowicz and Martinac, 2007; Le, Hollenhorst, Harris, McLaughlin and Shook, 2006; Scanlon, 2007); and tourism and biodiversity (Van der Duim and Caalders, 2002). The *social dimension* refers to the business and society linkage. Social dimensions in tourism are found in issues like sex tourism (Garrick, 2005; Kibicho, 2005; Montgomery, 2008); fair trade in tourism (Bohdanowicz and Zientara, 2009; Cleverdon and Kalisch, 2000); and pro-poor tourism (Mitchell and Ashley, 2010). The *economic dimension* of CSR focuses on the firm's contribution to socio-economic development, for example illustrated by the debate on linkages and leakages (Meyer, 2007). *Stakeholders* are identified when developing sustainable destinations (Jamal and Stronza, 2009) and sustainable businesses (Amaeshi and Crane, 2006; Cespedes-Lorente, Burgos-Jimenez and Alvarez-Gil, 2003). Finally, the *voluntariness dimension* refers to actions that firms are not legally obliged to take, as for example illustrated by the debate on Antarctic tourism (Haase, Lamers and Amelung, 2009).

Although CSR definitions thus have demonstrated congruence along these five dimensions, uncertainty remains with respect to what exactly constitutes social responsibility and how related challenges should be managed in practice. As argued by Dahlsrud (2008: 6): 'The only conclusion to be made from the definitions is that the optimal performance depends on the stakeholders of the business'. Hence, an answer to the question what CSR is, largely depends on stakeholders' expectations of the firm and the context in which the firm operates. To delineate the scope of action for CSR it is essential to consider the context of CSR . The core business activity of a sector and the context of a particular enterprise define the emphasis on particular issues of the people-planet-profit axiom (Mair and Jago, 2010). While the accommodation sector is predominantly concerned with issues of natural resource management, local procurement to reduce leakages, labour conditions and in some regions, the combat of child-sex tourism, the core issue for the transportation sector is climate change. The tour operating industry is somewhat different as its core activity is brokering and not physically accommodating or mobilising goods or people. This intermediary position in the tourism supply chain has long provided tour operators with an excuse not to accept their responsibility towards sustainability, '[claiming] to be simultaneously the innocent victim in satisfying existing consumer demand while helplessly responding to the existing supply stock' (Miller, 2001; 590). Nevertheless, tour operators are increasingly called upon action and to take CSR seriously (Font, Tapper, Schwartz and Kornilaki, 2008; Van Wijk and Persoon, 2006). In the next section, we will discuss what CSR entails in tour operations.

CSR in Tour Operations

Tour operators engage in the procurement of holiday package components such as accommodation, transport and excursions; they assemble these components in an attractive holiday package and then sell them by adding value in the form of pricing, convenience or expertise. In order to enhance their sustainability performance, tour operators may take action at three different levels: at the firm level, along their supply chain, and at the holiday destination level.

Firm Level

While tour operators previously considered sustainable tourism development the primary responsibility of the governments in holiday destinations (Forsyth, 1997), tour operators nowadays include sustainability in their business strategy (Font et al., 2006). In the context of UNEP's *Tour Operators' Initiative* numerous practical guidebooks with 'best practice' examples have been developed to help tour operators in establishing CSR policies and practices (for example, Font and Cochrane, 2005; Tepelus, 2005; TOI, 2003). Several programmes and management tools implemented in the last decade have improved the environmental performance of tour operators. For example, research by Van der Duim and Van Marwijk (2006) showed that in 2004 over 90 per cent of the tour operators in the Netherlands informed their clients about sustainability issues, 70 per cent separated waste and reduced the use of paper, almost 60 per cent lowered the distribution of brochures and almost 50 per cent informed or trained staff on CSR. Most likely these percentages will now be much higher. To illustrate their policy of 'buying, flying, selling, sharing and being green and good', recently TUI Nederland published, as the first Dutch tour operator, a sustainability report (TUI Nederland, 2011).

Supply Chain Level

Although the tourism sector includes many actors, to date tour operators still have significant power in selecting and assembling suppliers in a holiday package, as well in influencing consumers' choices with respect to destinations, accommodations and additional services (Font et al., 2008; Van Wijk and Persoon, 2006). Moreover, larger tour operators are also often in possession of hotels and airlines, as for example TUI Travel PC owning almost 150 airplanes, over 3,500 retail shops and hotel chains like Grecotel, Iberotel and Rui-hotels (Allart, pers.com. 2011). By virtue of these activities, supply-chain management is a key component of the tour operating business (Budeanu, 2009; Font et al., 2008; Schwartz, Tapper and Font, 2008). Supply-chain management can be defined as 'a philosophy of management that involves the management and integration of a set of selected key business processes from end user through original suppliers, that provides products, services and information that add value for customer and other stakeholders through the collaborative efforts of supply chain members' (Ho, Au and Newton, 2002, as cited in Schwartz et al., 2008: 299). The supply chain approach offers a more clearly delineated context and framework for tour operators to pursue CSR policies and practices, implying that the degree of supply chain sustainability depends on the performance of all the components, the suppliers and their links with the supply chain (Sigala, 2008).

The CSR performance of different suppliers poses several challenges. Many of the grassroots' suppliers in developing countries lack the capacity and ability to implement advanced techniques for waste management and pollution control. Dismissing them in favour of more environmentally friendly and often more wealthy suppliers would be unsustainable from a socio-economic perspective. In this respect the brokering role of inbound tour operators and local agents provides a great opportunity to pursue social and environmental responsibility along the chain. However, these local agents and inbound tour operators often lack the urge or capacity for taking on this role. More generally, local knowledge concerning sustainable development is often absent or minimal. In sum, although the concept of sustainable supply chain management has received increasing recognition and few doubt the importance of sustainable supply chain management for supporting CSR in the tour operating industry, for many companies pursuing genuine sustainable supply chain management is still a bridge too far.

Holiday Destination Level

Unsustainable development of tourism can have serious negative impacts on destinations, while tourism largely depends upon these destinations' natural and cultural resources. Therefore, tour operators increasingly engage in sustainable destination management. However, greening dFestinations requires significant investments, whilst returns will – if ever – generally pay off in the long run. Furthermore, the implementation of these greening efforts needs to be monitored and evaluated. The basic question therefore is: who is responsible for coordinating this endeavour and for bearing the costs? Destinations are *de facto* the products in tourism, but in contrast to products and services in other industries, tourism products are not completely controlled for in supply chains. Despite tour operators' key role in the supply chain, the relationship between tour operators and destinations at large lacks the necessary elements of mutual interdependency that determine business relationships. Although types of business relationships vary extensively in strength and duration, determinants of its success relate to its dyadic nature including reciprocity, balanced distribution of risks and benefits and intrinsic need (Dabholkar, Johnston and Cathy, 1994; Donaldson and Toole, 2000; Dwyer, Schurr and Oh, 1987; Holmlund, 2007). Starting with the latter, tour operators generally lack the intrinsic motivation to invest in sustainable development of a destination. Bluntly speaking, if tourism destinations tend to get overexploited, with all its social and environmental consequences, tour operators can easily shift their focus to other destinations, as can their competitors. Tour operators are thus not only in the position to *include* destinations in their offering, but also to *exclude* those that seem to lose their attractiveness for tourists. Conversely, destinations, being the producers and the product in one, do have intrinsic arguments to remain attractive, hence to prevent negative or downward exploitation of their natural and cultural beauty. But destinations are hardly ever corporate entities (with exceptions such as Disneyland); rather they are public domain.

In the case of tour operators being intrinsically motivated to invest in the sustainable development of destinations, they face particular risks that likely outweigh the benefits. Investing large sums of capital would need to be balanced with assurances that for the decades to come tour operators would be capable of sending vast numbers of tourists to the destination, or in financial terms: they should be sure about their return on investment. Therefore they would almost need to monopolise the destination, not being rivalled by competitors parasitising on the investment made, a phenomenon known as 'free riding'. Apart from competitors, externalities as for example terrorist attacks, political upheaval, and natural disasters pose another major threat to such investment. For example, the political unrest in Kenya after the 2008 elections resulted in a significant drop in the number of tourists to Mombasa and the outbreak of swine flu in Mexico in 2009 almost completely shut down tourism flows to Cancun. Lastly, due to the numerous interests and stakeholders at the destination level, a reciprocal relation between the tour operator and, for instance, local governments, NGOs, village councils, is not that obvious. If tour operators put serious efforts into sustainable destination development and attempt to partner up with different stakeholders, it is still unsure that their efforts will be met by similar constructive efforts from other stakeholders. There is no guarantee that partners stick to their agreements and or that tour operators have teamed up with the right parties.

Nevertheless, voluntary initiatives that aim at sustainable destination development are increasingly encouraged among tour operators, and these initiatives might even positively spin-off across the industry. For instance, the UK Travel Foundation is a charity that 'cares for the places tourists love to visit', running projects across the world to show the good "greener holidays" can do. They work closely with UK travel companies to encourage and support wider action. However, Miller (2001: 593) reminds us that the implementation of CSR in the tour operating industry should not be judged against the broader need of sustainable development at destinations, arguing that 'all steps are bounded by the limitations of the industry structure'.

Case Study: The Development of CSR in Dutch Outbound Tour Operations

The previous sections have introduced the concept of CSR in tourism in general and the scope of CSR activities in tour operations in particular. This section examines what CSR practices Dutch outbound tour operators have adopted over time. The case study is based on two dissertations (Van der Duim, 2005; Van Wijk, 2009), using interviews with tour operators, representatives of the trade association and sustainable tourism proponents; documentation like CSR reports, policy reports, newsletters, firm histories and trade journals; archival materials like minutes of meetings of the trade association's Executive Committee on Sustainable Tourism and the multi-stakeholder platform on sustainable outbound tourism; and participant observations. We extended these materials with more recent information drawn from secondary sources and expert interviews. In presenting this case study, we first provide a brief historical outline of why CSR (or more broadly: sustainable tourism) became an issue in this sector. Second, we list the main management tools developed and deployed in this industry. Finally, we assess the progress made in the transformation towards CSR and the prospects for further change.

Historical Outline

Similar to the emergent debate on the negative impacts of tourism and supported by evidence of environmental degradation in popular holiday destinations like the Mediterranean, in the early 1980s several individual and organisational actors challenged the Dutch tour operating industry to move towards sustainable tourism. These actors, for example, were concerned about the environmental impacts of mass winter sports holidays in the Alps as well as the social impacts of mass tourism to developing nations. They organised conferences, published articles and books, generated media attention for the topic and developed practices such as public information campaigns on how to behave as a responsible tourist (see for an overview: Van Wijk, 2009).

In the mid-90s the societal critique towards the negative impacts of holidays mounted, particularly after a publication by the Dutch Advisory Council for Nature Policy in 1994, tellingly titled 'Are we going too far?' The Council posed the provocative question: Do we have to go and see everything which seems attractive and interesting to us, and at what price do we allow ourselves the space and freedom to do so? The report, and particularly its proposal to introduce an eco-tax on holiday flights, caused a shockwave, resulting in a confrontation between the industry and environmental NGOs. In response to the report, together with other departments, the Ministry of Nature Conservation organised the first national conference on sustainable tourism in 1995 and launched the multi-stakeholder Platform IDUT in 1996 to spearhead the debate (now known as the Initiative Group for Outbound Sustainable Tourism. In Dutch: *Initiatiefgroep Duurzaam Uitgaand Toerisme*, IDUT). Members included representatives of the tourism industry, governmental organisations, NGOs and educational institutes. The Dutch Association of Travel Agents and Tour Operators (ANVR) took up and still is chair of the Platform.

Against the backdrop of this debate, ANVR formally installed an Executive Committee on Sustainable Tourism in 1995, as part of the Association of Tour Operators (VRO; *Vereniging Reisorganisaties*). It marked the official launch of sustainability in the tour operating industry and perhaps more importantly, the explicit acknowledgement of tour operators' and travel agents' responsibility towards sustainable tourism development. Soon after, the first policy paper on sustainable tourism was published, recognising the essence of sustainable development for the survival of the industry. The policy paper included two central assumptions; measures should be taken collectively, preferably at the international level, and consumers should continue to have the right to travel. Indeed, the ANVR called for the International Federation of Tour Operators (IFTO) to take appropriate action in 1995. Likewise, the Executive Committee made efforts to develop collective measures to facilitate ANVR tour operators to take action. For instance, information on the *Blue Flag* label for beaches and marinas was included in a database for ANVR members. However, in spite of this formal recognition of sustainability issues by the tour operators, governments in destinations were still seen as the stakeholders ultimately responsible for sustainable tourism development, and it was up to the tourists themselves to make informed decisions on responsible travel behaviour.

By the end of the 1990s, this view on the tour operator's role in sustainable tourism development significantly changed. Propelled by the continuous efforts of numerous advocates of sustainable tourism pushing for change and the potential threat of governmental interference, the ANVR started to demonstrate a more proactive attitude towards sustainable tourism. For example, in 1998, it published a brochure on tourism and the environment, publicly announcing the positive role that tour operators and travel agents have in sustainable tourism development. Together with various tour operators offering holidays in the Netherlands Antilles, the association also supported a project to promote sustainable diving holidays on these islands. In addition, responding to the critique on the detrimental impacts of air transport, policy documents in this period reported on sustainable holiday transportation. Hence, sustainable tourism increasingly became part of the tour operators' and travel agents' business agenda, with the trade association as one of the proponents of change. As expressed by the ANVR on its website: 'CSR in general and sustainable tourism entrepreneurship in particular […] signifies that besides profit and continuity, enterprises should also consider the effects of their operations on the natural and social environments'. The next section details how Dutch tour operators put these ideas into practice.

Overview of the Main Industry Tools

Over the past decades, the ANVR – in close cooperation with sustainable tourism proponents and frontrunner firms – has developed several programmes and management tools to assist its member tour operators to systematically and structurally incorporate sustainability issues in their strategy and daily operations. These initiatives intervene at the individual firm level (*POEMS* and *DTO*), in the supply chain (*Travelife* and *Intour*) and at the holiday destination level (*IDH*).

POEMS (1998-2008)

The development of a Product-oriented Environmental Management System (POEMS) (in Dutch: *Product georiënteerd Milieu Zorgsysteem*, PMZ) was announced in the 1998 policy document of the ANVR. POEMS structures the efforts and activities within a company in order to control, minimise and, where possible, prevent products and services within the chain from having environmental impacts (Berg, 2000 as cited in Van der Duim, 2005; 190). Existing initiatives like eco-labels, informative websites and carbon emission schemes were structured along the main elements of the tourism product (travel, accommodation, leisure). In this way, POEMS translated the existing initiatives into a language tour operators would understand. Pilot-projects among different tour operators were used to test the scheme. Although member tour operators agreed to make POEMS a mandatory standard for ANVR membership in late 2000, it would take until 2005 to have all tour operators awarded with the POEMS certificate.

In order to receive this POEMS certificate, a tour operator was required to (1) formulate an environmental policy statement, (2) formulate an environmental programme related to transport, accommodation, entertainment, internal actions, and communication, (3) appoint a POEMS coordinator who was trained and certified, and (4) refrain from offering travel products that were on the list of non-responsible or non-ethical products. Whereas the scope and impact of POEMS is arguably limited to some environmental aspects, it certainly demarcated a shift in thinking about the industry's responsibility. That is, sustainable tourism moved from a collective responsibility taken care of by the representative body ANVR to an individual firm responsibility. It should be noted that not all tour operators welcomed the POEMS scheme. Research into the implementation of POEMS in 2004 (Van der Duim and Van Marwijk, 2006) distinguished three groups of tour operators with different responses to POEMS (see Table 4.1).

The 'unconvinced minor participants', a relatively small group comprising approximately 10-15 per cent of the tour operators, never accepted the solution proposed by the ANVR. Initially, these tour operators were indifferent, but when the deadline for POEMS implementation came closer, the compulsory character of POEMS irritated them. They either did not show a real interest in solving the problem or they perceived a lack of power to improve their sustainability performance. A second group comprising 60-70 per cent of the tour operators and labelled 'open-minded yet sceptical participants', did put much more emphasis on the sustainability problems caused by tourism, principally thought POEMS was a good idea, but questioned its compulsory character and effectiveness. This group accepted the solution (although with mixed feelings) and took action, such as informing their clients on sustainable tourism or having another look at all offered products from a POEMS perspective. For 'loyal actors' (20-30 per cent of the tour operators), POEMS worked as a catalyst that structured and guided their efforts towards sustainability. This group includes the frontrunners that took action towards sustainability issues even before the POEMS scheme was introduced. It should be noted that the frontrunner firms consist of both specialist and mainstream tour operators.

Table 4.1   Typology of tour operators having implemented POEMS

Group	Key Defining Characteristics
Unconvinced minor participants	Do not accept the solution proposed by the ANVR, are opposed to the POEMS, acknowledge the problem but do not feel responsible or able to provoke change, take no concrete action to alter business practices.
Open-minded yet sceptical participants	Acknowledge the problem, accept the POEMS with mixed feelings, alterations of business practices directed predominantly towards information and informal procedures.
Loyal actors	Proposed solution accepted, the POEMS works as a catalyst, they make a range of alterations to business practices (information, employees, products), most procedures are formalised.

DTO (>2008)

In 2008 the DTO-programme (*Duurzaam Toeristisch Ondernemen*/Sustainable Tourism Entrepreneurship) replaced POEMS. In DTO the focus shifted from mainly environmental concerns as in the POEMS-scheme to the triple bottom line for sustainable development. The DTO-mission is to 'stimulate and support the development of sustainable tourism products and services, implying that positive impacts will be strengthened and enhanced, and negative social, cultural and environmental impacts of travelling will be reduced to a minimum' (ANVR, n.d.). DTO policy prescribes that all associated tour operators follow ANVR-DTO standards, including (1) the appointment of a DTO-coordinator, certified with a personal Travelife Exam certificate that remains valid for three years, (2) the formulation of a DTO-policy declaration, and (3) the delineation of a DTO-action plan. Tour operators are required to submit a bi-annual DTO-report to an independent DTO-foundation. By late 2010, all member tour operators appointed a certified DTO-coordinator and formulated a DTO-policy statement, and the majority submitted an action plan. Although the plans have not yet been analysed and evaluated, the ANVR recently confirmed that all plans fulfil the minimum ANVR requirements (see Table 4.2). Reporting standards, however, exceed these minimum conditions, as they require tour operators to report also on issues as philanthropy, internal labour policy, training and education, waste and energy management, CO_2 compensation initiatives, carrier selection and pro-active actions towards sustaining destinations. A number of tour operators already act and operate beyond these minimum standards and reporting requirements.

Although it is too early to assess the implementation of DTO, there is no reason to believe that the conclusions of the 2004 POEMS evaluation (Van der Duim and Van Marwijk, 2006) have fundamentally changed. Within current

Table 4.2   DTO requirements

Issue	ANVR DTO Requirement
Sustainability coordinator	Coordinator has been appointed and his/her role and actions are clearly delineated.
Coordinator training	The appointed coordinator holds a valid 3-year Travelife certificate.
Policy declaration	A formal sustainability policy (DTO) declaration has been drafted.
Internal communication	DTO policies and actions are internally communicated on a regular basis.
Action plan	A sustainability action plan has been drawn.
Monitoring and evaluation	An internal monitoring and evaluation system is in place in order to assess the progress made in implementing this sustainability action plan.
Management reporting	The sustainability action plan is resubmitted every 2 years to the special ANVR-DTO commission.
Child labour	Suppliers employing children below the age of 14 will not be contracted.
Child prostitution/abuse	Immediate termination clauses on sexual exploitation of children will be included in contracts with accommodation providers.
Prohibited souvenirs	Souvenirs made from endangered species as mentioned in the CITES-convention or the IUCN Red List will not be promoted.
Negative impact activities	Companies will not offer products or services that are damaging to humans, animals, natural or cultural environments.
Legislation	Activities or products that do not comply to national or international law and jurisdiction will not be offered.
Hunting	Hunting is not promoted, unless in compliance with environmental interests and with government permission.
Endangered areas	Extremely vulnerable or endangered areas, such as Antarctica or the Galapagos will not be visited unless performed in an ecologically responsible way.
Company policy and commitment	The sustainability policy will be publicly available and clearly communicated to Consumers.

initiatives, such as the Travelife programme, the same frontrunners are pulling the strings as in the process of introduction and implementation of POEMS. For those who are lagging behind in this process still the same arguments seem to count.

Travelife (>2008)

Another major development within the Dutch tour operating industry's transition towards sustainability has been the collaborative project of Travelife, under the umbrella of the EU-funded project of Tourlink. The UK Federation of Tour Operators (FTO) and Leeds Metropolitan University, in collaboration with ANVR, Platform IDUT and ECEAT-Projects have collectively developed a Sustainability Management System for the tourism sector, integrating prior certification and management systems from the tourism sector, other sectors and general systems such as the EU EMAS system (Environmental Management and Assessment System), ISO 14001 and the UN supported Global Reporting Initiative (GRI). The aim of the Travelife project is to render a method for coherent and easy assessment of sustainability performance of different suppliers in the tourism supply chain in order to improve transparency and stimulate the use of sustainable tourism products among suppliers and consumers. In short, Travelife is a web-based checklist on a wide range of sustainable tourism criteria and, according to the degree to which these are met by the accommodation provider, awards can be achieved, ranging from bronze, silver to gold. Awards are rewarded after inspection by an independent auditor. This information then becomes publicly available to all associated tour operators, helping and encouraging them to work with more responsible suppliers. By November 2010 in total 533 accommodations had been awarded out of 1,286 audits. In addition, 1,056 accommodations had performed a self-check (Hardeman, pers.com. 2010).

Dutch tour operators very much welcome the Travelife scheme. It provides them with a concrete tool to preferentially select suppliers. The firm-level DTO programme aims to institutionalise such choices and preferences at the firm level, embedding them into corporate policies and routines. Nevertheless, Dutch tour operators have expressed their fear of 'free riders' in using the Travelife system. To build up a database with certified hotels takes time, energy and costs, which later entrants can make use of without bearing these costs. Moreover, a business model for generating sufficient revenues in order to account for the enforcement and monitoring costs of the Travelife certificates has not yet been established. In light of this uncertainty of the prospects of Travelife, it is essential to question by whom these investment and enforcement costs should eventually be borne. Finally, environmental issues still tend to dominate the indicator sheets for sustainability. Although issues of waste and energy management are undoubtedly important, prioritising them might divert attention away from socio-economic dimensions of sustainable development that are particularly important in, for example, developing countries.

Intour (2010)

Recently, the industry has sought further collaboration with partner associations in other European countries through the Intour project. Intour is a market-led, cluster-based approach to EMAS III (third version of the Eco-Management and Audit Scheme) and eco-labelling. It aims at integrating sustainability tools with EU voluntary instruments and implementing them in the tour operator supply chain. The project runs from 2010-2013, is chaired by ECEAT-Projects and involves 11 European tour operators' associations (Intour, 2010). It aims to increase the number of certified accommodations, to develop the compatibility and sustainability of the sector, to support innovative initiatives and to develop a common strategy for European standards (Intour, 2010).

IDH (>2009)

ANVR has also partnered with the Dutch Sustainable Trade Initiative (*Initiatief Duurzame Handel*; IDH). The objective of the Dutch Sustainable Trade Initiative is to improve the sustainability of international supply chains, by tackling social, ecological and economical bottlenecks for chain actors in developing countries. The Initiative is a multi-stakeholder process in which actors from both Northern and Southern countries actively participate. The sectors that are already implementing a programme in the context of the Dutch Sustainable Trade Initiative are: tropical timber and other forest products, soy, nature stone, cocoa, tea, aquaculture, cotton and tourism. For tourism the idea is to eventually execute destination management projects and implement the Travelife management system in six popular tourism destinations for the Dutch, being Thailand, Brazil, Egypt, Turkey, Kenya and Tanzania. Although IDH ultimately aims at incorporating the whole tourism supply chain, it now primarily focuses on the accommodation sector, using the Travelife system. The audits and self-checks have delivered a significant volume of information concerning the environmental and social performance of the accommodations, however the translation of this information into viable action strategies and programmes, not only within the accommodations themselves but also at the level of the destination more broadly, still appears to be lacking.

CSR Assessment and Prospects

Overall, the development of CSR in the Dutch outbound tour operating industry has been a gradual process of attitudinal change. The five-stage model for firm's actions towards CSR developed by Zadek (2004) provides a sound framework for assessing the current CSR status of the industry. The model suggests that the adoption of CSR policies and practices is a process that every business goes through, albeit at a different pace. Zadek (2004) differentiates five subsequent stages starting with the defensive stage. In this stage organisations practically deny the problems or at least their responsibility for addressing them. After the stage of defence, organisations enter the compliance phase, where minimum efforts and costs are taken in order to comply with laws and standards. The first two stages can be earmarked as reactive or, at times, even ignorant. The third stage reveals a more proactive attitude, rather than organisations being forced to take action. In this managerial stage, organisations assign responsibilities for social and environmental issues, and their solutions, to operation managers, and responsible business practices are integrated into daily operations. The fourth stage is strategic, where responsibilities for today's and future social and environmental issues are taken up as a core business strategy. The ultimate fifth stage of CSR in organisations is the promotion of strategic CSR policies and practices across the entire industry.

Drawing on this model, we argue that the development of CSR in the Dutch outbound tour operating industry currently evolved into stage 3, with the trade association ANVR as a pivotal player behind this transition. By 2010, 213 tour operators, 124 business travel agents and 1463 travel agents were associated with the ANVR (De Reus, 2010), comprising roughly 90 per cent of the industry. Hence the ANVR has a solid and authoritative reputation within the industry. In addition, the ANVR is not only the representative of the industry; it also advocates the interests of the tour operators and travel agents to governments, NGOs and society at large. As such, the association has played a key role in the advancement of sustainable development policies and practices on the industry's agenda. While a frontrunner group has emerged, of which some have moved to Zadek's (2004) fourth stage, for many other firms in the industry full implementation of CSR is yet to come.

Nevertheless, the transition towards CSR is remarkable if we take into account that most of the driving forces that are generally considered to be relevant to a firm's CSR engagement, are almost absent in the Dutch setting or have waned over time. According to Bansal and Roth (2000) there are four drivers of greening businesses. The first driver is *legal requirements*, pointing to the legal framework in which organisations need to operate in order not to be fined, penalised or even sued. The report 'Are we going too far' in 1994 provided several recommendations to regulate the tourism industry and generated the threat of governmental interference into outbound tour operations. However, this threat did not materialise in regulations. Apart from some generic policy instruments and a short-lived introduction of eco-taxation for international flights in 2008, the Dutch Government did not send out a clear message that there is a need for changing practices – let alone stimulate and facilitate innovation in tourism in any substantial manner. Of course, some new initiatives and niches have been welcomed and supported, but usually not in an enduring way. Moreover, in the Netherlands the four most involved government departments and sectors (i.e. Economic Affairs, Nature Conservation, Development Cooperation, and Environmental Affairs) continuously have scratched each other's back when discussing primary responsibility. The global character of contemporary tourism, the consequent deadlock of national competition positions and confusion about accountability suggest that regulatory pressure is not likely to become a significant driver for greening the industry in the near future (Mair and Jago, 2010). Put differently, governments at different scales are caught in a catch 22. This was clearly demonstrated by the introduction of the 2008 flight eco-taxation, which was being reverted within a year. As many Dutch travellers started to book their flights from neighbouring airports in Germany and Belgium to avoid the taxes, the Dutch government cancelled the levy.

Beyond legal regulations, organisations can be pressured by *stakeholder groups* such as local communities, civil society organisations, customers or suppliers to adopt more responsible policies. In our case, stakeholder pressure has waned over time. One of the focal organisations in the Netherlands that consistently challenged the industry (*Stichting Retour*) ceased to exist after being very active in the 1990s, while other organisations that potentially could perform this role have joined collaborative arrangements with the industry, formalised in the IDUT Platform. Whereas broad-scale societal campaigns to create consumer awareness about unsustainable industry practices by, for example, Oxfam Novib have proven to be highly effective in other industries such as cocoa, similar initiatives have been absent in tourism. Contrary to the production of tangible goods, in the service industry responsibilities often are less overt (Mair and Jago, 2010). Nevertheless, NGOs could start to target consumers in their campaigns rather than the tour operators so as to enhance consumer understanding of how sustainable holidays differ from non-sustainable ones. By stimulating the market demand for sustainable products, commercial arguments for change will provide a stronger business case for CSR.

Thirdly, Bansal and Roth (2000) identify *economic opportunities*, such as scaling production, outsourcing and green marketing as a third corporate motive for thinking and acting responsibly. While Dahlsrud (2008: 6) argues that at the conceptual level CSR is nothing new since '... business has always had social, environmental and economic impacts, been concerned with stakeholders ... and dealt with regulations', corporations have come to identify the business case for explicitly addressing social and environmental issues. As Carrigan and Pelsmacker (2009: 683) argue: 'Those firms who treat sustainability as an opportunity, rather than a costly add on are most likely to reap the rewards long term by exploiting the opportunity it brings to differentiate, make cost savings, build consumer trust, and help consumers continue to make more sustainable purchasing decisions'. Obviously some of the frontrunners and especially tour operators in niche-markets have seen and capitalised on these opportunities. However the majority of the tour operators still face the absence of a clear business case. Although consumer awareness is on the increase, it is not yet translated into a clear quest for sustainable tourism (NBTC/NIPO, 2010). Other industries are confronted with more overt and strategic necessities for being concerned with environmental sustainability and social responsible practices, particularly where they depend on the increasing scarcity of natural resources (Dahlsrud, 2008; Mair and Jago, 2010). The fragmented and diverse nature of the tourism sector is one of the major limitations for adopting coherent CSR strategies in the tourism supply chain (Budeanu, 2009; Schwartz et al., 2008; Miller, 2001).

Despite this lack of clear-cut corporate motivations, as depicted above, in the last decade policies and practices associated with environmental and social responsibility have been institutionalised in the Dutch outbound tour operating industry. The *ethical or moral motivation* is the fourth and remaining driver to explain this change (Bansal and Roth, 2000). For the ANVR responsible business is 'the right thing to do' and therefore the association still actively promotes CSR among its members. In that sense the Dutch tour operating business indeed entered the third stage as depicted by Zadek (2004), where ANVR and the frontrunners actually take their responsibility, rather than being forced to do so. In this managerial stage, these organisations have attributed themselves responsibilities for social and environmental issues, and their solutions, and have integrated responsible business practices into daily operations. Although this undeniably is a major step forward, the question remains how solid these moral concerns are in running a business under challenging economic conditions.

Conclusion

This chapter briefly introduced the concept of CSR in tourism in general and tour operations in particular. We argued that tour operator's scope of action for CSR is to be found at three levels; the firm level, the supply chain level and the destination level. With regard to the tour operator's responsibility we noted that the industry is bound by the limitations of the industry structure (Miller, 2001). Tight margins, many, different and scattered suppliers and above all the exogenous factors composing the tourism product, make in all reasonableness that tour operators cannot be held accountable for the sustainable development, or lack thereof, of the *holiday destination* at large. Notwithstanding that, tour operators are increasingly encouraged to contribute to sustainable destination development. Tour operators also play a key role in *supply chains*, by assembling holiday packages, by selecting suppliers of accommodation and transportation, directing large flows of tourists, and marketing destinations particularly in mainstream tourism. Hence, tour operators do have a chain responsibility. However the principal driver behind broad-scale acknowledgement and action towards chain responsibility – the business case at *firm level* for 'going sustainable' – has not yet been clearly defined or made accessible for the majority of tour operators. Tour operators are to a large extent locked into existing technologies and old ways of doing (Van der Duim, 2005). According to Dodds and Kuehnel (2010), externalities seem to control most of the operations within the tour operating industry, whereas tour operators do not consider themselves in control of the content and resources (nature, culture, beaches, events) they 'sell'.

Nevertheless, the Dutch case study on outbound tour operations illustrates that tour operators do signal opportunities for change. Over more than two decades, serious efforts have been taken to endorse social and environmental responsibility across the industry, reflected by the adoption and implementation of the POEMS-scheme, followed by the current DTO-framework, and the Travelife management system and its implementation within the IDH framework. The merits of *people* and *planet* have thus become part of the commercial business agenda. While PR arguments in the anticipation of a market pull for sustainable holidays clearly play a role in the steps taken to date, many efforts are based on a strong sense of moral responsibility towards the natural environment and local populations. The major achievement in that respect has been the institutionalisation of this moral responsibility, beyond philanthropic support. As such, our case study nuances the negative portrayal of tour operators as irresponsible actors. Moreover, by showing how the trade association ANVR took and still takes the lead in pushing its members towards sustainable tourism, our study heeds Tyler and Dinan's (2001) call for more research on business-interest organisations in tourism. While Tyler and Dinan emphasise the role of trade associations in influencing public policies on tourism, our case study reveals the key role trade associations play in promoting CSR in the industry itself. As suggested by Gupta and Brubaker (1990), trade associations are in the position to develop and define CSR standards; to inform and convince their members on the need for CSR and to proffer possible solutions; to promote the diffusion of these solutions and monitor their implementation through the association's channels of communication and education; to safeguard the industry's green image; to educate the public about the relationship between tourism and society at large; and to actively engage in stakeholder consultations, here institutionalised in the IDUT Platform. While Dutch frontrunner tour operators suggest that it is possible to be successful in carving out a niche for sustainability, not all tour operators signal these opportunities as yet.

It is here that future research is warranted. Research on CSR in tour operating has tended to focus on frontrunner firms in order to identify 'best practices' (for example, Tepelus, 2005), leaving the motivations of laggards *not* to engage in CSR little understood. Are these firms differently positioned in the market, constrained by the type of holiday products they offer, the countries they operate in or the customers they serve? Moreover, a comparative case study of the driving forces behind CSR in the tour operations industry across different EU countries could enhance our understanding of external and internal drivers of CSR. For instance, it would be interesting to systematically compare the Dutch transformation process with the process unfolding in the UK industry where the NGO Tourism Concern has played a significant role in pressurising tour operators to act socially responsible. By understanding the driving forces behind CSR in outbound tour operations, interventions to instigate change can be better designed. Given the expected growth rates of tourism in the years to come, these interventions for sustainability are urgently needed and ask for bold actions. Indeed, as Zadek (2004) argues, making business logic out of a deeper sense of corporate responsibility requires courageous leadership and insightful learning, and a grounded process for organisational innovation.

References

Amaeshi, K.M. and Crane, A. (2006) Stakeholder engagement: A mechanism for sustainable aviation. *Corporate Social Responsibility and Environmental Management*, 13(5), 245-60.

ANVR (n.d.) *ANVR en Duurzaam Toeristisch Ondernemen*. Available at: http://www.anvr.travel/opreis_details.php?opreis_groep_id=19 [Accessed: 16 November 2010].

Bansal, P. and Roth, K. (2000) Why companies go green: A model of ecological responsiveness. *Academy of Management Journal*, 43(4), 717-36.

Bohdanowicz, P. and Martinac, I. (2007) Determinants and benchmarking of resource consumption in hotels: Case study of Hilton International and Scandic in Europe. *Energy and Buildings*, 39(1), 82-95.

Bohdanowicz, P. and Zientara, P. (2008) Corporate social responsibility in hospitality: Issues and implications: A case study of Scandic. *Scandinavian Journal of Hospitality and Tourism*, 8(4), 271-93.

Bohdanowicz, P. and Zientara, P. (2009) Hotel companies' contribution to improving the quality of life of local communities and the well-being of their employees. *Tourism and Hospitality Research*, 9(2), 147-58.

Budeanu, A. (2009) Environmental supply chain management in tourism: The case of large tour operators. *Journal of Cleaner Production*, 17, 1385-92.

Carrigan, M. and De Pelsmacker, P. (2009) Will ethical consumers sustain their values in the global credit crunch? *International Marketing Review*, 26(6), 674-87.

Cespedes-Lorente, J., Burgos-Jimenez, J.D. and Alvarez-Gil, M.J. (2003) Stakeholders' environmental influence: An empirical analysis in the Spanish hotel industry. *Scandinavian Journal of Management*, 19(3), 333-58.

Cleverdon, R. and Kalisch, A. (2000) Fair trade in tourism. *International Journal of Tourism Research*, 2(3), 171-87.

Cowper-Smith, A. and de Grosbois, D. (2011) The adoption of corporate social responsibility practices in the airline industry. *Journal of Sustainable Tourism*, 19(1), 59-77.

Dabholkar, P., Johnston, W. and Cathey, A. (1994). The dynamics of long-term business-to-business exchange relationships. *Journal of the Academy of Marketing Science*, 22(2), 130-45.

Dahlsrud, A. (2008) How corporate social responsibility is defined: An analysis of 37 definitions. *Corporate Social Responsibility and Environmental Management*, 15, 1-13.

Dodds, R. and Kuehnel, J. (2010) CSR among Canadian mass tour operators: Good awareness but little action. *International Journal of Contemporary Hospitality Management*, 22(2), 221-44.

Donaldson, B. and O'Toole, T. (2000) Classifying relationship structures: Relationship strength in industrial markets. *Journal of Business and Industrial Marketing*, 15(7), 491-506.

Dwyer, F.R., Schurr, P.H. and Oh, S. (1987) Developing buyer–seller relationships. *Journal of Marketing*, 51(2), 11-27.

Egri, C.P. and Ralston, D.A. (2008) Corporate responsibility: A review of international management research from 1998 to 2007. *Journal of International Management*, 14(4), 319-39.

Font, X. and Cochrane, J. (2005) *Integrating Sustainability into Business: A Management Guide for Responsible Tour Operations*. Paris: United Nations Environment Program – Tour Operators' Initiative.

Font, X., Tapper, R. and Cochrane, J. (2006) Competitive strategy in a global industry: Tourism, in P. Coate (ed.) *Handbook of Business Strategy*. Bradford: Emerald Group Publishing Limited, 51-5.

Font, X., Tapper, R., Schwartz, K. and Kornilaki, M. (2008) Sustainable supply chain management in tourism. *Business Strategy and the Environment*, 17, 260-71.

Forsyth, T. (1997) Environmental responsibility and business regulation: The case of sustainable tourism. *Geographical Journal*, 163(3), 270-80.

Garrick, D. (2005) Excuses, excuses: Rationalisations of Western sex tourists in Thailand. *Current Issues in Tourism*, 8(6), 497-509.

Gössling, S. and Peeters, P. (2007) 'It does not harm the environment!' An analysis of industry discourses on tourism, air travel and the environment. *Journal of Sustainable Tourism*, 15(4), 402-17.

Gupta, S.K. and Brubaker, D.R. (1990) The concept of corporate social responsibility applied to trade associations. *Socio-Economic Planning Sciences*, 24(4), 261-71.

Haase, D., Lamers, M. and Amelung, B. (2009) Heading into uncharted territory? Exploring the institutional robustness of self-regulation in the Antarctic tourism sector. *Journal of Sustainable Tourism*, 17(4), 411-30.

Henderson, J.C. (2007) Corporate social responsibility and tourism: Hotel companies in Phuket, Thailand, after the Indian Ocean tsunami. *International Journal of Hospitality Management*, 26(1), 228-39.

Holcomb, J.L., Upchurch, R.S. and Okumus, F. (2007). Corporate social responsibility: What are top hotel companies reporting? *International Journal of Contemporary Hospitality Management*, 19(6), 461-75.

Holmlund, M. (2007) A definition, model, and empirical analysis of business-to-business relationship quality. *International Journal of Service Industry Management*, 19(1), 32-62.

Intour (2010) *Eco-Innovation "INTOUR" project*: Summary.

Jamal, T. and Stronza, A. (2009) Collaboration theory and tourism practice in protected areas: Stakeholders, structuring and sustainability. *Journal of Sustainable Tourism*, 17(2), 169-89.

Johnson, D. (2002) Environmentally sustainable cruise tourism: A reality check. *Marine Policy*, 26(4), 261-70.

Kibicho, W. (2005) Tourism and the sex trade in Kenya's coastal region. *Journal of Sustainable Tourism*, 13(3), 256-80.

Le, Y., Hollenhorst, S., Harris, C., McLaughlin, W. and Shook, S. (2006) Environmental management: A study of Vietnamese hotels. *Annals of Tourism Research*, 33(2), 545-67.

Lynes, J.K. and Andrachuk, M. (2008) Motivations for corporate social and environmental responsibility: A case study of Scandinavian Airlines. *Journal of International Management*, 14(4), 377-90.

Mair, J. and Jago, L. (2010) The development of a conceptual model of greening in the business events tourism sector. *Journal of Sustainable Tourism*, 18(1), 77-94.

Mak, B. and Chan, W.W. (2006) Environmental reporting of airlines in the Asia pacific region. *Journal of Sustainable Tourism*, 14(6), 618-28

Meyer, D. (2007) Pro-poor tourism: From leakages to linkages. A conceptual framework for creating linkages between the accommodation sector and 'poor' neighbouring communities. *Current Issues in Tourism*, 10(6), 558-83.

Miller, G. (2001) Corporate responsibility in the UK tourism industry. *Tourism Management*, 22, 589-98.

Mitchell, J. and Ashley, C. (2010) *Tourism and Poverty Reduction: Pathways to Prosperity*. London: Earthscan.

Montgomery, H. (2008) Buying innocence: Child-sex tourists in Thailand. *Third World Quarterly*, 29(5), 903-17.

Mowforth, M. and Munt, I. (2009) *Tourism and Sustainability: Development, Globalization and New Tourism in the Third World*. Third Edition. London: Routledge.

NBTC/NIPO (2010) *Duurzame Vakantie: Ver van mijn bed of dicht bij huis*? *Presentation of Preliminary Conclusions*. Vakantiebeurs: Utrecht.

Reus, T. de (2010) Travel Top 50 2009. *Reisrevue*, 42: appendix (11 pages).

Scanlon, N.L. (2007) An analysis and assessment of environmental operating practices in hotel and resort properties. *International Journal of Hospitality Management*, 26(3), 711-23.

Schwartz, K., Tapper, R. and Font, X. (2008) A sustainable supply chain management framework. *Journal of Sustainable Tourism*, 16(3), 298-314.

Sigala, M. (2008) A supply chain management approach for investigating the role of tour operators on sustainable tourism: The case of TUI. *Journal of Cleaner Production*, 16, 1589-99.

Tepelus, C.M. (2005) Aiming for sustainability in the tour operating business. *Journal of Cleaner Production*, 13(2), 99-107.

TOI (2003) *Sustainable Tourism: The Tour Operators' Contribution*. Paris: United Nations Environment Program – Tour Operators' Initiative.

TUI Nederland (2011) *Samen het verschil maken: Duurzaam toerisme jaarverslag 2010*. Rijswijk: TUI Nederland.

Turner, L. and Ash, J. (1975) *The Golden Hordes: International Tourism and the Pleasure Periphery*. London: Constable.

Tyler, D. and Dinan, C. (2001) Trade and associated groups in the English tourism policy arena. *International Journal of Tourism Research*, 3(6), 459-76.

Van der Duim, R. and Caalders, J. (2002) Biodiversity and tourism: Impacts and interventions. *Annals of Tourism Research*, 29(3), 743-61.

Van der Duim, R. (2005) *Tourismscapes: An Actor-network Perspective on Sustainable Tourism Development.* PhD Dissertation. Wageningen: Wageningen University.

Van der Duim, R. and Van Marwijk, R. (2006) The implementation of an environmental management system for Dutch tour operators: An actor-network perspective. *Journal of Sustainable Tourism,* 14(5), 449-72.

Van Wijk, J. and Persoon, W. (2006) A long-haul destination: Sustainability reporting among tour operators. *European Management Journal,* 24(6), 381-95.

Van Wijk, J. (2009) *Moving beyond Heroes and Winners: Institutional Entrepreneurship in the Outbound Tour Operations Field in the Netherlands, 1980-2005.* PhD Dissertation. Amsterdam: VU University Amsterdam.

Zadek, S. (2004) The path to corporate responsibility. *Harvard Business Review,* 82(12), 125-32.

Chapter 5

CSR-inspired Environmental Initiatives in Top Hotel Chains

Paulina Bohdanowicz and Piotr Zientara

Introduction

It is hardly in dispute that environmental protection, with climate change to the fore, is one of the most important challenges facing policy-makers and ordinary citizens alike. Accordingly, ecological issues have become the focus of widespread public and policy interest. As a result, increasing attention has been paid to such concepts as "sustainable development", which is about ensuring that humanity "meets the needs of the present without compromising the ability of future generations to meet their own needs" (Kates et al. 2005: 10) or "eco-efficiency", which "prescribes reducing the amount of energy and natural resources used, as well as wastes and pollutants discharged in the production of goods and services" (Kelly et al. 2007: 377). At the same time, corporate social responsibility (CSR), which implies, among other things, that businesses should behave ecologically by minimising their environmental impact, has come to occupy a salient place in managerial thought (Porter and Kramer, 2006, Holcomb et al., 2007, Bohdanowicz and Zientara, 2008, Franklin, 2008). In point of fact, it is almost inconceivable today for a large international company to be without a CSR policy (Franklin, 2008) or a comprehensive sustainability programme (since in some firms, as will be indicated later, CSR and sustainability constitute separate domains).

This presumption also holds true for businesses operating in the hospitality industry (Knowles et al., 1999, Kalisch, 2002, Holcomb et al., 2007, Bohdanowicz and Zientara, 2008). Indeed, over the last two decades, most international hotel chains have carried out – within the framework of their CSR programmes – a variety of projects that aimed at reducing their environmental footprint and protecting the environment (Erdogan and Baris, 2007). Some hospitality companies even "embedded" CSR into their business models. Wyndham, for example, regards CSR not as a stand-alone programme to implement or a policy to follow, but as "a way of living, working and playing that embodies our vision and values, celebrates our diversity and supports a balance of professional and personal needs" (Wyndham Hotels and Resorts, 2009). This implies that environmentalism – alongside employee well-being and community development – underpins all decision-making processes and managerial practices. Equally importantly, various organisations and institutions have come up with a number of guidelines that are meant to help hotels "green" their operational modes (see, for instance, International Hotels Environment Initiative, 1996, Bass Hotels and Resorts, 2000, ITP, 2008, World Travel and Tourism Council, 2009).

All this is of great significance since tourism, of which hospitality is an integral part, produces substantial negative environmental impacts. For instance, the industry – which represents approximately 10 per cent of global GDP, or 5.8 billion dollars, and 8 per cent of employment worldwide, or 230 million jobs (World Travel and Tourism Council, 2009) – is thought to contribute five per cent of the total man-made CO_2 emissions (Chiesa and Gautam, 2009). In this context, one needs to realise that hotels still consume above-average amounts of natural resources and non-durable goods, at the same time turning out large quantities of waste (International Hotels Environment Initiative, 1996, Bass Hotels and Resorts, 2000, Erdogan and Baris, 2007). Indeed, although estimates vary (since much depends on the type and size of a facility), a typical hotel that uses fossil fuel-generated electricity usually emits more than 40kg of CO_2 equivalents per room per night and produces about three kilograms of waste per guest-night (Chiesa and Gautam, 2009).

That has far-reaching implications. For one, there is ample scope for improvement. For another, considering that an undamaged environment is simultaneously an essential constituent of service quality and a major factor determining the attractiveness of any tourist destination, it is in the interest of hospitality companies to promote environmental sustainability. But there is far more to it than that: in fact, the entire industry has a crucial role to play not only because of its direct contribution to the conservation of the environment, but also due to its interaction with (and, by extension, its potential impact on) millions of travellers and tourists each year (not to mention suppliers and subcontractors). This means that what hospitality businesses do in the area of environmental protection can influence – and hopefully change – attitudes of millions of people all over the world.

Such is the background against which the present chapter, which assumes the form of a positivist-empirical study, examines CSR-inspired environmental initiatives implemented by selected international hotel chains. Specifically, the chapter, employing the content analysis technique (Neumann, 2003), shows what selected international hotel companies have done within their CSR programmes to reduce their environmental footprint and to promote environmental sustainability. In doing so, it aims to answer the following research questions: (1) what do concrete projects consist in?; (2) how does CSR thinking influence the design and implementation of projects?; (3) what is the significance of new technologies?; (4) what sort of implementing difficulties can managers usually encounter?; (5) how can creativity help overcome certain problems?; (6) what role do employee empowerment and ecological awareness raising play in implementation processes?;

The structure of the chapter is as follows. The initial section offers a conceptual framework, which will provide an indispensable context in which to place the issues under consideration. In it, we first discuss the theoretical underpinnings and practical implications of CSR for corporate environmentalism and human resource management (HRM). Next the focus shifts to the critique of CSR. The subsequent part briefly describes the method and examines environmental initiatives implemented by selected hotel chains, with special emphasis on their activities in Europe. The chapter concludes by highlighting its limitations, suggesting further research directions and, critically, making a number of managerial policy recommendations. The study, by exploring the question of "greening" hotel operations, aims both to make an important contribution to the topical debate on corporate environmentalism and to disseminate best practice amongst hospitality practitioners.

CSR: Theoretical Underpinnings and Practical Implications

Corporate social responsibility – also known as corporate citizenship, corporate sustainability, corporate responsibility or responsible business (Kalisch, 2002, McIntosh et al. 2003) – has recently flourished both as an inspirational idea of societal character and an influential aspect of managerial thought (see, for instance, Crook, 2005, Jenkins and Yakovleva, 2005, Porter and Kramer, 2006, Holcomb et al. 2007, Bohdanowicz and Zientara, 2009, Franklin, 2008). A growing popularity of environmentalism and a surge of interest in sustainability development have coincided with mounting criticism of the corporate world. Generally, it is alleged that companies are to blame for climate change (greenhouse gas emissions), environmental devastation (rainforest logging, coal excavation, oil spills), human-rights violation in developing countries (collaboration with dictatorial regimes) and employee exploitation (use of child labour or failure to ensure adequate working conditions). At issue therefore is the perceived tension between private profit and public interest. So corporate misconduct has led some to believe that capitalism, if left unchecked, would be destructive and exploitative in its blind pursuit of profit (Solomon, 1992, Bakan, 2004). This means, by implication, that businesses – unable to abide by high ethical standards – should be checked by double-strength government regulation or, indeed, held to account by the public.

It follows that corporate responsibility is about producing "public benefit" (Business in the Community, 2009). In other words, companies should justify their existence in terms of (environmentally friendly) service to a wider public rather than mere profit (Crook, 2005). To take the argument to its logical conclusion, corporate social responsibility is in fact about the attitude firms adopt towards such stakeholders as workers, consumers, the broader society or even future generations. Thus, on the one hand, great stress is laid on dealing fairly with employees, suppliers and customers, and, on the other, on supporting (in assorted ways) local communities, respecting human rights (in undemocratic countries), giving donations to charitable causes and, crucially, preserving the environment and promoting sustainable development (Franklin, 2008, Bohdanowicz and Zientara, 2009, Dow Jones Sustainability Index, 2009). In other words, "socially responsible companies not only try to be economically sustainable and profitable, but also endeavour to work with their employees, families, local communities and nation states to improve the quality of life in ways that are both ethical and sustainable in relation to society and the environment" (Cacioppe et al. 2008: 684).

The focus on broadly-understood environmental protection is central to the concept of CSR. However, as mentioned in the introduction, there needs to be a recognition that in some companies (at Hilton, for instance) CSR and sustainability constitute separate domains (with the former concerning equity, fair treatment and other social aspects, and the latter – ecological issues). Sometimes CSR programmes and environmental initiatives are not linked in terms of philosophy and purpose. To put it differently, a firm may well devise an environmental programme and carry out some eco-friendly projects within its framework, but this does not necessarily have to mean that the programme in question is part of its CSR policy (or its CSR-inspired philosophy). That said, in most cases (at least in hospitality) corporate social responsibility and environmentalism are intertwined with each other (Zientara and Bohdanowicz, 2010).

Hence ecological issues, with climate change to the front, should be given top priority by any socially responsible company (Franklin, 2008, Dow Jones Sustainability Index, 2009). This is based on the premise that the functioning of most businesses – and, by and large, almost any economic activity – affects the earth's environment (thereby leading, *inter alia*, to the intensification of climate change). CSR proponents argue therefore that firms should restructure so as to function in line with the ideals of sustainable development. To that end, CSR-inspired companies ought to "green" their operations (Bohdanowicz and Zientara, 2008) through eco-efficiency (Kelly et al. 2007). In practice, this means that companies should, among other things, switch to renewable or low-carbon sources of energy (such as solar thermal, wind power and fuel cell technologies) as well as reduce the amount of resources by installing technologically-advanced efficiency-enhancing appliances and environmental management systems. Specifically, it is imperative to conserve water, which is increasingly regarded – due to its progressing scarcity – as "new gold". This might be achieved by reducing operational wastage and installing water-efficient appliances and equipment. Likewise, emphasis ought to be placed upon the reduction of (all sorts of) waste and material intensity (minimising the waste in the first place, avoiding packaging, reusing various items and prolonging their active life by maintaining them in good working order and repairing them, and then sorting, recycling and ensuring the appropriate disposal of waste).

But there is far more to it than that: such actions should be accompanied by initiatives aimed at raising ecological awareness among staff and customers alike. These should get them involved not only in creative ecologically-friendly undertakings (such as planting trees or protecting rainforests), but also in simple but useful daily activities (such as switching off lights whenever possible or ensuring that water does not drip from taps). One should realise at this point that, from a HRM perspective, hotels stand out amongst other workplaces. It follows that managing employees in hotels – due to the specificity of their functioning and the intrinsic nature of typical hospitality jobs – poses particular challenges (Magd, 2003, Furunes and Mykletun, 2005). For example, the relatively flat organisational structures of most hospitality facilities mean that employees are less likely to change positions and, critically, to be promoted (Furunes and Mykletun, 2005). This in turn does not facilitate the retention and recruitment of talented and ambitious people (see also Lehmann, 2009) as well as might negatively affect employee job satisfaction (Spector, 1997) and organisational commitment (Meyer and Allen, 1997).

And it is in this area that CSR could play a decisive role (Cooke and He, 2010). The idea is to project the image of an attractive employer that cares about his employees and, crucially, the environment – an aspect which for many ambitious and talented job seekers is an increasingly important issue (Albinger and Freeman, 2000). Cacioppe et al. (2008: 681), for example, found that well-educated managers and professionals are likely to take into account "the ethical and social responsibility reputations of companies when deciding whether to work for them, use their services or buy shares in their companies". Moreover, Roozen et al. (2001) point out that employees who work for organisations that behave in an ethical manner and pay due attention to the welfare of their stakeholders are more likely to abide by the principles of ethical conduct and to curb their self-interest for the greater communal good.

It follows that by embracing CSR companies might enhance their employees' job satisfaction and organisational commitment (Brammer et al. 2007, Valentine and Fleischman, 2008). And these work-related attitudes (Kirkman and Shapiro, 2001), albeit of great importance to any organisation, play a crucial part in the service sector and, by implication, in hospitality. This is because service quality, which is ensured by employees having direct contact with customers, is one of the major factors behind organisational performance (Kini and Hobson, 2002). Accordingly, customer satisfaction – conditional mostly upon staff behaviour – is critical to the success of hotels (Crawford and Hubbard 2008). In this sense, Baron (2001: 7) argues that CSR not only has "a direct effect on the costs of the firm", but also has "a strategic effect by altering the competitive positions of firms in an industry". Other studies also emphasis a link between CSR adoption and positive organisational outcomes (Hillman and Keim, 2001, Roozen et al., 2001).

The Nature of CSR Critique

Corporate social responsibility, however, has come in for heavy criticism. One school of thought points out that businesses are responsible, above all, to their owners (shareholders) rather than to society and other stakeholders (Beckerman, 2002). Equally importantly, it is argued that, given its overt aversion to profit-maximisation (Bakan, 2004), CSR undermines the fundamental principle of the free-market economy (Friedman, 1962, Henderson, 2001, Beckerman, 2002).

Friedman (1962), one of the first prominent critics of CSR, asserted that it is wrong to believe that profit-seeking – unless tempered and controlled by corporate responsibility (or double-strength government regulation) – *de facto* works against the public interest. To follow the line of his argument, "there is one and only one social responsibility of business – to use its resources and engage in activities designed to increase its profits so long as it stays within the rules of the game, which is to say, engages in open and free competition, without deception or fraud" (Friedman, 1962: 133). Still in a similar vein, the imposition under public pressure of assorted constraints on businesses is likely to have a negative impact on their operation and, potentially, competitiveness (Henderson, 2001). This applies especially to all sorts of obligations and restrictions (which, at least in the short run, mean higher operating costs) related to environmental protection and, by extension, sustainable development.

Others suggest that the implementation of CSR-driven schemes – in particular, those taking the form of high-profile, well-publicised public relations actions – is actually more about improving a company's image than *genuinely* helping anyone (Esrock and Leichty, 1998, Jenkins and Yakovleva, 2005, Rodriguez et al., 2006). So, in other words, it has more to do with brand management rather than true commitment to good causes (Rodriguez et al. 2006). This bears directly on the very quintessence of CSR: is it about proving that a business, having wholeheartedly embraced the philosophy of social responsibility, is genuinely committed to "doing good" or is it about showing that a business, aware that it pays to have a positive, eco-friendly image, is (more or less cynically) involved in "right" things (Holcomb et al. 2007).

Sometimes, truly well-intentioned initiatives have debatable or downright erroneous underpinnings and lead to unintended harmful outcomes (*Economist*, 2006). For instance, some argue that organic farming – which, being ideologically linked to environmental sustainability promotion, often features saliently in CSR programmes – is not as environmentally benign as its proponents claim. Borlaug (2007), the father of the "green revolution", points out that organic farming can be more harmful to the environment than traditional agriculture. This is because organic farming produces lower yields and hence necessitates more land under cultivation (to turn out the same quantity of food).

By contrast, traditional farming – more intensive thanks to (chemical) fertilisers or genetically modified crops (which do without chemical fertilisers) – uses up less land, which means that more land is left for rainforests (in developing countries in Asia and South America). Of course, in affluent countries (Europe, North America) forests are well-protected, but in an increasingly globalised and interconnected reality any big-scale action undertaken in one place of the world has implications for the rest of the planet. It follows that European and American companies that promote organic farming – by, for example, discriminating against suppliers which are dependent on traditional agriculture – could somewhat insidiously contribute to the deforestation processes. Likewise, it is suggested that organic farming may actually require '… more energy per tonne of food produced, because yields are lower and weeds are kept at bay by ploughing.' (*Economist*, 2006: 72) So its environmental impact (in terms of CO_2 emissions) might well be bigger than that of traditional farming. Moreover, the promotion by the green lobby of supposedly environment-friendly first and second generation bio-fuels is rightly seen to have been one of the major factors behind the spike in food prices in 2007-2008, which dramatically affected the situation of the poor in the developing world.

Furthermore, serious doubts are currently being cast over the effectiveness and actual "fairness" of Fairtrade schemes (Harford, 2005, *Economist*, 2006), which also come high on corporate CSR agendas (indeed, as it will be demonstrated, many hotel companies serve considerable amounts of organic food and Fairtrade products). The following excerpt illustrates the line of argument adopted by Fairtrade sceptics: 'The standard economic argument against Fairtrade goes like this: the low price of commodities such as coffee is due to overproduction, and ought to be a signal to producers to switch to growing other crops. Paying a guaranteed Fairtrade premium – in effect, a subsidy – both prevents this signal from getting through and, by raising the average price paid for coffee, encourages more producers to enter the market. This then drives down the price of non-Fairtrade coffee even further, making non-Fairtrade farmers even poorer. … But perhaps the most cogent objection to Fairtrade is that it is an inefficient way to get money to poor producers. Retailers add their own enormous mark-ups to Fairtrade products and mislead consumers into thinking that all of the premium they are paying is passed on. Mr Harford calculates that only 10 per cent of the premium paid for Fairtrade coffee in a coffee bar trickles down to the producer' (*Economist*, 2006: 72).

Admittedly, this reasoning cannot be easily refuted, which may put a question mark over CSR-motivated decision of various (hospitality) companies to serve Fairtrade coffee, tea and other products. All that is not to debase – or to make a case against – the very rationale of corporate social responsibility. Rather, this is to suggest that one should not unproblematically accept all its tenets. It follows that managers, while devising CSR programmes, should follow, above all, scientific evidence and common sense rather than political correctness and activist pressure. In fact, the above critical remarks just remind us that in today's complex, multifaceted reality, it is essential to weigh up particularly carefully the pros and cons of certain initiatives and to make an in-depth analysis of the potential consequences of concrete policy choices.

This is of crucial importance since a growing number of businesses from developed and developing countries alike are introducing comprehensive CSR programmes. To reiterate, no large company can nowadays afford to neglect the question of how its operations affect the environment. Arguably, this reflects a profound shift in societal perception of the role of the modern-day corporation (Dow Jones Sustainability Index, 2009). It follows that companies' approach to ecological issues is likely to make an increasingly significant impact on their competitiveness (Porter and Kramer, 2006). And this also applies to hospitality companies as more and more guests (and potential employees) pay attention to whether and how hotels they choose reduce their environmental footprint.

Method

As indicated in the introduction, to address our research questions, we employed the content analysis technique (Neuman, 2003). Specifically, we visited the websites of the following companies – Intercontinental Hotels Group, Wyndham Hotels and Resorts, Marriott International, Hilton Worldwide, Scandic Hotels, Rezidor Hotel Group and Accor – and analysed their CSR-related content. In the case of Scandic and Hilton, apart from analysing their corporate websites, we drew on internal documents (available online and offline) and personal correspondence with senior managers. We chose to focus on the aforesaid hotel companies because Intercontinental Hotels Group, Wyndham Hotels and Resorts, Marriott International and Hilton Worldwide, having comparable accommodation capacity (over half a million rooms or million beds) and scope of operation (worldwide), are listed as the top four hotel companies, according to the Hotel Giants list published by the Hotels Magazine (Hotels Magazine, 2009). On the other hand, Scandic – like Wyndham – made CSR the centrepiece of its business model (which means, to reiterate, that its corporate *modus operandi* is, to a large extent, determined by CSR-inspired environmentalism), while Accor and Rezidor Hotel Group, being well established in Europe, are also seen as pioneers in the area of CSR.

Analysis of Initiatives Implemented by Selected International Hotel Chains

InterContinental Hotels Group (IHG) is currently the largest hotel chain in terms of the number of rooms (Hotels Magazine, 2009). It manages seven brands, has 4,438 hotels (86 per cent of which are franchised) in 100 countries and employs 355,000 people. The company explicitly states that corporate responsibility is integral to how it conducts its business and that 91 per cent of its staff are proud to work for it (IHG, 2010). Like other big hotel chains, the company concentrates its environmental efforts on different areas. These include: (1) energy, water and waste; (2) global carbon and environmental footprinting; (3) siting, design and construction standards. IHG has been working on implementing responsible operation practices for a number of years now. Its flagship initiatives include: Green Engage, IHG Academies, Responsible Business Partnerships, and the Innovation Hotel. It has also set up a CR Committee at board level with a view to driving Green Engage and other schemes from the top of the organisation. Of special interest is the partnership with Oxford University, which aims to map biodiversity. More specifically, the idea is to create (and to improve) online "hot spot" maps that identify areas which are either suitable or unsuitable for (hotel) development. IHG has earmarked approximately one million dollars (over a five-year period) for this project.

The company also implemented a number of specific schemes. For instance, it launched the "Chase the Extraordinary" (CTE) campaign (in America). This initiative aims to get each IHG employee – whatever their place in the corporate hierarchy – engaged in new IHG projects. The most popular best practices carried out within the framework of the CTE campaign were: (a) moving to energy saving light bulbs (which in the USA saved 130.1 GWh of electricity worth over US$2.28 million annually and avoided the emission of around 90,610 tonnes of CO_2); (b) developing recycling programmes (as a result of which in 123 hotels over 554 metric tonnes of waste was recycled); (c) reducing the amount of printing; (d) reducing energy use; (e) improving community welfare. The company also developed an IHG Environmental Standard for hotel design and construction.

Interestingly, within the framework of the programme, a "CR in a Box", a set of Corporate Responsibility materials and posters, was delivered to all American hotels. This was meant to raise employee awareness, and was followed by two initiatives. The first tool is "Green Engage", an online environmental reporting tool (which has over 1,400 individual users), while second, the "Green Aware" (About Water, Air, Recycling and Energy), is a course aimed at providing practical examples of more responsible hotel operations to hotel General Managers, Chief Engineers, Executive Housekeepers, Directors of Operations and Owners.

The "Green Engage" was coupled with an ESCAP Enviro, a management tool to measure and internally benchmark the environmental performance of IHG hotels in terms of energy usage, water consumption and waste production. This internet-based system, which in 2010 was in place in 900 hotels (indicated on the online map), allows individual hotels to enter data on a monthly basis, which can then be reported over time (IHG, 2010). Individual hotels' benchmarking results are easily understood by the use of a dashboard display system for the key indicators (such as utility consumption/waste or CO_2 generation per rented room, guest-night or square metre of hotel floor area). A particularly important communications aspect of ESCAP Enviro is its ability to show data as "equivalents to". For example, when highlighting good environmental performance to guests, hotels are able to describe water savings in terms of the numbers of Olympic-sized swimming pools, washing machine loads or toilet flushes. Thanks to this, the human scale of IHG actions can be better understood. To further the understanding of a hotel's impact on its surroundings and possible responsible actions, "Innovation Hotel" was developed. It is an interactive online tool allowing employees as well as the general public to take a tour of a virtual hotel (which encompasses a number of best practices) and comment on each of them. Currently version 2 of the "Innovation Hotel" is available on the company website (IHG, 2009).

A number of sub-initiatives have been launched overtime. In 2007, for example, a comprehensive waste management project was implemented. Its aim was to identify opportunities for reducing the amount of waste IHG sends to the landfill, thus reducing environmental impacts (which, of course, adds value to the business from reduced costs). In a similar vein, a water reduction project, called "Conserving for Tomorrow" (CFT), was put into place in the same year. The main idea behind CFT, used in over 50 per cent of its US hotels, is to ask guests to use their linens and towels more than once to save on water, detergent, energy, labour and replacement linen. The programme has an 80-90 per cent participation rate from hotel guests and for each average-sized 100-room hotel it saves 22,000 litres of water and 150 litres of detergent each month (IHG, 2009).

With regard to the reduction of CO_2 emissions, IHG worked with a UK-based sustainability consultancy, Best Foot Forward, to "footprint" its hotels. It was estimated that the company is annually responsible for about 9 million tonnes of carbon dioxide from direct and indirect emissions (an average of 59 kilograms of CO_2 per occupied room, and 51 per cent being accredited to energy consumption) (IHG, 2009). It is also worth noting that in 2008 the company initiated its GRI reporting to increase the transparency of its responsible business practices, and, as things stood at the end of 2009, it achieved 60 GRI indicators.

To summarise, in 2007-2009 IHG's (owned and managed) hotels reduced their energy consumption by 9.3 per cent per available room night. In 2009, the total use of energy in all the establishments amounted to approximately 18.2 billion kWh, which translated into a total energy bill of 1.9 billion dollars (at 2009 prices). In 2010 IHG intends to make an average hotel (in a temperate zone) conserve 10-20 per cent of its water usage. Furthermore, it plans to achieve an energy savings of 6-10 per cent over the next three years (2010-2012) on a per available room night basis. Finally, let us mention some of the awards the company received in 2009 alone in recognition of its environmental efforts: National Business Travel Association Award, Hotel Visionary Award (from *Hospitality Technology Magazine* for Green Engage), CSR Innovation Award (from *Hotel Magazine*), Eco-lodging Award (at the China Hotel Investment Summit) and Worldwide Hospitality Award (for the best initiative in sustainable development). In the light of the above analysis, it is justified to claim that IHG – while acting on different levels and implementing a variety of initiatives – is making constant progress in the area of CSR-inspired environmental protection.

As mentioned in the introduction, Wyndham Worldwide Corporation decided to embed CSR values into its business model (Wyndham Hotels and Resorts, 2009). In other words, it sees corporate social responsibility as an integral part and an organising principle of its operation rather than as a stand-alone policy. Specifically, the company concentrates on six main areas: (1) energy conservation; (2) water conservation; (3) recycling/re-use; (4) education; (5) community; (6) innovation. Equally importantly, Wyndham established two bodies – Worldwide Green Team and Green Council – which are responsible for co-ordinating eco-friendly activities and implementing concrete green projects.

Wyndham's environmentalism is guided by its "WyndhamGreen" programme, which focuses on 10 initiatives that should be followed by the management and hotel employees alike (Wyndham Hotels and Resorts 2009). These include, *inter alia*, such schemes as: (1) EarthSmart® linen and towel programme; (2) the

"Reduce Energy" initiative, which consists in installing energy-efficient bulbs (or sensors) in guest rooms and public spaces; (3) the "Reduce Water" project, which focuses on the installation of low flow faucets, shower heads and toilets as well as ozone laundry systems; (4) the "Recycle" initiative, which promotes recycling paper, bottle, plastics, batteries or cell phones; (5) buying eco-friendly cleaning and laundry products as well as organic coffee; (6) community programmes, which involves co-operating with local charities; (7) "Energy Tracking", which is about using the ENERGY STAR® tracking programme to monitor and to reduce energy consumption; (8) green training for employees, hotel owners and developers.

Wyndham also established a number of important partnerships. For example, Ecolab is providing its range of environment-friendly detergents and cleaning products to Wyndham Hotels worldwide, while a co-operation with Cintas is meant to deliver a range of employee uniforms featuring eco-friendly fabrics such as recycled polyester (Wyndham Hotels and Resorts, 2009). On the other hand, a partnership with Starbucks will result in serving organic food and fair-trade coffee at participating hotels (whose rationale, as indicated earlier, is open to question, though). The Blue Harmony spa and fitness centres will be designed, constructed and operated with the environment sensitiveness in focus with a view to making the interior design eligible for Leadership in Energy and Environmental Design (LEED) standard (awarded by the U.S. Green Building Council). Also worth emphasising is the company's ecological programme for children, called "Wyndham Green Kids". It is devised to teach children about the world in general and the environment in particular. The idea is to provide young people – in an interesting and interactive way – with the basic knowledge of how to take care of the planet.

As for tackling climate change, Wyndham committed itself to offsetting a portion of its carbon footprint, equal to 150,000 pounds (68 tonnes) of CO_2 via a partnership with the Native Energy. Crucially, all guests and the general public are invited to face the challenge and increase this number to one million pounds (454 tonnes) (Native Energy, 2009). As things stood in July 2009, the number of offsets bought globally in the name of Wyndham amounted approximately to 260,000 pounds (118 tonnes) (Wyndham Hotels and Resorts, 2009).

As for concrete achievements, due to the "Go Green" energy tracking programme, Wyndham reduced its energy use by nine per cent over the July 2008-March 2009 period. It also reduced its production of water pollutants (to 40,823 kilograms) through utilising low or no phosphate detergents. As a result of the "Paper Reduction Challenge" project, its main offices cut the consumption of paper by 36 per cent and saved 477,499 sheets. Moreover, Wyndham hotels and Wyndham Vacation Resorts increasingly use the green Front Desk uniform made from 25 two-litre plastic bottles. So far, 10,850 bottles have been recycled, saving around 4,200 kWh (14.4 million BTUs) and 2,275 kilograms of CO_2 emissions. Each uniform requires 66 per cent less energy and 90 per cent less water to produce than a standard uniform at Wyndham. The company also informed more than 20,000 of its associates about the "WyndhamGreen" programme through its website, training sessions and conferences.

Although the company finds itself at the early stage of responsible action implementation, it seems to be moving fast and in the right direction. Its efforts have been recognised and the Newsweek magazine ranked Wyndham Worldwide first among the top 100 greenest companies in America, and the top 10 of its Media, Travel and Entertainment category (Newsweek, 2009). What needs to be emphasised is Wyndham's creativity and innovativeness, as manifested in its recycling/uniform scheme. However, little is known about its partnerships with ecological NGOs and institutions.

Marriott International's activities in the area of environmental sustainability are carried out within the framework of the "Spirit to Preserve" programme, which focuses on the following areas: (1) water, waste and energy reduction; (2) the supply chain; (3) buildings; (4) employee and guest engagement; (5) community involvement (Marriott, 2009). The programme is comprehensive in character, has clearly defined goals and a very active communications team. As for resource and waste reduction (1), Marriott is committed to: (a) reducing its fuel and water consumption by an additional 25 per cent per available room over the next 10 years; (b) installing solar power in up to 40 hotels by 2017; (c) expanding existing "reduce, reuse, recycle" programmes. In this context, Marriott points out that, over the last decade, 450,000 light bulbs were replaced with fluorescent ones reducing lighting energy use in guestrooms by 65 per cent and 400,000 low-flow showerheads were installed saving on average 10 per cent of hot water use annually (Marriott, 2009).

As far as the supply chain is concerned, Marriott teamed up with its suppliers to introduce the following environmentally-friendly solutions (Marriott, 2009): (a) greener key cards; (b) eco-pillows (filled with material made from recycled bottles); (c) coreless toilet paper: (d) eco-friendly towels (that do not need to be pre-washed); (e) recycled pens; (f) low Volatile Organic Compounds (VOC) paint; (g) biodegradable laundry bags; (h) eco-friendly laundry detergent. With regard to buildings (3), Marriott empowers its hotel development partners to design and construct greener hotels. And it is in this domain that Marriott is really making spectacular progress. Symptomatically, in April 2010 it opened a green hotel prototype (created for its Courtyard brand) that is pre-certified with LEED®. The building is endowed with such eco-friendly features as improved energy savings, better indoor air quality and reduced CO_2 emissions, easy access to public transportation, in-room recycling and light sensors in the guest rooms. All this will help to reduce the hotel's consumption of energy and water by 25 per cent. One needs to recognise in this context that Marriott already has 50 hotels registered for LEED, with 15 open or bound to open by the end of 2010 (note also that Marriott employs more than 20 LEED-accredited specialists). According to Arne Sorenson, the company's President and Chief Operating Officer, "the green hotel prototype gives Marriott a competitive edge with guests who prefer a green hotel experience, and with the growing number of owners and franchisees who want to provide it"

(Hotels Magazine, 2009). In a similar vein, Doug Gatlin, Vice President of the U.S. Green Building Council (USGBC), points out that 'Marriott's commitment makes it among the first in the world to commit to implementing green buildings on this scale' (Hotels Magazine, 2009).

Significantly, Marriott earmarked two million dollars for (and invited its customers, suppliers and other stakeholders to contribute to) a special fund, which is administered jointly by the Amazonas Sustainable Foundation and Brazil's State of Amazonas (Marriott, 2009). The principal idea behind the scheme is to monitor and to enforce the protection of 1.4 million acres (589,000 hectares) of endangered rainforest in the Juma Sustainable Development Reserve with a view to reducing greenhouse gas emissions (from avoided deforestation). Yet the programme goes far beyond rainforest protection. In fact, it attempts to ensure long-term sustainability by helping – and empowering – Juma residents; for example through distributing mosquito nets and "Bolsa Floresta" stored value cards to each of the local families for protecting the rainforest. The initiative is worth emphasising because, while combining the ideal of environmental sustainability with help for local community, it involves local authorities, the private sector and inhabitants of a protected area (note that Marriott entered into other partnerships such as Conservation International and International Tourism Partnership). What is more, guests can "Green Their Hotel Stay" and offset their carbon footprint by making a donation to the fund. In 2008, Marriott launched the "Spirit to Preserve the Rainforest" promotion: for meetings or stays of 10 rooms or more booked during select dates, participating Marriott hotels around the world contribute funds equal to five per cent of the total cost of the group's guest rooms to protect the Juma rainforest (Marriott, 2009).

Furthermore, Marriott employs a wide variety of modern-day instruments to communicate its environmental efforts and concrete achievements. Hence apart from using such "traditional" means as conference presentations, guest room materials and internal newsletters, Marriott is particularly active in the cyberspace (website, blogs, email, online media releases, Facebook, YouTube and Twitter). This is testament to the weight the company attaches to projecting its image as an ecologically responsible business. To this end, Marriott also attempts to raise green awareness amongst its employees. For meeting planners, for instance, Marriott introduced Eco-Events, a menu of eco-friendly products and services including recycle bins in meeting rooms, pens and notepads made from recycled material, organic flowers, linen-less tables, re-usable name tags and leftover food donations.

To conclude, in 2006 alone, the combined efforts of management and employees resulted in the reduction of energy use by 8,600 million kWh, equivalent to the greenhouse gas emissions of 70,000 tons (Green Lodging News, 2007). Two years later the company saved – thanks to its energy-saving procedures at all its hotels – one million dollars. Not coincidentally, the American Environmental Protection Agency conferred its "2008 Sustained Excellence" award to Marriott and placed the ENERGY STAR label on more than 250 of its hotels (the most of any hotel company). Recently, the World Travel and Tourism Council (WTTC) selected Marriott as the recipient of the "2009 Tourism for Tomorrow Award for Sustainability" in the Global Tourism Business category (CSRwire, 2009).

Hilton Worldwide hotels across the globe have been implementing measures aimed at environmental efficiency and sustainability for many years. These were typically focused on on-site energy and water conservation as well as interacting with local communities to improve the quality of the relationship. In June 2008, recognising the role the hospitality industry may have in promoting sustainability, Christopher Nassetta, the CEO of Hilton Worldwide announced the Global Sustainability Commitment and Mission Statement. The company promises to integrate sustainability into its operational practices. By implementing various innovative actions, it aims to enhance the experiences of guests, to engage its employees (called team members), to serve the communities and to protect the global environment.

To further the Sustainability Mission Statement, between 2009 and 2014 Hilton Worldwide will commit itself to a range of measurable sustainability improvements from the direct operations of the hotels and corporate offices worldwide. The short term goals are to reduce energy consumption by 20 per cent, to cut carbon dioxide emissions by 20 per cent, to reduce the output of waste going to landfill by 20 per cent and to minimise fresh water consumption by 10 per cent. The commitment was also made to focus on some high-impact areas of hotel operations that offer significant long-term sustainability opportunities and benefits, such as sustainable building design and construction, more responsible operational practices as well as chemicals management and purchasing. Awareness raising and engagement of employees, customers and suppliers alike are also high on the company agenda. The company attempts to attain its green objectives through partnership and co-operation (note that Hilton Worldwide is a founding member of the International Tourism Partnership and locally co-operates with the Travel Foundation).

A number of tools have been developed to help individual hotels and team members implement sustainability-oriented projects. Sustainability policy, commitment and mission statement are available in many local languages and displayed at premises. Educational and engagement programmes, including online ecoLearning courses, centralised intranet web content and various training modules are available to all team members. Sustainability is about the involvement of every individual, it is very much a grass-root initiative. There are green teams and champions working at hotels. Among assorted engagement programmes, intra-departmental and regional competitions stand out for their innovative character and effectiveness. For example, in Europe, since 2006 a mountain bike was promised to each team member in the best performing hotel in each operational region. This has been found to be a good incentive to encourage team members to take part in the programme and, over the four year period during which the competition was on, more than 4,000 bikes were given to team members at hotels across Europe.

In a more top-down fashion, brand, operational, and design and construction standards have been revised to ensure that both internal and external best practices are shared and adopted across the portfolio. Renewable energy is regarded as a source of power for hotel operations. But the idea is not only to reduce the company's carbon footprint, but also to develop a viable commercial infrastructure for powering buildings. Hilton suppliers are likewise encouraged to improve their environmental responsibility. This is done by sharing best practices, reviewing the availability of more sustainable product and service alternatives as well as supporting environmental initiatives at a community level.

The company management firmly believes that without accurate, data-driven metrics that allow for performance review and feedback, sustainability can never be truly embedded in the business. To this end, LightStay, a proprietary system was developed by Hilton Worldwide to calculate and analyse the company's environmental impact (for history of one of LightStay's predecessors, see Bohdanowicz, 2007). LightStay measures energy and water use as well as waste and carbon outputs at company facilities around the globe (Hotel Online, 2010). By providing the environmental performance feedback to all hotel teams, the tool proves to be instrumental in raising ecological awareness and in fostering a sense of responsibility for the hotel performance in individual properties. The system further analyses performance across 200 operational practices, such as housekeeping, paper product usage, food waste, chemical storage, air quality and transportation and reports the feedback in the form of a hotel sustainability profile. It also allows each hotel to communicate progress in their resource efficiency to team members and customers alike. A unique feature of LightStay is a "meeting impact calculator" that measures the environmental impact of any meeting or conference held at a Hilton Worldwide property. This enables meeting planners and corporate travel managers to consider the environmental impact of hotel stays and meetings when making purchasing decisions. In addition, it provides corporate customers with the opportunity to include meeting impact data in their own sustainability reporting (Hotel Online, 2010).

By 31 December 2011, all 3,500 properties within Hilton Worldwide's global portfolio of brands will use LightStay, making the company the first major multi-brand company in the hospitality industry to require a property-level measurement of sustainability (Hotel Online, 2010). Consequently, measurement of sustainability performance will become a brand standard, on a par with service, and will be accordingly evaluated as part of regular, property-level reviews.

The company firmly believes that integrating sustainability into daily business practices supports both the provision of highly satisfactory guest experience and improvement of operating performance. This assumption is borne out by the results from 1,300 Hilton Worldwide properties that have actively used LightStay tool over the past 24 months. On average, hotels that have embraced sustainability reduced energy use by five per cent, carbon output by six per cent, waste output by 10 per cent and water use by 2.4 per cent in 2009, as compared to 2008. On a global scale, these reductions translate into enough energy to power 5,700 homes for a year, enough water to fill more than 650 Olympic-size pools and reduction in carbon footprint equivalent to taking 34,865 cars off the road. These savings in utilities further translate into dollars saved, with estimated avoided costs of more than 29 million dollars in utility costs in 2009 (Hotel Online, 2010).

To recapitulate, the above analysis suggest that the investment of mainly time and human effort in sustainability does makes good business sense and improves the triple bottom line. Hilton Worldwide, like its direct competitors, goes to great lengths to ensure the environmental sustainability of its operations. To further this end, it acts holistically, combing introduction of innovative, technology-driven measures with ecological awareness raising (admittedly, the LightStay system – though it has yet to prove its cost-effectives and viability over a longer period of time – can already be held up as an instrument with which to reduce the environmental footprint and to make people sensitive to ecological issues). Its senior managers are fully aware that failure to act responsibly (at different levels) *vis-à-vis* the environment is bound to affect the company's competitiveness.

Now, having seen what the largest hotel chains have done in the area of environmental protection, let us move on to discuss CSR-inspired initiatives carried out by its smaller counterparts with stronger European presence (Scandic, Accor and Radisson Blu of Rezidor Hotel Group). As we will see, they focus their eco-friendly efforts on similar areas and are no less innovative. First, it might be instructive to analyse Scandic – one of the pioneers of CSR-underpinned environmentalism.

In the early 1990s, Scandic, which now has almost 160 hotels across Scandinavia and Easter Europe and is one of Scandinavia's largest hospitality companies, faced serious economic problems and strategic dilemmas. This accentuated the need to come up with a new strategy. In the words of Jan Peter Bergkvist (former Vice President Sustainable Businesses), "the decision was made to build up a strong brand that the employees could be proud of and guests could identify with. A value community" (Personal communication). The company decided to emphasise its commitment to environmentalism and turn itself into "one of the most environmentally friendly and most resource-efficient hotel chains". In the event, in 1993 Scandic declared that it intended '… to lead the way and work continuously to promote both a reduction in our environmental impacts and a better environment' (Scandic, 2003). As a result, environmentalism took centre stage in the company's philosophy. The initial idea of eco-friendliness was subsequently expanded to holistically cover all dimensions of sustainability with the introduction of "The Compass" and, critically, the concept of "Omtanke" in 1998 (Scandic 2007, Bohdanowicz and Zientara, 2008).

Within economic sustainability, the efficiency of operations and salesmanship are seen as the major factors leading to profitability (which, of course, underpins the *raison d'être* of any for-profit business). Ecological sustainability covers the issue of reducing the environmental footprint of the company itself and its co-operators as well as refers to the need to offer guests and employees (like at Hilton, also called team members) the opportunity to lead a healthy life. Since the launch of the initiative, thousands of activities – which are reported online to be shared with other hotel teams – have taken place in the Nordic. They are meant to reinforce the feeling of unity and shared values between hotel employees and residents of host communities (Bohdanowicz and Zientara, 2009). It is also believed that they will project the image of Scandic as a more attractive employer for local inhabitants and a reliable partner in co-operation deals.

More specifically, Scandic set out to increase efficiency and conserve resources within the framework of the so-called "Resource Hunt" programme. Its central feature was a special online database, the Scandic Utility System, created for the monitoring of resource consumption. Currently, the upgraded version of the database, the Scandic Sustainability Indicator Reporting (ScandicSIR) is used, followed by hotel performance results being displayed on the internet as Scandic Sustainability Live Report (Scandic, 2010).

Scandic also committed itself to purchasing products with a low (lifecycle) environmental impact. To further that end, it decided to involve their suppliers in the environmental programme and accordingly developed the Scandic Supplier Declaration. At the outset of the millennium, corporate management decided to eco-certify facilities with the Nordic Swan eco-label. As things stood in 2010, over 100 Scandic hotels were Nordic Swan labelled (Inger Mattsson, Sustainability Coordinator at Scandic Sweden, personal communication, 3 April, 2010). A network of environmental coordinators was created to facilitate participation of individual hotels in various activities, and feedback on facility performance is continuously provided to team members.

On the other hand, it is essential to realise that Scandic typically rents the building from an owner, which often makes it hard to reconcile both stakeholders' diverging interests. In practice, this means finding a compromise between the goals of the stakeholders in respect to resource utilisation and necessary investments in modernisation of the building systems. Thus Scandic first decided to focus on improvements that could be achieved by altering team members' behaviour (such as switching off unused equipment, water conservation during housekeeping and replacing light bulbs). Once the benefits of such actions were documented, the next step involved talking to building owners about possible cooperation in implementing concrete solutions (replacement of boilers, installation of heat exchangers, etc.). This is of significance since continuous retrofitting of facilities is viewed as an opportunity to reduce environmental impacts. To this end, the Scandic Environmental Construction Standard was developed. The document lists materials that should not be used in the facilities and specifies acceptable alternatives. To further minimise the amount of waste generated on site, the company came up with comprehensive waste sorting and recycling guidelines and eliminated the use of single packaged items, where possible.

Scandic also recognises the need to educate its team members, to assist them in everyday choices and to help them improve their job performance. To further this end, it introduced a new interactive training programme on ecological sustainability into its "check-in@Scandic" welcome pack. This training, addressed to all new team members, is accompanied by classroom-like courses conducted at Scandic's internal university (the Scandic Business School). All those employees who are interested in expanding their knowledge can attend them. Moreover, fully aware of the potential waste of energy and other resources involved in sending out Christmas cards (which are usually thrown away after a while), Scandic decided to earmark the money that would otherwise be spent on sending cards to its corporate customers and partners for a more worthy cause. Since 2003, these financial resources have been donated to various youth projects in Estonia though the Save the Children organisation. In 2007, money was given to the World Wildlife Fund and the Baltic Sea Project, too (Bohdanowicz and Zientara, 2008).

Of special interest is Scandic's recent initiative concerning bottled water (Green Lodging News 2009). This scheme, marked by a combination of simplicity and innovativeness, stands out amongst typical eco-friendly projects. Scandic used to transport nearly four million bottles of water to its hotels a year, which translated into a sizeable carbon footprint and therefore was deemed unsustainable (Zientara and Bohdanowicz forthcoming). Hence a decision was taken to invest in bottling its own water. In the event, since autumn 2008, all Scandic hotels, having been equipped with water dispensers, sell its own bottles of filtered and chilled water (still and sparkling). It is worth noting that the shape of the bottle was designed by Therese Alshammar, a Swedish swimmer, and is made from hand-blown recycled glass with recycled plastic cap. In this way, the company not only reduces its carbon footprint, but also ensures that valuable minerals and salts are kept in the water its guests drink. Scandic used to sell around 1.2 million litres of water a year at its hotels, which is an equivalent of 3.6 million 0.3-litre bottles. Due to its own bottled water, it now cuts its carbon emissions by 160 tonnes per year. But there is also another dimension to this scheme (which earned Scandic the Environmental Initiative of the Year award in 2008). The proceeds from each bottle sold (10 euro cents) goes to the Scandic Sustainability Fund, which aims to support initiatives that actively contribute to a more sustainable society. Both organisations and individuals can apply for grants from the Fund for projects that support sustainable development (understood in a broad sense). The Scandic Sustainability Award financed from the Fund and worth 100,000 euro, is given to the best project every year (Scandic, 2010).

Furthermore, every year Scandic serves four million organic breakfasts, 1,000 tonnes of organic food, nine million cups of Fairtrade coffee, four tonnes of organic apple purée and 32 tonnes of organic muesli (Scandic, 2010). Even though, referring back again to the arguments adduced in the theoretical section, one can put a question mark over the actual rationale of such activities, it is hard to deny that the company is truly committed to propagating this sort of food. It follows that, while the merits of organic food and Fairtrade products remain a matter of dispute, Scandic considers it worthwhile to consistently pursue such a strategy. To advance the concept of healthy lifestyle, back in 2009 Scandic initiated a 3-year cooperation with Jamie Oliver to develop menus for the hotels (Scandic, 2010). The first year saw Jamie Oliver creating dishes for children, while 2010 marks new menu options for the meeting guests.

Finally, it needs to be stressed that Scandic has ambitious plans for the future (Scandic, 2010). In 2007 the company announced that it intended to halve its CO_2 emissions by 2011 and that it aspired to operate on a carbon-neutral basis (that is, with zero CO_2 emissions) by 2025 (to achieve this objective, all Norwegian and Swedish Scandic facilities have been supplied with "green/non-fossil" electricity since 2004). The company also wants to be the first hotel chain in the world with all its employees wearing a completely organic uniform (designed by a leading fashion designer). By the company's own admission, the uniform, endowed with "its own personality and soul", will show the scope of the new Scandic and will cause team members to be proud to wear it (HospitalityNet, 2010).

More than a decade of sustainability work at Scandic has resulted in a significantly reduced environmental impact (Scandic, 2010). The energy saved is enough to provide electricity and heating for 9,000 households for one year, water would fill 683 Olympic swimming pools, while the avoided waste would require 2,770 lorries to be moved. The amount of fossil CO_2 avoided is equivalent to 270,000 return drives between Stockholm and Gothenburg in a petrol-driven car. All these further translate into significant cost savings, yet again proving that pursuing sustainability makes good business sense.

French Accor, with a particularly conspicuous presence in western and eastern Europe, has of late come up with the "Earth Guest" policy, which is founded on eight priorities falling into two categories: (1) enhancing the well-being of the earth's populations (EGO) and (2) preserving the planet's resources (ECO). Within the first category, the company has set itself the following priorities: local development, child protection, fight against epidemics and food. Equally importantly, energy, water, waste and biodiversity are Category 2 priorities (of special interest to the present study). At this juncture, it is necessary to mention that Accor's ecological efforts are guided by the Hotels Environment Charter, developed back in the mid-1990s (Accor, 2010).

The charter recommends 19 energy-optimising measures to be implemented in each facility. These include, among others, the use of energy-efficient refrigerators, optimised outside lightning and solar panels to heat the water in swimming pools. To date, installation of low-consumption bulbs in 2,300 hotels saved 72 million kWh of electricity in a year. Moreover, 64 hotels (against 41 in 2006) were equipped with thermal solar panels to produce hot sanitary water. There is a wide plethora of great case studies within the portfolio, with two facilities standing out for the utilisation of their state-of-the-art technologies. The Ibis Paris Hotel (opened in 2004) is the first hotel in France equipped with photovoltaic panels that, being integrated in the building façade, directly converts solar radiation into electricity. The Etap Hotel Toulouse Airport (built in 2008) uses cutting-edge insulation and renewable energy technologies (a geothermal probe, a heat pump and solar panels). Consequently, it uses 30 per cent less energy than required by French thermal regulations. The company's objectives for 2010 in the area of energy include a 10 per cent reduction in energy use per room as compared to

2006 performance, installation of energy efficient lights in all owned properties, and expanding the solar thermal systems to 200 hotels (Accor, 2010).

As far as water is concerned, Accor's charter recommends 10 measures to reduce water consumption and four for the treatment of waste water. The 2010 water goals include: installation of water flow reducers in all owned properties and making sure that these hotels consume 10 per cent less water per occupied room than in 2006 (Accor, 2010). The latest statistics showed 0.6 per cent reduction in water use in 2008, while installation of water flow reducers in 2,300 hotels has saved almost four million cubic metres of water over one year. More specifically, in the UK the Etap Hotel Birmingham City Centre installed in 2007 a rain water recovery system, which saves the hotel the hotel approximately 780 million cubic metres a year. In France the Ibis Ménimur installed a 10,000 litre tank (in 2008) to recover rain water, which is then used for watering plants and grass, and for washing guests' cars. Furthermore, some Accor hotels have signed partnerships with eco-friendly innovative laundries, which use a patented detergent-free cold water system (Greece and France) or operate on o-zone (the USA).

As regards waste, the 2010 goal is to have 70 per cent of the Accor hotels recycle paper, cardboard and glass while 95 per cent of them should sort and responsibly dispose of batteries and compact fluorescent light bulbs (Accor, 2010). In 2006-2008 all Accor hotels in France set up comprehensive programmes to reduce the volume of unsorted waste products by 10 per cent. In France the Pullman Paris Rive Gauche hotel established "a performance agreement" on waste performance with a service provider. The objective is to reduce the volume of waste and to innovate in selective sorting, while controlling waste management costs. In Brazil and Africa, glass, plastic and metal packaging is regarded as a valuable secondary (recoverable) material. These containers are carefully sorted to be reused and resold.

With regard to biodiversity, Accor is committed to preserving the richness of the planet's environment. To this end, it has teamed up with the IUCN with the aim of producing a guide for industry professionals which specifies how a facility can make a concrete contribution to conserving local biodiversity. The French League for the Protection of Birds and the Etap Hotel Brand have collaborated with a view to enhancing employee and guest awareness on the necessity of protecting biodiversity. In France the Novotel brand offers its hotels an interactive guide to transform their green spaces into "nature gardens". These areas are more respectful of nature, less dependent on human inputs and richer in biodiversity. Also, Accor places great emphasis on the significance of reforestation. Hence all its hotels participate in environmental-protection and tree-planting initiatives.

The company's efforts were recognised with the 2010 "Tourism for Tomorrow" awards given by the WTTC, where Accor received the Global Tourism Business award for its Earth Guest Program and company-wide philosophy based on "hospitality, respect for diverse cultures, environmental best practices and the social welfare of local people" where they operate (TravelBreakingNews, 2010).

Rezidor Hotel Group, which owns the Radisson Blu brand, introduced the "Responsible Business" programme in 2001 in response to increasing demands from guests, corporate clients, employees and owners (Rezidor Hotel Group, 2009). However, an environmental programme – which aims to reduce the company's negative impact on the environment as well as to raise employee green awareness – has been in place since the mid-1990s. Now all its environmentalist efforts are conducted within the framework of the aforesaid "Responsible Business" programme. The social and ethical aspects are also very high on the company agenda. Like all other global companies, Rezidor aims to reduce its carbon footprint. The company's overall decarbonisation strategy consists in reducing energy use and shifting to renewables as well as in complementing these activities by carbon offsetting. In 2007, more than 50 per cent of the company's hotels took some energy saving measures. These encompassed the installing of sensors and motion detectors as well as low energy demand equipment, upgrade of heating and ventilation systems and performance of energy audits. The Radisson Blu Royal Hotel Brussels, for instance, installed new energy efficient chillers which not only provide return on investment (due to energy savings), but also are ozone-friendly and silent. Besides, Rezidor promotes the re-use of rain water for irrigation (in place in seven per cent of the company's hotels) and grey water systems, in which shower water is used to flush the toilets (in place in six per cent of the hotels) (Rezidor Hotel Group, 2009).

In 2007, 279,128 tonnes of CO_2 equivalents were emitted from all the company's operations, which implies that, compared with 2006, its carbon footprint increased in absolute terms (Rezidor Hotel Group, 2009). A strong growth in hotels opened, especially in countries outside Western Europe, might go some way towards explaining this away. Yet, when measured by room nights, Rezidor's carbon footprint went down by five per cent in 2007, compared to 2005. What is more, 93 hotels are third party environmentally certified (Rezidor Hotel Group, 2010). Also worth mentioning is the fact that the company attempts to raise ecological awareness among its employees and customers by involving them in various green undertakings. In 2007, a unique database was created that now holds nearly 450 proven examples from the past five years, from more than 40 countries in Europe, the Middle East and Africa. It demonstrates the practical ways in which hotels have attempted to reach out to a local community, to reduce their environmental footprint, to share the Responsible Business message and to ensure the health and well-being of guests and employees. To convey the message to guests, a set of posters was printed and distributed within hotels. Also, some Rezidor hotels offer all guests the possibility to offset the carbon emissions associated with their trip through its specially-designed loyalty programme. In Poland Radisson SAS hotels distributed to their guests specially designed posters and leaflets with pictograms ("beware of the global warming", "charity actions" or "health food").

Tellingly, the Radisson Blu Hotel Ålesund was the first hotel in the group to hold a carbon neutral event for guests. It was co-ordinated with a ceremony during which the hotel received the prestigious Nordic Swan eco-label – one of the world's most respected eco-labels and marks of quality control in the area of environmental sustainability. The hotel offset the carbon emissions by donating money to The CarbonNeutral Company, which in turn financed a Solar Electrification project in India and a Tree Planting project in Uganda. In a similar vein, in September 2007, employees of the Radisson Blu Hotel in Edinburgh went to Dumfries and Galloway to work on a native woodland reforestation project (the area was once wild woodland, yet deforestation was brought about by inordinate logging and cattle grazing). In the event, the hotel's staff joined a group of volunteers who worked on reforesting the area and repopulating its wildlife.

Besides, Rezidor was among the first international hotel companies to join the United Nations Global Compact project, and more recently signed the "Caring for Climate" initiative. Its efforts to operate in a more responsible manner are widely recognised. Accordingly, Rezidor can be regarded as a company that authentically strives to put CSR ideas into practice. In this way, it meets the high environmental standards which, as has been shown throughout the chapter, have recently come to characterise the operation of most top hotel chains.

As we can see, all the companies seem to be committed to environmental sustainability. What is worth noting is the comprehensive character of their efforts. All the international chains focus upon various aspects of the hotel operating mode: from resource-consumption reduction and environmental awareness raising to green building design and local community development. In other words, they combine investment in modern resource-saving technical solutions and active employee engagement with ecological education (for staff and guests alike) and help (of both charitable and environmental nature) for localities. Of course, it is still open to question whether they are *genuinely* committed to green ideals. But the fact remains that, on the face of it, the companies have gone to great lengths to promote environmentally responsible behaviour. It follows that the entire sector can be held up – to firms from other industries – as a model of responsible behaviour *vis-à-vis* the environment.

Conclusion

In this chapter, we have focused upon CSR-inspired efforts at environmental protection in selected top hotel chains. The study's major limitation is that we have based our analysis on the information and data provided by the parties concerned. It follows that doubts might be cast over the objectivity and veracity of our source material. Still, there are reasons to believe that now – at a time when most information can be relatively easily verified and, thanks to activist pressure, monitoring corporate conduct is far more effective – no serious company can afford to provide the public with inaccurate or false data. On the other hand, we have not shown how all those initiatives translated into financial results. Hence other researchers might consider looking into the cost-effectiveness of concrete eco-friendly measures by calculating their impact on a company's (or an individual establishment's) financial performance in the short and long term. It could also be instructive to see whether company-led "green education" actually influences employees' and guests' stance towards environmental protection (this should be done, preferably, by means of a Likert scale survey). Moreover, one might examine what smaller independent hotels, which usually (but, admittedly, not always) do not pay as much attention to CSR as their larger counterparts, have done in the area of environmentalism.

Admittedly, CSR – despite certain justified criticisms and reservations – is bound to be increasingly embraced by businesses operating in different sectors all over the world. This is due, *inter alia*, to a shift in societal perceptions: nowadays more and more people simply expect companies to behave ethically and ecologically. If they fail to do so, they might be literally punished by citizens-consumers, who – using internet social networks – can urge their friends to boycott the products and services of *eco-unfriendly* businesses. As we have argued throughout the chapter, CSR has a special role to play in the tourism industry in general and the hospitality sector in particular: the success of hotels hinges – in function of the type and location of a concrete facility – on the state of the environment and, crucially, on the quality of service. The implication is that getting employees (most of whom have direct contact with guests) truly engaged in CSR-inspired activities seems of great importance. Not only can this help the implementation process, but also is likely to enhance their job satisfaction and reinforce their organisational commitment, which in itself constitutes a vital aspect of human resource management.

Indeed, referring to managerial experience, our analysis offers a number of practical guidelines. Thus managers in charge of devising CSR programmes and implementing concrete projects should:

1. Make sure that the programme is – and the projects carried out within its framework are – well-thought-out.
2. Provide subordinates with a clear explanation of the rationale of concrete projects and set attainable objectives.
3. Make projects look interesting and encourage the spirit of competition.
4. Provide employees with *authentic* support and make sure that the programme is not a one-off project but a continuous effort and an integral part of corporate philosophy.
5. Engage employees and guests in innovative and learning-oriented activities that raise ecological awareness and monitor their reactions.
6. Create and put into place environmental (sustainability) management IT systems (such as ESCAP Enviro and LightStay) that, using meaningful indicators (energy in kWh per guest-night or energy in kWh per m^2 of floor area), monitor and show in comprehensible and vivid fashion the environmental performance of particular establishments.
7. Give feedback on performance to all the concerned.
8. Persuade suppliers and subcontractors to pay attention to environmental issues and to comply with green legislation (for instance, co-operate with

those taxi and car-rental firms that use hybrid, electric or bio-fuelled vehicles and with those developers that, while designing and constructing new buildings, use state-of-the-art energy-efficient technologies).
9.   Co-operate with external organisations and institutions that have experience in innovative projects that aim at environmental conservation in different places all over the world.
10. Consult their ideas and activities with local communities.

To sum it up, embracing CSR in general and being green in particular bring concrete cost savings and are good for the triple bottom line. The cost savings come in various forms: some are evident and easily noticeable (a reduced use of resources translating into lower bills), some are a bit less obvious and harder to quantify. For instance, employees who are convinced that their employer behaves ethically and ecologically are, *ceteris paribus*, less likely to leave. This leads to a lower staff turnover, which in practice implies non-negligible savings (as both the training and recruitment of new employees is costly). In a similar vein, employees who are satisfied with their jobs and feel motivated usually tend to put on greater effort, which in turn translates into better service quality for customers (and this, as already indicated, conditions customer loyalty and, par extension, financial performance). Also, the fact that more and more suppliers and subcontractors decide to buy (and to use) more environmentally sustainable products can cause their price to fall in the longer run (due, among other things, to the economies of scale and scope).

While discussing private-sector eco-friendly initiatives, it is also essential to recognise that, to effectively protect the environment, co-ordinated action is required both at governmental and corporate levels. This is because there is a strong interconnectedness between government-led actions and corporate behaviour. For example, installing energy-efficient appliances and switching to low-carbon energy sources can be spurred – and facilitated – by the introduction of tax breaks or subsidies or, conversely, penalises can be imposed if certain initiatives are not implemented and norms are floated. This means that the issue of environmental protection and the implications of corporate social responsibility are likely to remain the focus of public and managerial interest in the near future. In this sense, the chapter, offering insights into CSR-inspired environmentalism in top hotel chains, both helps disseminate best practice amongst hospitality practitioners and makes an important contribution to the on-going debate.

References

Accor (2010) *Sustainable Development* [Online]. Available at: http://www.accor. com/en/sustainable-development.html/ [Accessed: 25 June 2010].

Albinger, H. and Freeman, S. (2000) Corporate Social Performance and Attractiveness as an Employer to Different Job Seeking Populations. *Journal of Business Ethics*, 28(3), 243-53.

Bakan, J. (2004) *The Corporation: The Pathological Pursuit of Profit and Power*. New York: Simon & Schuster Inc.

Baron, D. (2001) Private Politics, Corporate Social Responsibility, and Integrated Strategy. *Journal of Economics and Management Strategy*, 10(1), 7-45.

Bass Hotels and Resorts (2000) *Energy and Water Management Manual*. London: Bass Hotels & Resorts.

Beckerman, W. (2002) *A Poverty of Reason: Sustainable Development and Economic Growth*. Oakland, CA: Independent Institute.

Bohdanowicz, P. (2007) A Case Study of Hilton Environmental Reporting as a Tool of Corporate Social Responsibility. *Tourism Review International*, 11(2), 115-31.

Bohdanowicz, P. and Zientara, P. (2008). Corporate Social Responsibility in Hospitality: Issues and Implications. A Case Study of Scandic. *Scandinavian Journal of Hospitality and Tourism*, 8(4), 271-93.

Bohdanowicz, P. and Zientara, P. (2009) Hotel Companies' Contribution to Improving the Quality of Life of Local Communities and the Well-Being of their Employees. *Tourism and Hospitality Research*, 9(2), 147-58.

Borlaug, N.E. (2007) Sixty-two Years of Fighting Hunger: Personal Recollections. *Euphytica*, 157(3), 287-97.

Brammer, S., Millington, A. and Rayton, B. (2007) The Contribution of Corporate Social Responsibility to Organizational Commitment. *International Journal of Human Resource Management*, 18(10), 1701-19.

Business in the Community (2009) *Corporate Responsibility*. [Online]. Available at: http://www.bitc.org.uk [Accessed: 28 March 2008].

Cacioppe, R., Forster, N. and Fox, M. (2008) A Survey of Managers' Perceptions of Corporate Ethics and Social Responsibility and Actions that May Affect Companies' Success. *Journal of Business Ethics*, 82(3), 681-700.

Chiesa, T. and Gautam, A. (2009) *Travel and Tourism Climate Change Report: Working Towards a Low Carbon Travel and Tourism Sector*. Geneva: World Economic Forum.

Cooke, F.L. and He, Q. (2010) Corporate Social Responsibility and HRM in China: A Study of Textile and Apparel Enterprises. *Asia Pacific Business Review*, 16(3), 355-76.

Crawford, A. and Hubbard, S.S. (2008) The Impact of Work-Related Goals on Hospitality Industry Employee Variables. *Tourism and Hospitality Research*, 8(2), 116-24.

Crook, C. (2005) The Good Company. *Economist*, 8410, 3-18.

CSRwire (2009) *World Travel and Tourism Council (WTTC) Honors Marriott with "Tourism for Tomorrow Award for Sustainability"* [Online, 18 May]. Available at: http://www.csrwire.com/press_releases/ [Accessed: 20 May 2009].

Dow Jones Sustainability Index (2009). Available at: http://www.sustainability-index.com [Accessed: 11 May 2010].

Economist (2006) Food Politics. 8507, 71-3.

Erdogan, N. and Baris, E. (2007) Environmental Protection Programs and Conservation Practices of Hotels in Ankara, Turkey. *Tourism Management*, 28, 604-14.

Esrock, S. and Leichty, G. (1998) Social Responsibility and Corporate Web Pages: Self-presentation or Agenda-setting? *Public Relations Review*, 24(3), 305-26.

Franklin, D. (2008) Just Good Business. *Economist*, 8563, 3-22.

Friedman, M. (1962) *Capitalism and Freedom*. Chicago, IL: The University of Chicago Press.

Furunes, T. and Mykletun, R.J. (2005) Age Management in Norwegian Hospitality Businesses. *Scandinavian Journal of Hospitality and Tourism*, 5(2), 1-19.

Green Lodging News (2007) *Marriott Reduces its Greenhouse Gases 70,000 Tons in One Year* [Online, 1 November]. Available at: http://www.greenlodgingnews. com [Accessed: 5 May 2009].

Green Lodging News (2009) *Scandic's New Bottled Water Program is a Smash* [Online, 5 January]. Available at: http://greenlodgingnews.blogspot. com/2009/01/scandics-new-bottled-water-program-is.html/ [Accessed: 4 July 2010].

Harford, T. (2005) *The Undercover Economist: Exposing why the Rich are Rich, the Poor Are Poor and Why You Can Never Buy a Decent Used Car!* Oxford: Oxford University Press.

Henderson, D. (2001) *Misguided Virtue: False Notions of Corporate Social Responsibility*. London: Institute of Economic Affairs.

Hillman, A. and Keim, G. (2001) Shareholder Value, Stakeholder Management, and Social Issues: What's the Bottom Line? *Strategic Management Journal*, 22(2), 125-39.

Holcomb, J.L. and Upchurch, R.S. and Okumus, F. (2007) Corporate Social Responsibility: What Are Top Hotel Companies Reporting? *International Journal of Contemporary Hospitality Management*, 19(6), 461-75.

HospitalityNet (2010) *Scandic Becomes First Hotel Chain to Launch an Organic Uniform*. [Online, 15 June]. Available at: http://www.hospitalitynet.org/news [Accessed: 4 July 2010].

Hotel Online (2010) *Hilton Unveils LightStay Sustainability Measurement System*. [Online, 20 April]. Available at: http://www.hotel-online.com [Accessed: 20 April 2010].

Hotels Magazine (2009) *Marriott Accelerates Green Hotel Development*. [Online, 11 November]. Available at: http://www.hotelsmag.com [Accessed: 11 November 2009].

InterContinental Hotels Group (2009) *Corporate Responsibility* [Online]. Available at: http://www.ihgplc.com [Accessed: 30 January 2009].

InterContinental Hotels Group (2010) *Corporate Responsibility* [Online]. Available at: http://www.ihgplc.com [Accessed: 20 June 2010].

International Hotels Environment Initiative (1996) *Environmental Management for Hotels: The Industry Guide for Best Practice.* 2nd ed. Oxford: Butterworth-Heinemann.

International Tourism Partnership (2008) *Environmental Management for Hotels: The Industry Guide to Sustainable Operation.* 3rd ed. London: International Business Leaders Forum.

Jenkins, H. and Yakovelva, N. (2005) Corporate Social Responsibility in the Mining Industry: Exploring Trends in Social and Environmental Disclosure. *Journal of Cleaner Production*, 14(3/4), 271-84.

Kalisch, A. (2002) *Corporate Futures: Social Responsibility in the Tourism Industry.* London: Tourism Concern.

Kates, R.W., Parris, T.M. and Leiserowitz, A.A. (2005) What Is Sustainable Development? Goals, Indicators, Values, and Practices, Environment. *Science and Policy for Sustainable Development*, 47(3), 8-21.

Kelly, J., Heider, W., Willimas, P.W. and Englund, K. (2007) Stated Preferences of Tourists for Eco-efficient Planning Options. *Tourism Management*, 28, 377-90.

Kini, R.B. and Hobson, C.J. (2002) Motivational Theories and Successful Total Quality Initiatives, *International Journal of Management*, 19(4), 605-13.

Kirkman, B. and Shapiro, D. (2001) The Impact of Cultural Values on Job Satisfaction and Organizational Commitment in Self-Managing Work Teams: The Mediating Role of Employee Resistance. *Academy of Management Journal*, 44(3), 557-69.

Knowles, T., Macmillan, S., Palmer, J., Grabowski, P. and Hashimoto, A. (1999) The Development of Environmental Initiatives in Tourism: Responses from the London Hotel Sector. *International Journal of Tourism Research*, 1, 255-65.

Lehmann, S. (2009) Motivating Talents in Thai and Malaysian Service Firms. *Human Resource Development International*, 12(2), 155-69.

Magd, H. (2003) Management Attitudes and Perceptions of Older Workers in Hospitality Management. *International Journal of Contemporary Hospitality Management*, 15(7), 393-401.

Marriott (2009) *Spirit to Preserve* [Online]. Available at: http://www.marriott.com/ [Accessed: 30 January 2009].

McIntosh, M., Thomas, R., Leipzinger, T. and Coleman, G. (2003) *Living Corporate Citizenship.* London: Prentice Hall.

Meyer, J.P., and Allen, N.J. (1997) *Commitment in the Workplace: Theory, Research, and Application.* Newbury Park: Sage.

Neuman, W.L. (2003) *Social Research Methods: Qualitative and Quantitative Approaches.* Boston: Allyn and Bacon.

Newsweek (2009) *Green Rankings 2009* [Online]. Available at: http://greenrankings.newsweek.com/ [Accessed: 3 July 2010].

Porter, M. and Kramer, M. (2006) Strategy and Society: The Link between Competitive Advantage and Corporate Social Responsibility. *Harvard Business Review*, 84(12), 78-89.

Rezidor Hotel Group (2009) *Responsible Business* [Online]. Available at: http://www.rezidor.com/ [Accessed: 30 January 2009].

Rezidor Hotel Group (2010) *This is How We Do Business – Responsible Business Report 2010.* [Online]. Available at: http://www.rezidor.com/ [Accessed: 4 July 2010].

Rodriguez, P., Siegel, D., Hillman, A. and Eden, L. (2006) Three Lenses on the Multinational Enterprise: Politics, Corruption, and Corporate Social Responsibility. *Journal of International Business Studies*, 37(6), 733-46.

Roozen, I., Pelsmacker, P., and Bostyn, F. (2001) The Ethical Dimensions of Decision Processes of Employees. *Journal of Business Ethics*, 33(2), 87-100.

Sharpley, R. (2000) Tourism and Sustainable Development: Exploring the Theoretical Divide. *Journal of Sustainable Tourism*, 8(1), 1-19.

Scandic (2003) *Environmental Common Sense – That's Sustainability in Practice.* Stockholm: Scandic AB, Hilton International Nordic Region.

Scandic (2007) *Omtanke – a Day in the Life of a Scandic Hotel.* Stockholm: Scandic.

Scandic (2010) *Sustainability and the Environment* [Online]. Available at: http://www.scandichotels.com/ [Accessed: 4 July 2010].

Solomon, R.C. (1992) *Ethics and Excellence: Cooperation and Integrity: Cooperation and Integrity in Business.* New York: Oxford University Press.

Spector, P.E. (1997) *Job Satisfaction: Application, Assessment, Cause, and Consequences.* Thousand Oaks, CA: Sage Publications, Inc.

TravelBreakingNews (2010) *Tourism for Tomorrow Winners Announced* [Online, 27 May]. Available at: http://www.breakingtravelnews.com/news/article/tourism-for-tomorrow-winners-announced/ [Accessed: 4 July 2010].

Valentine, S. and Fleischman, G. (2008). Ethics Programs, Perceived Corporate Social Responsibility and Job Satisfaction. *Journal of Business Ethics*, 77(2), 159-72.

World Travel and Tourism Council (2009). *Leading the Challenge on Climate Change.* London: WTTC.

Wyndham Hotels and Resorts (2009) *Wyndham Green* [Online]. Available at: http://www.wyndhamworldwide.com/wyndham-green/ [Accessed: 11 January 2009].

Zientara, P. and Bohdanowicz, P. (2010) The Hospitality Sector, in J. Jafari and L.A. Cai (eds) *Tourism and the Implications of Climate Change: Issues and Actions* (Bridging Tourism Theory and Practice, vol. 3), 91-111.

Chapter 6

Environmental Management and Accommodation Facilities in Slovakia

Jana Kučerová

Introduction

Slovakia, prior to independence in 1993, was a part of the territory of Czechoslovakia. It shares borders with Austria, Czech Republic, Poland, Ukraine and Hungary and has a population of approximately 5.5 million people living in an area of 40,000km². Since 1989 (after the "Velvet Revolution") it has undergone substantial changes; the transition from a centrally planned economy to a market economy involving numerous reforms; predominantly in the public sector. It became an EU member state in 2004 (together with 10 other countries) and in 2009 joined the Euro zone. Today, Slovakia is considered to be one of the fastest-growing market economies in Central Europe.

The country has a diverse geography, contained within a comparatively small territory of which 40 per cent is forested, and temperate climate. The central and northern areas are mountainous whilst to the south and east is lowland wherein flows the river Danube which connects the capital, Bratislava, with neighboring capital cities of Vienna and Budapest. Recognition of the quality of the country's natural resources and biodiversity (see Slovakia Travel, 2011) is manifest in the extensive areas covered by various forms of protected designation status (in total some 12,000km²), including nine national parks. Areas designated under NATURA 2000 status account for approximately a quarter of this territory. Furthermore, of the 198 recognised biotopes in Europe, 63 are situated in Slovakia. The country is also know for its substantial range of caves and has more than 1,300 mineral and hot springs waters, acclaimed for their curative effects, which accounts for the presence of 23 spas. Aligned with these diverse natural resources is a rich cultural heritage. There are numerous designated historical sites, castles and mansions, which bear witness to the past, and cities with designated heritage status (mainly due to their historical squares). Over 300 wooden churches have survived to represent the religious architecture. This cultural heritage is further represented through over 70 museums, 19 galleries and more than 100 other expositions. To date, eight sites, representing the natural and cultural heritage, have gain UNESCO Heritage status.

In total, this combination of natural and cultural diversity accounts for much of the tourism in Slovakia and holds tremendous potential for development. But such touristic development needs to be developed with due consideration to the environment as well as the community – in addition to the economy. Thus, the objective of this chapter is first to provide a brief introduction into the characteristics of tourism development in Slovakia and then to identify contemporary problems in the implementation of environmental management in accommodation facilities. In the process drawing on earlier as well as current research involving criteria, drawn from both the accreditation process involved in EU's Community Environmental Management and Auditing System and ISO 14001, to investigate and establish the overall environmental performance of the accommodation sector, primarily hotels, in Slovakia.

Tourism Development

An initial problem with any discussion of the past development of tourism in Slovakia is a lack of statistical data and research, particularly prior to the current century. However, what we can establish is that in 1989 there were 32.7 million visitors, which represents a 250 per cent increase on the numbers cited for 1983 (Malachovsky, 2000: 19). This growth is largely attributed to the political change within Slovakia post-the-"velvet-revolution", the extensive media attention and the interest stimulated on the part of mainly western Europeans. During the 1990s (except 1994) the average annual decrease was seven per cent. A period during which Slovakia had the lowest tourism revenues amongst the central European countries and was the only one to experience such a long term decline in tourism demand (Kučerová et al., 2001: 28). This decline is due to a combination of factors including less media attention and also a lack of quality in the provision of tourism products and services offered to satisfy the needs of tourists from western European countries. This situation was certainly not helped by the fact that Slovakia did not (and still does not) have a comprehensive tourism policy. The lack of marketing effort also accounts in part at least for the limited awareness of the country on the part of many potential tourists, especially within western European countries, the USA and Asiatic countries. This is in spite of the existence of Slovak Tourism Agency, which is responsible for promotion of Slovakia in the international marketplace, but it has struggled due to a very limited budget (the lowest amongst its neighbours). The situation improved post-2004 when the agency gained funding from the EU pre-accession and later through structural funds to support better marketing activities. In the 2007 the new national web portal www.slovakia.travel was launched, again greatly aided through EU financial support.

After some early variations, the period 2001-2007 witnessed a steady increase in visitor numbers, attaining the previous high of 1989 in 2007 (see Table 6.1); albeit about 54 per cent of all visitors are either in transit or day visitors. The consistent increase from 2003 coincides with becoming a Member state of the EU and serves to demonstrate improvements that have been made in the provision of

Table 6.1   Tourism Development in Slovakia (2001-2008)

Indicator/year	2001	2002	2003	2004	2005	2006	2007	2008
Incoming Tourism (Tourist Arrivals) (millions)	27.70	26.40	24.90	26.40	29.40	30.60	32.60	x
Outgoing Tourism of Slovakian Inhabitants (millions)	18.30	17.60	18.30	20.40	22.40	22.70	23.80	x
Incoming Tourism (base index 2001)	-	0.95	0.89	0.95	1.06	1.10	1.17	x
Outgoing Tourism (base index 2001)	-	0.96	1.00	1.10	1.20	1.20	1.30	x
Number of Accommodated Tourists (millions)	3.10	3.40	3.40	3.20	3.40	3.60	3.80	4.00
Average Length of Stay (overnights)	3.60	3.60	3.60	3.30	3.10	3.10	3.10	3.10

Source: Derived from http://www.economy.gov.sk/index/go.php?id=129.

Note: x – data not available.

tourism products and services. The main markets for international visitors have changed little over this period namely the Czech Republic, Germany, Hungary, Poland and Austria; latterly there has been increased demand from the UK and Italy. However, since joining the EURO zone in January 2009, there has been a decline in visitors from the Czech Republic, Hungary and Poland, which correlates with a drop in the respective national currency exchange rates.

The average spend per visitor increased from the equivalent of $23 in 2001 to $61.7 in 2007. This development was not only influenced by a change in the exchange rate of the Slovak currency favourable to Slovakia thus increasing per visitor expenditure but also due to the remarkable increase in the quality of tourism services and development of new tourism products (new ski resorts, aqua parks, spa centre); and since 2004 the status of being a member of the EU. Countering such growth in economic terms has been a rise in outbound tourism over the same period (see Table 6.2). A factor that affirms the country's growing prosperity during this period. This demand has been facilitated by the extensive number (approx. 400) of travel agents and tour operators in the country.

The data in Table 6.2 demonstrates the relatively fast growth of outbound tourism. Also the eightfold increase in tourism revenue between 2001 and 2008. However, the share of tourism as a proportion of the country's GDP has been mainly stable at approximately 2.7 per cent. This is substantially lower than the average share for many other destinations throughout the world (4.1 per cent) (Gúčik, 2004: 132), which demonstrates the fact that Slovakia does not utilise its potential for tourism development.

Table 6.2   Tourism Incomes and Expenditures in Slovakia (2001-2008)

Indicator/year	2001	2002	2003	2004	2005	2006	2007	2008
Incomes ($m)	638.5	724.0	863.0	901.2	1209.8	1513.4	2013.2	2583.7
Index (base 2001)	-	1.1	1.3	1.4	1.8	2.3	3.2	4.0
Expenditures ($m)	266.7	442.2	572.2	745.1	845.7	1054.7	1526.4	2150.9
Index (base 2001)	-	1.6	2.1	2.8	3.1	3.9	5.7	8.0
Index (base 2001)	-	0.7	0.8	0.4	1.03	1.3	1.4	1.2
Average Income per Incoming Tourist ($)	23.0	27.4	34.6	34.1	41.1	49.5	61.7	x
Share of Incomes on GDP (%)	3.1	3.0	2.7	2.1	2.6	2.7	2.7	2.7

Source: Derived from http://www.economy.gov.sk/files/cestruch /4stvrtrok05.doc.

Note: x – data not available.

The objective for tourism development in Slovakia should be in concert with the objectives of sustainable development, which comprises an ongoing increase in quality within the context of the three pillars of sustainability and thus not quantity per se, which manifestly is the objective of the Government's tourism policy. A notable factor in this to date is the total absence of mass tourism. The majority of facilities are small or medium-sized enterprises with little foreign investment. About 70 per cent of all hotels and hospitality enterprises are small, locally owned. However, the start of the 21st century has seen a growing presence of international chain hotels (for example, Holiday Inn, Sheraton, Carlton, Kempinski); not surprisingly these are mainly located in the capital.

Accommodation Facilities

The capacity, location and structure of accommodation facilities are all-important factors that influence tourism development in any country. In Slovakia, this sector has been influenced by the reforms involved in the process of transition to a free market economy, which included the privatisation of accommodation and restaurant facilities, for example the national hotel chains Interhotel, Javorina, and Restauracie. Analysis of the available capacity is also fraught given the lack of comprehensive data. What we can establish is the growth in provision since 2005 What is notable about these statistics is the trend to decreasing room and bed capacity, which is connected with the aim of improving the quality of provision. In 1993 the average number of beds per facility was 83 and by 2006 it was 50 beds. This is partly due to the introduction of the Standardisation of Accommodation and Restaurant Facilities (Number 125/1995, Collection of Law) implemented in 2001 (Number 419/2001) and furthered in 2008 (Number 277/2008). The standardisation

Table 6.3   Accommodation Facilities in Slovakia (2005-2008)

Indicator/year	2005	2006	2007	2008	2008/2005
Facilities	2,446	2,490	3,182	3,434	1.4
Rooms	47,666	48,173	56,525	58,182	1.2
Beds	122,612	124,323	146,655	151,991	1.2
Rooms/Facility	19.5	19.3	17.8	16.9	0.8
Beds/Facility	50.1	49.9	46.0	44.3	0.9

Source: Derived from http://www.economy.gov.sk/files/cestruch/4stvrtrok05.doc.

Note: There is still a relatively high share of 'recreational facilities', which date from the last century. They have a comparatively large capacity, which was designed for the recreation of staff from large, industrial companies and/or trade unions. They are known for their lower standard of services. However, they are gradually being developed into hotels. Many independent providers consider they should have a minimum of 40 beds so that they can accommodate one tour bus.

introduced in 2001 established minimum standards for accommodation facilities across a range of services including the size of a room in relation to bed capacity. This lead to many accommodation facilities having to reduce the number of beds per room. A further outcome was that many accommodation facilities (mainly hotels) had to review there 'star' rating, which lead to a loss of one star in many cases such that now the majority of hotels are 2 star or 3 star hotels. Another factor accounting for the reduced capacity is the increased number of "para hotels" (these are similar to Guest Houses and have less than 10 rooms; there were 197 in 1998, which had risen to 717 by 2008), bed and breakfast operations and private rooms. Table 6.4 also shows the growth in demand in recent years. A downside to this increase in provision, fuelled as it is by the entry of new, invariably small, enterprises, is that their managers often lack knowledge of key environmental issues and associated management systems (Kučerová, 1999; Gunther, 2002). A relatively negative feature is the increasing number of places in camping sites of lower quality standards, which may partly be attributed to their high seasonality. But, it is also recognised that some of these sites clearly have negative impacts on the physical environment.

The overall shift towards smaller units is also an indication of the trend towards more personnalised leisure behaviour (Gúčik et al., 2010). In contrast, a decline in quality hotel capacity could be a concern as many tour operators bringing in international visitors favour hotel accommodation and so too many independent visitors on their first visit.

Despite the progress made in the last few years the general quality of services and tourism products still needs to be improved. Enhanced quality is certainly present in new tourism products based on the resources of mineral and hot springs waters; for example, reconstructed wellness centers, the 10 new aqua parks

Table 6.4   Share of particular accommodation facilities on total capacity of beds (%)

Category/year	2003	2004	2005	2006	2007	2008
Hotel, motel, botel*	42.9	42.7	42.8	41.7	38.4	38.4
Pensions	9.8	10.7	11.0	12.3	14.6	15.2
Hostels	16.5	15.3	14.0	13.7	14.1	13.6
Chalets (self-catering)	5.6	5.2	5.6	5.5	5.0	4.4
Recreational facilities, camping sites**	21.9	22.6	23.1	23.2	24.0	23.8
Private rooms, flats (apartments)	3.3	3.5	3.5	3.6	3.7	4.5

Source: Derived from http://www.economy.gov.sk/files/cestruch/4stvrtrok05.doc

Note: *Botel = hotel located on a boat ** Recreational facilities = accommodation of large capacity and limited services.

and the improvements made in a number of ski resorts, which are well placed to attract more visitors and make more of a contribution to the local economy and community. The exemplar for both progress and quality is Aquacity Poprad, has achieved a number of ecolabel awards – "Green Apple", "Green Globe" in 2005 and in 2007, and a World Travel Award as "World's Leading Environmental Resort" in 2008.[1]

However, the ongoing development of tourism needs to incorporate addressing the environmental performance and the adoption of environmental management systems by tourism businesses. Thus, we now turn to examine to what extent this is already happening in the tourism sector.

Implementation of an Environmental Management System

International standards designed to promote the introduction of environmental management systems play a significant role in reducing negative impacts of human activities on the quality of the environment. Slovakia, in line with international agreements, adopted the standard ISO 14001 "Systems of Environmental

---

1   Green Apple is awarded by the Green Organisation as an independent, non-political, non-activist, non-profit environment group dedicated to recognising, rewarding and promoting environmental best practice around the world. The International Green Apple Environment Award campaigns are for environmental best practice and also for enhancing the built environment and architectural heritage. Green Globe award is the most prestigious environmental award presented by King County every two years. World Travel Award is considered to be like an "Oscar's award in tourism and travel industry worldwide. The AquaCity Poprad has achieved this award for the highest environmental standards, its contribution to sustainability of local economy and environment.

Management" in 1996. In 2010, there were 461 accredited organisations with ISO 14001 of which two are considered to be within the tourism sector, namely the Dudince Spa and the Thermal Swimming Pool Podhajska (see http:/www.sazp. sk, 2010). The promotion of ISO 14001 appears to be more successful than that of the Community's Environmental Management and Audit Scheme (EMAS), which was introduced in 1993 and in 2001 EMAS II was implemented. Notably, EU member states should support small and medium-sized enterprises in the implementation of EMAS (Brňák, 2005: 24). The legal framework for this scheme was accepted in Slovakia (Code No. 491/2005 Z.z) and subsequently further incorporated in the regulations of the Slovakian Ministry of the Environment (Code No. 606/2006 Z.z) and implemented in the legal system. Even so, the adoption by businesses has been very limited. To date there are four organisations registered under EMAS; none of which are in the accommodation sector.

In the 1996, Slovakia accepted the "National Program of Environmental Evaluation and labeling of the Products". Based on this programme the Slovak Association of Hotels and Restaurants established a national eco-label for Slovakian hotels, based on meeting a relatively small number of criteria, and providing basic information on environmentally friendly management practices for its members. The "National Program" was subsequently updated in 2004 with the objective of synchronising procedures for the environmental label "Environmental friendly product" with the European label "European flower".[2] The organisation with responsibility for accreditation is the Ministry of the Environment. Since 2007, this award has included accommodation services. The first hotel to gain such accreditation was the Ma Maison Residence Sulekova in Bratislava, which is entitled to use the label 'European flower'.

Research Methodology and Methods

To investigate the current situation in the implementation of the principles of environmental management, a representative sample of hotels in the Banska Bystrica region (including the Dudince Spa resort), where researched involving interviews with the managers and a survey, based on criteria drawn from ISO 14001, comprising 76 questions divided into six main fields – the management system, energy, water, chemical materials, waste and other services. This also

---

2   "The European Ecolabel is a voluntary scheme, established in 1992 to encourage businesses to market products and services that are kinder to the environment. Products and services awarded the Ecolabel carry the flower logo, allowing consumers – including public and private purchasers – to identify them easily. Today the EU Ecolabel covers a wide range of products and services, with further groups being continuously added. Product groups include cleaning products, appliances, paper products, textile and home and garden products, lubricants and services such as tourist accommodation". http://ec.europa.eu/environment/ecolabel/promo/flash_en.htm.

included compulsory and obligatory criteria used for the European Flower accreditation label. The key findings are presented according to the six main categories identified above. In the process, and as appropriate, drawing on the outcomes of two earlier studies. The first of these involved a representative cross section of hotels in the cities of Kosice, Humenne, Presov and Bardejov with the objective of establishing the extent to which they had introduced environmental management practices. This involved interviews with the managers of the hotels and a survey comprising 80 indicators informed by the International Hotels Environment Initiative (IHEI, 1996). The second study mirrored the earlier study in that the objective was the same. However, this time the focus was on selected accommodation facilities in two tourist resorts. Donovaly, which is situated in the Low Tatra National Park and is a 'typical' mountain tourist resort and Slnava, which is a 'typical' summer season resort adjacent to a lake. In the case of Donovaly, a range of accommodation operations, representative of the resort, were selected (mix of hotels, pensions, two chalets and one camping site). Whilst for Slnava, all the accommodation operations participated (all two star hotels with an average of 135 rooms). The relationship between the standard of the hotel (number of stars) and implementation of environmental performance measures was tested by correlation coefficient. The result at 0.5231, means middle direct dependence thus those hotels with higher standards are more likely to implement principles of environmental performance and related practices.

Environmental Management System

One hotel was ISO 14001 accredited and their environmental policy, which is well publicised, comprises clearly elaborated objectives, an environmental programme and action plan for the achievement of these objectives. When selecting suppliers they seek to establish if a supplier has an environmental policy; favouring those who are can demonstrate appropriate accreditation. None of the other operations, including those enterprises in the earlier studies, indicated any attention to supply chain management. This hotel compared with the other operations has the highest standard of services. A finding that was also present in the first study which identified that the hotel gaining an outcome of greater than 75 per cent for adopting environmental management practices was ranked as a 3 star. However, whilst this may be taken as a general indication for the performance of 3 star operations it is not always so as the performance of one other 3 star hotel was found to be little better than average. Though none of the other hotels had any form of EMS accreditation or a clearly defined environmental policy, they do regularly monitor their energy and water consumption and try to identify potential savings. However, such attention does not include detail as to variance in energy consumption between different operational areas and so forth. These findings are all very similar to the outcomes of the preceding studies.

None of the hotels explicitly encourage their customers to support the environmental initiatives they may have introduced. All the managers were found to consider this approach too intrusive. It emerged through the interviews that they think (and in most cases stressing this point) that to provide more information and encourage guests to savings in the energy consumption and so forth is too like "education" and creates pressure on guests. Therefore they seek to make all measures "invisible" to their guests. Further, such actions as promoting these practices may be seen as contrary to the overall ambience they seek to create for their guests.

Overall, with but one exception, the hotels have not introduced an EMS. Basically, the hotels tend only to do what is required by government legislation, which is "Regular maintenance and checking of the heating system by authorised professionals; minimal once per year". Thus all the hotels meet at least one criterion; an outcome very similar to the earlier research studies.

Energy

All the hotels receive some of their energy needs from renewable sources due to the fact that the main energy supplier in the region derives 20 per cent of its total energy supply from renewable resources. Gas is the main source of energy for heating though some also use coal or wood frass (reconstituted ground wooden waste). None of the hotels has a heating system designed to utilise waste heat generated by boiler systems. The hotels are generally well insulated; the major exception to this is seeking a grant, under EU Structural Funds, for the thermo-insulation of buildings. None of the hotels undertake a regular (i.e. every two years) independent energy audit, which would probably lead to savings in fuel costs. The criteria to achieve a minimum of 50 per cent of energy from renewable resources was considered by all the managers to be unrealistic in the short-term.

In most cases, the hotels have more than 80 per cent of their light bulbs in the A category and also their dish washing machines; approximately 50 per cent use fridge's in the A+ category.

Energy consumption is further increased by the presence of a sauna [approximately two-thirds of cases], which is usually in continual operation. A few of these hotels operate their saunas on a request basis, which has been found to be more energy efficient. A quarter of the hotels have swimming pools, for which solar panels are used for heating the water but this is not utilised elsewhere within the hotel due to the high initial investment costs involved. None of the hotels provide information for guests as to how they could contribute to reducing energy consumption during their stay.

Overall, most of the hotels were found to perform above the average benchmark in this area. This is a better overall performance than for the businesses in the Donovaly and Slnava study and suggests that more attention is now being given to energy management.

Water

All the managers consider water costs to be high yet less than 50 per cent of them have introduced measures to decrease water consumption and consider the cost of introducing a Water Regulatory System as being too expensive. Even so, the number of operations which are taking appropriate measures is higher than found in the Donovaly and Slnava study.

The majority of hotels provide lists in strategic places detailing chemicals that must not be discharged into the waste water systems [guest are not similarly advised]. Approximately a quarter of the hotels (predominantly those in spa resorts) use environmental friendly materials, that is, sand or specially ground stone rather than chemical salt, for clearing snow and ice, which is necessary given the comparatively hard winters. However, the use of such materials is also by local measures put in place by the municipality; for example, in environment protected areas only sand or ground stone may be used and in some places only mechanical diggers may be used.

Due to the hardness of the water, which varies across the country, there are automatic 'dosing systems' for dishwashers and washing machines. But few hotels operate such systems.

In general, they all provide the necessary information and training for their employees in the use of chemicals, for example, cleaning materials.

In the light of the increasingly common practice of inviting guests not to seek daily changes of bed linen and towels, it is surprising that so few of the operations were found to have adopted this practice. Interestingly, a third of the managers indicated that now they know of this practice they are likely to implement it in the near future.

Overall, the hotels were found to perform poorly in the management of water resources. An outcome which contrasts with a generally better performance in this area in the first study.

Chemicals

The majority of the hotels were found to use 'strong' disinfectants and in higher than the manufacturers' recommend strengths – as opposed to environmentally friendly cleaning products. The main reasons given for this approach were to achieve better standards of hygiene and at the same time reduce the time needed for cleaning. Few of the hotels monitor the type and consumption of cleaning agents they use and seek to eliminate "aggressive" chemicals and try to buy environmental friendly products for washing and cleaning.

Again, we find that the hotels performed poorly in their use of chemicals, whether for cleaning or in washing systems.

Waste Disposal System

The hotels, with one exception, separate their waste (paper, glass, plastic, metal, organic waste and hazardous materials), which is greatly facilitated by their municipal authority. A factor also present in the Donovaly and Slnava study. The exception is in an area that has yet to introduce such a system despite the existing legislation. Although the manager indicated a willingness to separate waste, they have not presented a written request to their municipality, which might help to stimulate the appropriate action by their local government authority. Though none of the hotels provides the possibility for guests to separate their waste in their guests' rooms, a number of the hotels do separate such waste after collection.

The majority of hotels use individually wrapped portions in guestrooms and to a lesser extent in restaurants (similar to the Donovaly and Slnava findings). One hotel avoids small packaging throughout its operations and has found that this has reduced waste and purchasing costs.

In one case, items not required are passed to charity whilst other hotels seek to reuse such products were possible (for example, old towels for cleaning).

In the area of waste disposal systems, all the hotels achieved above a comparatively above average performance.

Other Services

Approximately 50 per cent of the hotels implement a non-smoking policy throughout the hotel whilst others allow smoking in some guestrooms.

Few of the hotels provide information to guests about local biodiversity and measures in conservation though they may display such material when provided by other organisations.

One hotel provides information on access by public transport and also tries to motivate guests and employees to utilise public transport. In contrast, improvements in road infrastructure and a decline in public bus services has lead to cars increasingly being used as the chosen means of transport for visitors to Donovaly/Slnava. One in five hotels has bicycles available for guest hire but due to a lack of demand some of the hotels have subsequently withdrawn this service. In marked contrast, a number of the other hotels are planning to introduce such a service.

The use of local produce is limited with none of the hotels meeting the criteria of a minimum of two local products on their menus. This is partly due to contracts with suppliers who may not supply such products. No one seeks to establish if the produce ordered is grown by methods of ecological agriculture, for example, organic.

One hotel does consider the environmental labeling of purchased products important. Approximately 25 per cent of the hoteliers purchase toilet tissue made from recycled paper. This finding is in contrast to the Donovaly and Slnava study wherein none of the operations used toilet tissue made from recycled paper, which is attributed to a lack of supply at that time. Few hotels use recycled paper for administrative purposes due to problems with printers and the higher price of this paper but do use renewable toners in their copy machines and printers.

None of the hotels were found to use eco-labeled paint.

Overall, the majority of the hotels achieved under-average values in the field of 'other environmental services'.

Conclusion

Slovakia as a small country, with extensive (often unspoiled) natural and cultural resources with substantial tourism potential, which compared to western European countries is comparatively undeveloped. This unrealised potential is partly due to its earlier history but arguably more so due to the absence of a comprehensive tourism policy and associated destination marketing. Thus, it is not surprising perhaps to find that it is still an unknown tourism destination for many potential tourists.

What development in tourism we have seen is largely characterised by quantitative growth and arguably, a relative decline in the socio-economic benefits of tourism in the context of the national economy. This quantitative growth is most remarkable in the development of accommodation facilities; the largest share of which is concentrated in those areas with the largest national parks and most valuable natural resources. Therefore it is especially important to pay due attention to environmental protection. As such, the promotion of tourism and associated development needs to be carefully considered such that it is attuned to environmental initiatives, informed by best practice and EU tourism policy, which aims to promote more considerate, more locally orientated and community lead development (see Leslie, 2010). Within this context the promotion of environmental management practices is very much to the fore; for example, the European Flower certification scheme.

However, as the research findings discussed above and those of earlier studies attest (Kučerová, 1999; Gunther, 2002) the implementation of the principles of environmental management in accommodation facilities in Slovakia is, at best, limited. Those operations that have implemented an environmental management system are predominantly to be found in the larger tourism businesses – spas, hotels recognised for higher standards of quality and aquaparks. A finding that mirrors other studies (Maráková and Faksová, 2009). However, the majority of operations are addressing and seeking to meet EMS criteria relating to their energy usage and waste management. An outcome, which is not unexpected given the strict legislation, introduced in Slovakia as an EU member state on waste management and in the light of increasing energy costs. Findings which reinforce the view that for substantive results to be achieved in environmental performance then legislation is required or at least a substantial increase in costs catalysing responsive action. The greatest problems are thus in the areas of creating an environmental policy, water management, chemical usage and general services. The operations generally do not play an active role in informing their guests about environmental issues nor do they seek to encourage their local community to introduce the environmental measures, especially in the area of waste management. However, the adoption of such standards and implementation of an environmental management system in tourism businesses is not only strongly influenced by the values of senior management and employees but also by a country's environmental policies and regulatory frameworks, local community initiatives and visitor attitudes.

Even so, the greatest challenge appears to be implementation of environmental management in small accommodation facilities, which are increasing in number. Generally their owners/managers evidence a lack of knowledge relating to best practices in resource management in spite of the activities of the Slovak Association of Hotels and Restaurants. Therefore it appears necessary to formulate an information campaign and training courses for the owners and managers in not only hotels but all other enterprises involved in tourism with the objective to increase their awareness and knowledge in the field of environmental management and ideally stimulate positive action.

References

Brňák, R. (2005) Co nevidiet v novom zakone o EMAS-e. *Enviromagazin*, roc. 10, c. 4, s. 24-5. *What can not be seen in the New EMAS Legislation.*

Gúčik, M. (2004). Nevyhnutnosť zmien v štátnej politike cestovného ruchu na Slovensku ako nového člena Európskej únie. *Ekonomická revue cestovného ruchu*, roc. 37, 2004, c. 3, p. 131–9. *The Necessity of Changes in National Tourism Policy in Slovakia as the EU Member State.*

Gúčik, M. (2010). *Manazment cestovneho ruchu*. Banska Bystrica: (EDS DALI-BB, s.r.o. pre Slovak – Swiss Tourism Banska Bystrica, 2010. *Tourism Management.*

Gunther, K. (2002) Analýza uplatnovania ekologického manazmentu v slovenskom hotelierstva. *Ekonomická revue cestovného ruchu*, roè. 35, c. 3, 131–41. *Analysis of Environmental Performance in Slovakian hotels.*

IHEI (1996) *Environmental Management for Hotels – The Industry Guide to Best Practice*. Oxford: Butterworth-Heinemann.

Kučerová, J. (1999) *Ekologický manazment podnikov cestovného ruchu v koncepcii trvalo udrzatelného rozvoja cestovného ruchu*. Habilitacna praca. Banska Bystrica: Ekonomicka fakulta UMB *Environmental Management of Tourism Businesses in the Sustainable Approach to Tourism Development.*

Kučerová, J., Malachovský, A. and Maráková, V. (2001) Sustainable Tourism Development in Slovakia, in *BADANIA NAUKOWE* Zeszyt 1. Kielce: Wysza Szkola Ubezpiecezn, 2001, 25-33.

Leslie, D. (2010) The European Union, sustainable tourism policy and rural Europe, in D.V.L Macleod and S.A. Gillespie (eds) *Sustainable Tourism in Rural Europe: Approaches to Development*. Oxon: Routledge, 43-60.

Malachovsky, A. (2000) Strategická analýza vývoja cestovného ruchu na Slovensku. *Ekonomická revue cestovného ruchu*, roc. 33, c.1, 28-32. *Strategic Analysis of Tourism Development in Slovakia.*

Maráková, V. and Faksová, R. (2009). Development Trends of Wellness Tourism in Selected European Countries. *Finance i Marketing w Sporcie*. Bialsko Biala: Redakcija Naukowa Janusz Klisinski, 183-92.

Chapter 7

From Eco-ignorance to Eco-certificates: Environmental Management in Slovene Hotels

Sonja Sibila Lebe and Saša Zupan

Introduction

Slovenia is one of the smallest EU countries, yet one which has potentially the richest bio-diversity per square kilometre due to its geographic diversity. In an area of approximately 20,000km^2, 60 per cent of which is covered in woodland, which places the country in third place (after Sweden and Finland) for forest cover in Europe, four major features of Europe's geographical characteristics are fusing: the Mediterranean, the Alps, the Great Pannonia Plane and the Karst region. To maintain and to protect this biodiversity has become one of the main goals of Slovenia since independence in 1991. Sustainability is now considered an obligatory part of all government policies, of every strategy and development plan – including the tourism sector – although not all sectors of economy are achieving these goals at the same pace and equally successfully. Overall the economy has seen major growth since the early 1990s as noted in Table 7.1, which shows that the GDP has more than tripled since 1995 and actually doubled in the last 10 years. Furthermore, the GDP per capita growth in Slovenia in the last decade (2000-2010) has almost tripled from 10,900 Euro in 2000 to 27,500 Euro in 2010 (SORS, 2011).

The most important part of the country's economy is the service sector, contributing approximately 61 per cent to the GDP, followed by industry (37 per cent) and agriculture (two per cent) (SORS, 2011). According to the last World Economic Forum report (WEF, 2009), tourism contributed 11.9 per cent to the country's GDP, accounting for 44 per cent of services exports and contributed 68 per cent to the overall surplus in trade of services (Bank of Slovenia, 2011). Tourism is clearly seen in Slovenia as an important provider of employment for the local population. Since 1995 tourism demand has experienced a steady increase. By 2010 the number of international visitors had nearly tripled and overnights doubled (see Table 7.2)

Government responsibility for tourism lies in the Directorate for Tourism and Internationalisation (DTI) within the Ministry of Economy. It is responsible for issuing tourism related laws as well as development strategies and policies for tourism. The main doctrine of the current Tourism Strategy (MG, 2011) is the

Table 7.1   Gross domestic product (GDP), 1995-2010 (000 €)

Year	GDP
1995	10,357
2000	18,566
2005	28,722
2010	35,974

Source: http://www.stat.si/eng/novica_prikazi.aspx?id=3941.

Table 7.2   Tourist flows in Slovenia, 1995-2010

	Arrivals			Overnights		
Year	Total	Domestic	International	Total	Domestic	International
1995	1,576,672	844,569	732,103	5,883,046	3,447,579	2,435,467
2000	1,957,116	867,567	1,089,549	6,718,999	3,314,901	3,404,098
2005	2,395,010	840,041	1,554,969	7,572,584	3,173,338	4,399,246
2010	2,963,595	1,120,032	1,843,563	8,771,666	3,848,403	4,923,263

Source: SORS (2011).

development of niche tourism and stimulation of tourism development in less developed rural regions. The primary government objective for tourism is to develop green and more environmental-friendly tourism products and services. To achieve these goals the Ministry has established a programme of quality augmentation, which encompasses two major themes: development of human resources and development of eco-tourism (MG, 2011).

The EU stated in their Agenda 2000 (EC, 1997) that a complex and integral environmental policy was required of Slovenia given that in their judgement the country was lagging considerably behind the most developed EU countries. By its accession to the EU, Slovenia was advised to direct its ecological policy towards governmental incentives that would foster the introduction of environmental management measures in all sectors of the economy. The first step in this process was the need for Slovenia to harmonise its policies and laws concerning the environment in line with all EU directives and normative documentation in the field of environmental protection. One of the main principles of its development policy established from the outset was that the objectives of sustainable development thus sustainability would be embedded in all the states' development policies. This has since been reaffirmed in the State Development Programme for Slovenia for the period 2007-2013 (SVLR, 2011), which serves as the umbrella document for all sector strategies and development plans and all sub-Departmental strategies (for example, tourism) are also based on sustainability. The institutions responsible for tourism (Ministry of Economy/DTI and Slovenia's National Tourist Organisation [STO]) have made substantial efforts towards the development of quality and responsible tourism; including a diverse range of activities (for example, elaboration of product strategies, surveys on customer behaviour regarding specific tourism products, targeted research programmes on human resource development and research programmes on the environmental performance of the tourism sector (see STO, 2011; MG, 2011). It is this latter aspect that is the focus herein.

This chapter primarily addresses the problems and potential barriers to the introduction of environmental management systems (EMS) in accommodation establishments in Slovenia. First, we discuss EMSs, which serves to provide the context for the subsequent discussion on the eco-labelling of accommodation facilities; in other words accredited certification schemes for hotels that have formally introduced an EMS. This is followed by more detailed consideration of the EU's Eco-Flower label for accommodation services. We then present the case study "Slovenia Green", which is based on research into Slovene hotels and their progress in the implementation of environmental management practices and the implementation of the environmental management system accredited though the Eco-Flower scheme.

Environmental Management Systems (EMS) in Tourist Accommodation Services

For a long time services have been considered as less critical to the environment than production processes. Yet today we know that albeit tourism supply is dominated by SMEs that use comparatively few resources at the individual level, collectively in global terms tourism is a major polluter, contributing around 10 per cent to global greenhouse gas emissions; three quarters of which is due to travelling to and from the holiday destination (Kajfež-Bogataj, 2009). Only hospitals have more of a negative impact on the environment than hotels. This is mostly due to their very high consumption of energy and water; for example, a typical hotel uses (per square metre) more energy than an industrial building whilst food waste is estimated at an average of 15 per cent (Ball et al., 2003). Energy costs are often critical to the profitable operation of a hotel, especially in countries where hotels need to be heated or cooled very intensively and also in the case of luxury hotels (Ball et al., 2003, Bogdanowicz et al., 2004; Bogdanowicz, 2005). It is thus not surprising that EMS systems are more likely to be found in large companies (see Chapter 5); corporations are generally much quicker to introduce an environmental policy and are concerned to maintain a positive environmental image.

As tourists become more environmentally conscious so too is demand for hotels with accredited EMSs. This is well illustrated in Greece, where hotels show signs of progress in the introduction of EMS which arguably is primarily influenced by one of their major tourist markets namely tourists from Germany who are generally recognised as being comparatively highly ecologically conscious. It is not only potential guests but investors, and possibly local communities, who support the concepts of eco-management in "their" hotels (Sloan et al., 2009). In Europe, the highest level of eco-consciousness is found in the northern countries, like Scandinavia, Netherlands and Germany (the Southern- and Eastern-European countries are lagging behind) (Sloan et al., 2009). Consequently even hotel chains that in the past have paid little attention to environmental issues have begun to change their attitudes: to be ecologically conscious has become smart. Hotels have found out that environmental management does not necessarily involve major investment in new technologies but rather more efficient management of resources and costs. To a large extent this is due to the age of the buildings involved where quite often the architecture, design and structure only allows for limited changes in contrast to the major savings in energy which can be achieved through the design of properties in such a way as to minimise energy consumption.

In general terms hotels have responded in different ways to environmental pressures of state regulators through, for example, policy initiatives and the concerns of potential guests. But by and large these are variances based on the fundamental principles of an EMS; for example, Total Quality Environmental Management, international standards such as the ISO14001 and European Union's Environmental Management and Audit Scheme (EMAS) (For a comprehensive discussion of these and other environmental auditing systems see Goodall [2004]). These latter systems are not that well suited to the vast majority of hotels given their small size and limited financial resources. Thus, we identify the emergence of accommodation specific schemes such as the Nordic eco-label Swan, which is the best known eco label in Scandinavia (Vähätiitto, 2010) or the Green Business Scheme Eco-label which was first developed in Scotland and now covers the UK and Ireland (Leslie, 2012). The reasons for hotels implementing an EMS and striving to obtain the appropriate eco-certification are varied and include the belief that this is a means to differentiate the hotel from their competitors (Ball et al., 2003). However, often a major factor for a hotel deciding to "go green" is that it can expect to gain financial benefits as a result (predominantly in cost savings on energy use) in a relatively short period of time. The overall approach and credo of a hotel deciding to become more environmental responsible and friendly means adopting the 3Rs: *reduce*, *reuse*, and *recycle*. Practically all eco-labels in the world are following this paradigm.

European Eco-labels for Tourism

The globalisation of society has led to the evolution of a new business paradigm. Striving for profit has gained a new and quickly growing partner namely corporate social responsibility (CSR) of which sustainable development is an eminent part. Public opinion was and continues to be increasingly concerned about environmental issues, which is having some influence on tourism demand. Tourism managers, to varying degrees, are aware that their guests are part of this more and more demanding and eco-conscious public that is asking for environmentally responsible tourism products services (Bohdanowicz et al., 2004a). Thus today the number of guests who expect their hotel to be environmentally friendly is increasing (see Chapter 1). The extent of such demand depends to some extent on their location, the type of accommodation offering and the context of that offering if part of a package. Demand will also vary whether it is for business (for example, institutional purchasers) or individual travellers. The availability of such eco-friendly hotels also varies considerably from country to country. There is thus a need for environmentally friendly hotels, which for clarity and simplicity we will adopt the term 'eco-hotels', to be promoted appropriately. The prospective tourist should be able to find the information about the sustainability and eco-friendliness that they are seeking. But, it is argued, the more mature consumer expects *reliable proof* that the hotel is not only advertising messages relating to its environmental performance but also wishes to see reliable evidence that the hotel is actually managed in an environment-friendly manner. One, out of many, possible ways of providing such evidence is through participation in an accredited EMS eco-certificate scheme. For example, tourists who want to find a "green" lodging property can search the internet for this information provided by organisations such as the "Green Meeting Industry Council" (see www.greenmeetings.info), the "Environmentally friendly hotels" (that have obtained one out of several existing environmental labels) (see www.environmentallyfriendlyhotels.com), or through the association "Green Hotels" (see www.greenhotels.com). These sites, amongst others, provide some degree of confidence by way of establishing the green credentials of the hotels listed. But what if such an opportunity is not available? How does the consumer potentially faced with a number of hotels with potentially different accreditation select which one is best based on such criteria? This is quite likely to be the case in Europe which has far more "green" certification programmes than any other region of the world. Environmental certificates and awards in Europe are designed for all types of tourism suppliers in the accommodation sector and also a host of other areas such as beaches, marinas, restaurants, handicrafts, golf courses, camping sites, tour operators (see Chapters 2, 3, 4). More than 40 schemes certify accommodation services: hotels with or without restaurants, camping sites, youth hostels, farm houses, alpine huts, holiday houses, guest houses, bed and breakfast lodgings and others (see www.eco-tip.org).[1]

Many member states have introduced an accredited EMS, promoted by their respective National Tourist Organisation, which invariably is limited to that country; notable exceptions being Nordic Swan, Green Globe and the Eco-Flower (see below). Furthermore there may be more than one accredited EMS scheme operating within a country. This situation has created a problem. In effect, it has

---

1   The ECO-TIP site was created in the 1990s by ECOTRANS, the European network for sustainable tourism development as a good practice examples and eco-labels for environmentally friendly tourism in Europe.

Table 7.3   Members of the VISIT initiative (as in 2010)

Country	Label	Certificates	Web-page
International	Blue Flag	over 3,450 beaches and marinas in 41 countries across Europe, South Africa, Morocco, Tunisia, New Zealand, Brazil, Canada and the Caribbean	www.blueflag.org
Switzerland	Steinbock	15 hotels in 6 Swiss cantons	www.oe-plus.ch
Italy	Legambiente Turismo	300 eco-friendly accommodation businesses	www.legambienteturismo.it
France	La Clef Verte	500 tourist accommodations had this label, among them 236 camping sites, 210 hotels and 54 rural accommodations	www.laclefverte.org
Austria	Das Österreichische Umweltzeichen für Tourismus-betriebe	Approximately 200 places to stay of all kinds, as well as restaurants	www.umweltzeichen.at
Latvia	Zalaissertifikats	53 accommodation businesses in the Latvian countryside	www.eco.celotajs.lv
Spain	El Distintivo de Garantia de Calidad Ambiental	70 accommodation businesses in Catalonia	www.gencat.net/mediamb/ qamb/inici.htm
Denmark Estonia Greenland Sweden	Den GroenneNoegle	Over 100 accommodation businesses from youth hostels to 4 star luxury hotels	www.dengroennenoegle.dk
Sweden Denmark Iceland Finland Norway	Nordic Swan	79 hotels in Sweden, Denmark, Norway, Finland and Iceland	www.svanen.nu
The Netherlands	Milieu-barometer	230 camping sites, holiday resorts, hotels, group accommodation and attraction parks	www.milieubarometer.com
United Kingdom	Green Tourism Business Scheme	348 visitor attractions, 101 Tourist Information Centres, 45 restaurants/cafés 4 shops, 1 other place to visit	www.green-business.co.uk
Luxembourg	Eco-label Luxembourg	23 places to stay in town and country	www.emweltzenter.lu/ emweltzenter/oekofonds/ ecolabel/virstellung.htm
27 EU-members	Eco-label (EU Eco-Flower)	Tourist accommodation services and tourist camps	http://ec.europa.eu/ environment/ecolabel

Source: http://www.indexmundi.com

become practically impossible for tourists to distinguish between different eco-labels and certificates, or to know at least the main criteria for each of them in order to make a suitably informed decision with some degree of confidence. In contrast to Europe, the USA appears to have a less complicated approach which is considered partly to be the result of the Green Seal, launched in 1989, which has been a pioneer in promoting sustainability in the economy in the USA (see www. greenseal.org). This long-standing eco-label is partly seen to be responsible for the many tourists travelling from the USA who are asking for eco-hotels in Europe.

An initiative which has sought to address this difficulty is VISIT – the Voluntary Initiative for Sustainability in Tourism (VISIT, 2011), which aims to bring together under one umbrella eco-certification labels for European countries (see Table 7.3). The organisation is coordinated by ECOTRANS, ECEAT, and partners and not only seeks to promote sustainability in tourism but also works as a marketing organisation to promote the accredited eco-labels and the enterprises involved. To be included, the schemes must meet similar criteria and standards and participation includes on-site inspections.

This potential confusion and diversity of accreditation programmes for EMS undoubtedly is one of the reasons why the European Commission decided to introduce an EU-wide eco-label – the Eco-Flower designed for hotel enterprises. It guarantees the implementation of the same criteria and the same level and intensity of environmental management performance among tourist accommodation providers in all EU member countries.

The European Eco-label for Tourist Accommodation Services

The European Eco-label, established in 1992, aims to encourage business to develop and market more environmental-friendly products and services. The scheme is open to firms throughout the European Union and the EEA countries (Norway, Iceland and Liechtenstein) can apply for the Flower logo for their products and services. The EU member states individually choose their own pace of promoting the EU Eco-label in their country. The number of applications and the intensity of implementing the label are thus varying considerably from one member state to another. The Eco Flower label is only awarded after verification that the product or service meets clearly defined criteria covering environmental and performance standards and based on life-cycle analysis (see Fouhy, 1993). Products and services awarded the Eco-label carry the flower logo. It is a rapidly growing brand and many producers appear to consider that it gives them a competitive advantage.

Today the EU Eco-label covers a wide range of products including cleaning materials, appliances, paper products, textiles and more recently services such as tourist accommodation services (since 2003) and camping sites (since 2009). Each product group has specific criteria and measures that are verified during the certification process. The 90 criteria for accommodation services (97 for camps)

Table 7.4   Six groups of criteria for tourist accommodations and tourist camps

Section	Short description of testing areas
Energy	Alternative/renewable sources of energy, energy saving equipment and machines, electricity saving programmes and measures for employees and guests.
Water	Limiting fresh water consumption, appropriate waste water management, awareness raising information for employees and guests.
Detergents and disinfectants	Biodegradable, forbidding or limiting use of disinfectants to the level prescribed by national legislation.
Waste	Preventing waste, wet and dry waste separation, no one way package products.
Other services	No smoking in common areas, encouraging staff and visitors to use public transportation.
General management	Maintenance and servicing of technical equipment, environmental programme and policy setting, staff training, information to guests, gathering energy and water consumption data, other environment relevant data collection – e.g. use of chemicals.

are divided into 29 mandatory criteria, the rest are optional, varying according to the product/service offer - the more diverse the more criteria that have to be met. In all, the criteria are grouped into six areas (see Table 7.4).

The foregoing discussion raises a number of issues that lead to the following questions.

- What are the differences between the various schemes and which are better in terms of positive environmental impacts?
- Does such certification generate benefits for the certified enterprise; tangible positive impacts on employees, on the local community, the environment on the one side, and on the other their finances when compared with enterprises without certificates?
- For whom are these schemes predominantly created? Is it, for example, for local providers as an obligation to reach a certain level of quality (thus similar to hotel grading criteria), or for tourists who would like to rely on the organisation/enterprise's promises that their offering is reliably environmentally friendly/responsible because it is certified or a combination of these?
- How can the Government of a country seeking to promote the greening of hotels assess which one might be the most appropriate to adopt?
- With cognisance of such questions the Ministry of Economy commissioned detailed research in order to establish how best to promote their objective

of progress in relation to sustainability issues and the greening of hotels, that is, the wide scale implementation of an EMS.

"Slovenia Green"

In 2006[2] the Ministry of Economy commissioned a survey to investigate the awareness and knowledge of environmental management systems amongst Slovene hotel managers. The Ministry was aware that a major barrier to the introduction of an EMS is a common belief that environmental measures are expensive. Thus the survey also sought to establish the kind of support hotel managers would need, as appropriate, to encourage them to introduce environment management practices into their establishments. In the process, the research was expected to evaluate the current extent of such practices implemented in Slovene hotels. Further the study aimed:-

- to establish primary motivators to encourage accommodation managers who have previously not thought of implementing an EMS into their establishments to change their minds and join the Government's eco-initiative;
- to establish whether Slovenia should develop its own eco-label for tourism enterprises (for example, accommodation) or rather adopt an existing and internationally renowned one;
- and to elaborate a platform/programme for further governmental measures and incentives in the field of ecotourism development, applicable to accommodation businesses.

Preliminary research involved an extensive review of the most common eco-labels, eco-schemes and eco-awards (with special attention given to the EU Eco-label – the Eco Flower), used for certification of EMS practices by accommodation operations. A complex benchmark analysis was undertaken involving countries that shared comparable destination attributes with Slovenia; thus Austria and Switzerland as Alpine countries, Italy and Croatia as Mediterranean countries, Hungary for its strong thermal spa offer, and Denmark and Ireland for being either very successful in terms of the number of EMS accredited hotels or a very successful tourism destination.

---

2 The first author of this chapter and her expert team on behalf of the Ministry of Economy has led research described in this section. The complete research documentation (detailed report on research) and the Manual for eco-label implementation for accommodation services can be accessed on the webpage of the ministry and downloaded for free: http://www.mg.gov.si/si/delovna_podrocja/turizem_in_internacionalizacija/turizem/zagotavljanje_kakovosti/

The primary stage of the research involved a survey conducted on the theme of environmental management involving all Slovene hotels (191 including those hotels which are part of a group). The survey was designed to capture general data about the hotel (size – including number of beds and of employees), the hotel's specialisation (for example, wellness hotel, sport hotel, congress hotel etc.), implementation of environmental management measures introduced (for example, energy, water and waste management), potential interest in introducing an EMS into the hotel (and under what conditions) and a range of opinion based questions to explore further their attitudes towards EMS certification (as, for example, shown in Table 7.5). The questionnaires were distributed through the postal system to the address of the general manager of each hotel. However, in the case of hotel groups the person responding was usually the environment officer for the hotel group; the latter responding on behalf of all the hotels in that group. After 14 days the researchers followed up as necessary to encourage additional responses by telephone contact and in a number of cases arranged for completion of the questionnaire via telephone. In this way, the survey achieved 63 completed questionnaires (a 39 per cent response rate). However, because of the collective response on the part of hotel groups, the overall sample represented approximately 75 per cent of Slovene hotels.

Main Findings

The majority of hotels did not have an environmental management plan. Five hotels did prepare annual environmental reports; two firms involving several hotels did have environmental management plans and one enterprise prepared and undertook an annual eco-accounting plan. An important factor to note, particularly as regards energy management (for example, for heating/air conditioning systems) is that most of the properties were old thus pre-date current designs and methods for energy management. Many were not built on the principles of bio-climatic architecture (using natural materials) and few identified that they were using natural materials to any extent. However, 22 per cent had introduced additional insulation and six hotels were regularly checked by a dowser for pathogen zones. Interestingly a quarter of the hotels were partly using the principles of Feng Shui. Overall, the findings in most areas, as briefly presented below, were discouraging.

- Energy: Most hotels were employing energy-saving equipment (for example, energy-saving light fittings, automatic turning off of lights, heating and air conditioning systems). Few (4) hotels were using alternative sources of energy and, of concern, 33 per cent of the hotels were still using oil with Sulphur content greater than 0.1 per cent or coal as their primary energy source.
- Water: Approximately a quarter of the hotels has introduced water flow restrictors for showers and taps and also water saving measures for urinals,

washing machines and dishwashers. A small majority (56 per cent) took active care over waste water management, though only two hotels, where appropriate, were recycling the water.

- Waste management: Waste separation was found to be very good in all cases primarily because the municipalities have introduced regulations on waste recycling and facilitated waste separation and collection. The use of the correct procedure for the removal of hazardous waste was also notably high (88 per cent), which is perhaps not to be unexpected given that by and large the hotels (90 per cent) were avoiding the use of chemical substances or hazardous products.

- Information for employees and guests: The one element of information dissemination that worked very well in but a few cases were instructions for cleaning personnel regarding the correct use of detergents (it is noted though that the use eco-labelled products – cleaning, disinfection, varnishes, lubricants – was limited). Employees were also given guidance on water and energy saving measures (82 per cent). Most hotels encouraged their guests in water and energy saving by re-using their towels. Less common was the availability of information for guests on local ecological programmes (38 per cent) or about measures of environmental protection (33 per cent).

- Organic produce:Many hotels (55 per cent) were using organic products only partially. The main reason, as cited by respondents, was the insufficient year-round supply of such products. Two hotels had made contracts with local farmers for the supply of organic produce. Interesting 18 per cent of the hoteliers were convinced that guests would not ask for a better provision of organic produce. Half of the hotels were using to varying extents, individually portioned packages for food service.

- Managers' views:As shown in Table 7.5, whilst the majority of managers indicated they were paying attention to environmental problems fewer indicated that they knew of the EU Eco-label. A finding which also evidenced the highest standard deviation and variance across all the statements. Knowing and adopting are clearly separate! There is evident agreement that seeking eco-label accreditation would incur costs whilst the possibility of charging more for their services as a result gained less agreement. The conclusion is that the managers expected to pay more expenses than they could expect to gain through financial benefits arising from eco-label certification. Support for adopting an internationally recognised eco-label is substantial and further affirmed by the lack of support for Slovenia developing its own eco-label certification programme. Further exploration of this data found no variances based on a range of variables such as size, type or grading of the hotels.

The managers were asked a range of questions designed to establish in what way(s) they considered that the Government could become active through supporting "going green" and the adoption of EMS. In response, approximately

Table 7.5   Managers' responses to attitudinal questions

	Statements	Average	Standard deviation	Variation
1	Our firm is paying a lot of attention to the eco problematic.	3.95	0.85	0.72
2	We know the EU Eco label (EU Eco Flower).	3.00	1.4	1.95
3	Hotels using any eco-label have a better market position.	3.43	0.96	0.92
4	Slovenia should adopt on the state-level one of the already existing international eco-labels (no own eco-label development.	4.18	1.01	1.02
5	Slovenia should develop an own eco-label.	2.45	1.22	1.49
6	An eco-label can positively influence Slovenia's image.	4.23	0.733	0.97
7	Applying for an eco-label would represent a big financial burden for our hotel.	3.43	0.98	0.97
8	Applying an eco-label would allow higher prices for our services.	2.95	1.15	1.33
9	We'll apply for the eco-label in case it should be developed for Slovenia.	3.33	0.90	0.81

Note: Based on scale of 1 = least agree to 5 = very much agree.

half (55 per cent) suggested financial incentives whilst one in five proposed a tax incentive for environmental-friendly hotels. The majority (76 per cent) of the managers considered that it was the role of the Government to provide the necessary information and introduce workshops to further this for hotel personnel at no charge to the hotels.

In total, these findings were not necessarily surprising and in many ways are similar to the outcomes of other such studies (see Chapter 6, Leslie, 2012) but even so they were discouraging. The level of awareness and knowledge of environmental management systems was predominantly lower in smaller hotels, which is largely attributed to the absence of an employed specialist in environmental matters, and their environmental performance was comparatively generally poor. Overall, few of the hotels were intensively and systematically implementing environmental management systems into their business. The level of knowledge of the positive benefits attributable to the introduction of an EMS was also limited. Furthermore, and the most significant in this context, they demonstrated a clear gap between government policy and "Slovenia green" and the hotels environmental management practices. In response to this the Ministry launched a series of measures to raise the awareness of the hotel managers and to stimulate the implementation of environmental management systems in hotels. The measures were three-fold:

- Workshops: organisation of four workshops annually on environmental management for accommodation properties; including information about the EU eco-label and how to apply for it (see: http://www.mg.gov.si). The workshops were free of charge and very practically orientated. A crucial part of each workshop was making participants aware of how they can use the knowledge gained in the workshop in their private lives (for example, when building or renovating their own flat/house) on the premise that the best promoter of an idea is a person who is "living" this idea in their private life. The first year gained a very limited response (two, four, and the maximum of six participants respectively). However, participation increased in the workshops in the following years to the extent that in the fifth consequent year (2011) some requests to attend the first spring workshop on environmental performance had to be refused because more than 30 managers wanted to attend.
- Finance: financial support for the costs involved in attaining a renowned eco-label. A year after the results were published, the Ministry of Economy introduced a grant scheme to provide financial support for those hotels seeking eco-label certification with a budget based on potentially 10 successful applications. This initiative was promoted in the media and to the hospitality sector and did gain "positive curiosity". However, although the grant was available for a period of almost two years, only two hotels (both new and built in a very eco-conscious way, with eco materials) have applied for the reimbursement of their expenses: one for the EU eco-label and one for the Green Globe. At the end of 2010, the scheme was re-launched and the Ministry allowed this time for seven awards. However, this time the response has been far more positive. In the first half of the year, five firms have applied for EU Eco Flower certification and at least five more are preparing applications (among the bidders there is a thermal spa, a mountain hotel, a holiday camp, a city hotel and a tourism farm). The consequence of this development is that in 2012, the Slovene NTO will have enough partners within the hospitality sector to be able to promote Slovenia as a green destination with sufficient green accommodation properties.
- Tourism Forum: the organisation of an annual Tourism Forum under the motto "Green and sustainable tourism" by Slovenia's Tourist Organisation. The Tourism Forum is a yearly meeting for all managers in hospitality, tourism, and managers of Destination Marketing Organisations in Slovenia – it is thus the ideal opportunity for launching ideas and placing information. The outcome of these Forums has been extremely positive. By the end of 2010, all hospitality managers in Slovenia were familiar with eco labelling and with the introduction of EMSs into hotels. Even if "only" 10 additional

accommodation services should apply for the EU eco-label, the key point is that all accommodation providers are now aware that much can be done to improve the environmental performance of their operation at little or no extra cost. As a result, they can gain various benefits; for example reduce resource costs, enhance reputation and gain a higher corporate social responsibility profile and improve the working conditions for and motivation of employees.

Conclusions

As in all other tourism destination around the world, Slovenia has been faced with the development of social responsibility and increasing demand by ecologically conscious consumers for environmentally responsible tourism services. Hotels today have to consider on the one side push factors, arising from the influence of green organisations and political agendas driven by sustainability issues and on the other side pull factors arising from competition in the marketplace.

Although hotels, some little time ago, started to distinguish their offering from 'less environmentally friendly' enterprises through introducing EMSs and gaining the appropriate eco-label accreditation – the significant increase in such eco-labels witnessed in the last decade means that it has become very difficult for the average tourist to distinguish between them. Consequently the Government questioned whether it made sense to develop a new, additional certification system for Slovene tourism enterprises or adopt a recognised, renowned scheme, for example, Eco-Flower? The participants in the survey commissioned as a result, clearly think not. Indeed, the smaller the country, the less wise it would be to fund the development of a new brand given limited resources and limited promotional budget to ensure good visibility for such a scheme. The Eco Flower label therefore presents the ideal choice for Slovenia and arguably for Europe; and not only for tourism. The main benefit with this brand is its wide visibility and major possibilities for cross- and co-branding, which is potentially constrained by the fact its promotion is left to individual member states. Arguably this label, which fosters economisation of resources, is not being given enough support (including financial) to become a really Europe-wide well-known brand. The European Commission as the authority standing behind this Eco Scheme should therefore launch promotional campaigns at least in relatively new EU countries, which have to catch-up with over a decade of development since the label has first been introduced.

Overall, the case study demonstrates that a well-designed governmental programme can trigger a considerable shift in the level of understanding and the willingness to implement priority strategies. As such it exemplifies best practice in the way forward of achieving progress in the implementation of a governmental programme in the field of promoting sustainability in the management of tourism enterprises.

In Slovenia, the breakthrough for the EU Eco-label was the result of a very well planned programme by the Ministry of Economy. The tourism sector expressed a willingness to apply for the brand when the Government decided to provide active support. Today even those enterprises that can not rely on financial support through the available grant scheme have decided to start the certification process. The idea of "Slovenia green" has successfully found its way from theory to practice.

References

Ball, S., Jones, P., Kirk, D. and Lockwood, A. (2003) *Hospitality Operations: A System Approach.* New York: Continuum.

Bank of Slovenia (2011) Available at: http://www.bsi.si/financni-podatki. asp?MapaId=138 [Accessed: 15 June 2011].

Bohdanowicz, P., Simanic, B. and Martinac, A. (2004a) *Sustainable Hotels – Eco-certification according to EU Flower, Nordic Swan and the Polish Hotel Association.* Regional Central and Eastern European Conference on Sustainable Building (SB04), 27-29 October, 2004, Warsaw, Poland.

Bohdanowicz, P. (2005) European Hoteliers' Environmental Attitudes: Greening the Business. *Cornell Hotel and Restaurant Administration Quarterly*, 46, 188.

EC (nd) Available at: http://ec.europa.eu/environment/ecolabel/about_ecolabel/ what_is_ecolabel_en.htm [Accessed: 15 June 2011].

EC (1997) *Agenda 2000.* Available at: http://ec.europa.eu/agenda2000/public_ en.pdf [Accessed: 15 June 2011].

EC (2011) Available at: www.ec.europa.eu [Accessed: 15 June 2011].

Fouhy, K, (1993) Life Cycle Analysis. *Chemical Engineering*, July, 30-34.

Goodall, B. (2003) Environmental Auditing: a means to improving tourism's environmental performance, in C. Cooper (ed.) *Classic Reviews in Tourism* Clevedon: Channel View, 192-226.

Green Seal (2011) Green Seal. Available at: http://www.greenseal.org/ AboutGreenSeal.aspx [Accessed: 15 June 2011].

Kajfež Bogataj, L. (2009) Turizem v času gospodarske in podnebne krize (*Tourism in the Era of Economic and Climate Crisis*). Turizem, okt/nov 2009, letnik 13, št. 100; str. 8- 9.

Leslie, D. (2012) Key players in the environmental performance of tourism enterprises. in M.V. Reddy and D. Wilkes (eds) *Tourism, Climate Change and Sustainability*. London: Earthscan.

MG (2011) Ministrstvo za gospodarstvo (Ministry of Economy, Slovenia). Available at: http://www.mg.gov.si/si/delovna_podrocja/turizem/zagotavljanje_kakovosti/ [Accessed: 10 April 2011].

Sloan, P., Lengrand, W. and Chen, J.S. (2009) *Sustainability in the Hospitality Industry: Principles of Sustainable Operations*. Oxford: Butterworth-Heinemann.

STO (2011) Slovenska Turistična organizacija (Slovene NTO). Available at: http://www.slovenia.info/si/Poslovne-strani.htm?_ctg_professional_pages=0&lng=1 [Accessed: 15 June 2011].

SORS (2011) Statistical Office of the Republic of Slovenia, Statistični urad Republike Slovenije) Available at: http://www.stat.si/eng/novica_prikazi.aspx?id=3941 [Accessed: 15 June 2011].

SVLR (2011) Služba vlade za lokalno samoupravo in regionalni razvoj (Government Office for local self-government and regional development) Available at: http://www.svlr.gov.si/si/zakonodaja_in_dokumenti/zakonske_podlage_s_podrocja_politike_spodbujanja_skladnega_regionalnega_razvoja/drzavni_razvojni_program [Accessed: 13 January 2011].

Vähätiitto, J. (2010) *Environmental Quality Management in Hospitality Industry – Case Hotel K5 Levi.* Master's thesis. Aalto University School of Economics.

VISIT (2011). Available at: http://www.yourvisit.info [Accessed: 15 June 2011].

WEF (2009) *Competitiveness Report.* Available at: http://www.weforum.org/issues/travel-and-tourism-competitiveness/ [Accessed: 15 June 2011].

Chapter 8

Entrepreneurship and Local Resources

Alina Badulescu and Daniel Badulescu

Introduction

Today it is largely recognised that SMEs and entrepreneurship represent main drivers of economic growth, employment and social development. Within the European Union, about 99 per cent of all non-financial businesses are SMEs, of which the majority (92 per cent) are micro enterprises and account for approximately 67 per cent of employment (European Commission 2010a). Between 2002 and 2008, the number of SMEs in the EU increased by 13 per cent and related employment by 1.9 per cent, compared with an increase in the number of large enterprises by five per cent and 0.8 per cent in employment. Given that tourism is the third largest socio-economic activity in the EU (after trade and distribution and constructions) (European Commission, 2010b), developing and improving the competitiveness of tourism are crucial concerns and objectives to be reached mainly by supply-side measures: improving product quality, fostering innovation, diversifying services, promoting and supporting entrepreneurial activity and measures to reduce the negative impact of seasonality. However, the competitiveness of tourism more and more relies on its sustainability, on the quality of the natural and cultural environment of destinations and their integration into a local community. The sustainability of tourism not only involves the responsible use of natural resources, the environmental impact of activities, the use of 'clean' energy, protection and preservation of the natural and cultural integrity of destinations but also the quality and sustainability of jobs created (see Chapter 10), local economic fallout and customer care (European Commission 2010b). Thus, SMEs have not only to respond to environmental requirements and issues of sustainability, but also to the necessity to be flexible and ability to specialise and adjust to changes in the production of the products and services provided. Indeed, an ideal model of sustainable development for SMEs is the integration of quality management, environmental management and flexible specialisation techniques. Therefore the objectives of a successful small business are to be '… profitable; environmentally friendly; competitive in the longer term and produce a quality good or service' (Welford and Gouldson, 1993: 176-7).

The European political responses to the needs of SMEs are included in the Small Business Act for Europe (SBA). The SBA is a set of 10 principles to guide the conception and implementation of SMEs policies at EU and national level, in order to allow these enterprises to realise their full potential for employment creation, innovation and growth. The very first principle is promoting entrepreneurship through various programmes to foster and support entrepreneurial initiatives among different groups of people (for example, young people, women, minorities).Particularly in times of recession, promoting entrepreneurship and SME creation is a major factor for economic recovery. Coherent and incentive policies to foster entrepreneurship, such as encouraging start-ups, removing bureaucratic and administrative burdens, improving business environment and labour market flexibility, facilitating their access to finance, and developing a more entrepreneurial culture are all particularly necessary.

This chapter first discusses briefly the concept and approaches of *entrepreneurship* and *entrepreneur*, terms, which are often used but rarely conceptually clarified. The second part explores specific issues in tourism entrepreneurship with the focus on sustainable entrepreneurship, which is subsequently illustrated through a range of examples prior to a more in-depth discourse on wine tourism as a sustainable tourism form and potential entrepreneurial field.

Entrepreneurship, Entrepreneur and the Entrepreneurial Process

Entrepreneurship theory is one of the most fragile sections of modern economic theory. Despite a rich and diverse literature, capturing the essence of entrepreneurship seems to be a difficult step for economists, who never cease to invoke it, but less to explain and even less to agree on it. The main lines of thought define entrepreneurship in a general and quite superficial way, as a result of the difference between business management and ownership (Hirshleifer, 1976) and describe it as a production factor, related to risk assuming and compensation, innovation, mitigation of uncertainties and generating profits. At the same time, the entrepreneur '… is at once one of the most intriguing and one of the most elusive in the cast of characters that constitutes the subject of economic analysis' (Baumol 1993: 8).

Among the first to deal with entrepreneurship, Adam Smith (1776) clearly acted against any kind of absenteeism of the owners in companies where they hold shares. He considered that directly involving the capital owners in the business administration is extremely important. The company is to be run by the owner, who shows responsibility and a direct interest in the efficient use of capital, unlike the appointed managers, who, although they may have personal qualities, skills or experience, have no connection with that property.

According to Knight (1942), entrepreneurs are the owners of the company (called "residual claimants") and thus they are entitled to profit. In order to gain profit, the entrepreneur shall initiate useful changes or innovations, adapt to changes in the economic environment and assume for his/her enterprise the consequences of uncertainty. The fact that entrepreneurs are owners at the same time does not mean that entrepreneurship and (small) business ownership are one and the same. It is argued, first that small business owners see their company as rather static, maintain the *status quo*, have a local market and limited growth prospects. Second, entrepreneurs see the business developing; they search opportunities and go beyond local conditions in a continuous desire for expansion (De Clerq et al., 1997). Conversely, Kirzner (1973) sees the entrepreneur as the "sole decider and arbitrator" and has no ownership. As Salerno (2007) argued, '... ownership and entrepreneurship are to be viewed as completely separate functions. ... Purely entrepreneurial decisions are by definition reserved to decision-makers who own nothing at all' (Salerno, 2007: 4-5).

Timmons and Spinelli (2003) and Nieman (2001) help to clarify this dichotomy through their consideration of entrepreneurship as the business launch (exploiting an identified opportunity), followed by growth and development of a specific area. Small business owners are seen as business starters, who consolidate and develop their business up to a stage, where they lose their willingness, ability and entrepreneurial intuition. Trevisan and Grundling (see Krueger, 2004) refer to a particular attribute: the inventiveness of entrepreneurs, which makes the difference between entrepreneurs and small business owners; in effect, the argument is that small business owners lack inventiveness. A further view on entrepreneurs is that they are leaders and key agents of creative destruction. This is perhaps explained by reference to the Schumpeterian approach of production function (Iversen et al., 2008). Unlike the manager who combines the production factors in the production function in order to achieve the highest technical efficiency, the entrepreneur goes outside of the production function through his or her innovations. The entrepreneur moves the economic system out of equilibrium, through creating new products or production methods, and therefore others become outdated. This is the process of "creative destruction", which Schumpeter views as the driving force behind economic development. Schumpeter pointed out that the entrepreneur does not necessarily discover things, goods, but operates in an innovative way with things which have already been invented. Combining the existing inventions, the entrepreneur and his creative destruction create new industries, while old industries are withdrawn, destroyed or have disappeared. They are also the destabilising agents, because they change the relationship and production techniques, and lead the economy toward a better use of capital and knowledge, ultimately leading to improved macroeconomic growth and productivity. They search opportunities and innovate to meet the society's needs, without taking into account limitations of the currently available resources. The Schumpeterian entrepreneur applies knowledge of inventions to create new combinations; s/he is the most entitled to decide which new combinations are profitable. The Knightian (Knight, 1942) entrepreneur foresees a unique situation that will arise and decides on how best to exploit this situation. Both theories contend that while entrepreneurs are *decision-makers*, many decision-makers are not entrepreneurs. Casson (2003) attempts to unify the definitions of Schumpeter and Knight by stating that the entrepreneur is that person specialised in decision-making, possessing many skills allowing them to make value judgements for an intelligent use of scarce resources. According to Casson, the entrepreneur operates with a set of technological conditions, faces some tough decisions, anticipates demand and supply under uncertain conditions, and, therefore, is able to claim a profit as a reward.

Although comprehensive and meeting the analysts' consensus, the behavioural theories are to be criticised at least in two respects. First, it is difficult to test these skills, especially to demonstrate that they comprehensively define entrepreneurship, and second these traits can exist in many people who are not necessarily entrepreneurs. As a conciliatory approach, we can say there is a general understanding that most of the above traits accompany a continuous business activity in most entrepreneurial types known over time. Nevertheless, to be an entrepreneur is the result of a very personal decision, generated by both push factors and pull factors. Among the push factors usually mentioned are redundancy, previous employment, financial needs whilst pull factors include working from home, own boss, lifestyle, location and natural progression (Sweeney 2008, quoted by Lee-Ross 2008: 56). For example, the last survey on the "Factors of Business Success" (EC, 2011) carried out in EU in 2005 has found that the main start-up motivations were: "desire to be one's own boss", "prospect of making more money" and "desire for new challenges"; other motivations include "avoiding unemployment", "combining work and private life", "desire to make a living from a hobby activity" and "realising an idea for a new product or service".

The actual entrepreneurial process comprises several stages, starting with idea and identification of the opportunity for exploitation and thus the business creation (Chell, 2008). The emergence of the idea is the first stage, necessary in any entrepreneurial activity. Opportunity identification is a prerequisite of any entrepreneurial activity about which entrepreneurship itself is built. The subsequent phase is opportunity identification and recognition, which involves taking into account, and related analyses, social-economic and contextual aspects (Chell, 2009: 44). Opportunity recognition is the result of prior experience and knowledge of the domain (Shane, 2000). Timmons et al. (1985) argued that understanding opportunity is the key factor for entrepreneurial success. This stage is particularly related to the ability of the entrepreneur to identify new opportunities, to be alert to specific useful information. Opportunity identification is not only a stage in the entrepreneurial process, but also distinctive entrepreneurial behaviour. The idea of opportunity brings into context the difference between on the one hand Kirzner's approach that entrepreneurs are to *identify* the *existing and waiting to be discovered* opportunities and on the other hand, Schumpeter's approach that they should *create* opportunities by innovation and "creative destruction". Whichever one ascribes to the reality is that not many persons will readily recognise an opportunity in a specific market or context: those possessing entrepreneurial orientation: autonomy, innovativeness, risk-taking, pro-activeness and competitive aggression (Lumpkin and Dess, 1996).

Following recognition, the next stage is opportunity formation and evaluation. This stage implies different characteristics of the entrepreneur: not only imagination and creativity, but also judgement, social and networking abilities and strategic thinking. Opportunity formation is the stage going beyond the inside thinking of the entrepreneur, in which he or she acts explicitly, evaluates the situation, the market and the potential of the idea, identifies networks, identifies human resources, partnerships, financial sources etc. It is the point at which the entrepreneur decides to apply the idea, after a comprehensive process of analysis and synthesis of the information. The final stage is that of exploitation, when the entrepreneur puts the idea into practice, by attracting and using resources: knowledge and capability. It is the stage when they become confident and aware they are on the right track, but also the time when they face the difficulties of identifying resources.

Many tourism enterprises whilst entrepreneurial ventures are also family businesses; often motivated by opportunity for example lifestyle and/or locational preferences (Getz and Carlsen, 2005); and demonstrate intergenerational ownership transference, which accounts for about 20 per cent of family businesses (Getz and Carlsen, 2000). A lot of advantages come with family businesses: commitment and reliability on family members, knowledge and know-how protected within the family, more flexibility in communications, employment, customer management and initial financing availability (see Deakins and Freel, 2006; Leach, 1996). Nevertheless, in addition to "real entrepreneurs", Shaw and Williams (1998) argued that the sector consists also of "non-entrepreneurs" and "constrained entrepreneurs". The "non-entrepreneurs" are mostly retired or semi-retired people using family capital and engaged in limited product development and marketing. Often, they are not motivated by economic reasons and they are not driven by a desire to develop the business, but they wanted to be self-employed, had personal reasons to change their life and improve their lifestyle or simply preferred the location of the business (Shaw and Williams, 1998). The predominance of lifestyle motives was noticed by Getz and Carlsen (2000), after analyzing 200 family businesses involved in tourism and hospitality in Western Australia: the main motive for starting or buying the business was lifestyle enhancement, including moving to or remaining in a rural area. This lifestyle motivation proves to be very important in the long run, as this kind of entrepreneur faces long-term survival problems. Shaw (2003) makes the distinction between business-orientated and lifestyle-orientated entrepreneurs, while Williams et al. (1989) sees lifestyle firms as a form of production and consumption at one and the same time.

Moreover, Getz and Petersen (2005) surveying family business owners in tourism in Canada and in Denmark, found out that lifestyle and autonomy goals predominate in the industry. These "lifestyle and autonomy-oriented" family businesses involve more females than males, are little or no growth-oriented (they create few or no jobs for non-owners), driven by self-employment and self-control motives. Finally, many small businesses in tourism represent additional sources of income during summer (Ioannides and Peterson, 2003); for example, the diversification of farming into tourism is driven by the need to find an employment for other family members or simply to gain more money, by fiscal incentives or developing a hobby (Nickerson et al., 2001). "Constrained entrepreneurs" are younger and more professional people but lack the resources necessary for development, acting as entrepreneurs in businesses with fewer capital requirements that others (Shaw and Williams, 1998). Shaw and Williams (1998) briefly characterise small-scale entrepreneurs as follows: they have no or little formal qualification, they use family labour and other resources, they do not have business plans and do not use management or marketing strategies, and of course, they are driven by non-economic motivators, as we already have stated.

We can conclude therefore that economic motivators of entering entrepreneurship are less important in tourism. Other reasons, such as the desire to be self-employed, to make a change in lifestyle, change of location are also important, and the businesses themselves are less profit more family oriented. Tourism enterprises also differ from other ventures in many other sectors due to the ease of entry as regards the resources required for start-up and later for successfully running the business. Usually, finding start-up funding is one of the first challenges the entrepreneur has to face and overcome. Most small firms use both internal and external sources of finance, but the most important are bank loans and hire purchase/lending (Deakins and Freel, 2006). However, in tourism the financial barriers to entry and start up costs are comparatively low and entrepreneurs often require but a small capital to start-up a business, fund through their own personal (or family) sources and possibly leasehold agreements. The result is a considerably large number of entrepreneurial enterprises are set-up in tourism and thus there is a high degree of competition. But whilst comparatively easy to start-up they can be difficult to control and to manage; as evident in the high number of reported failings. The sector experiences different causes of business failures than other sectors (Stoy Hayward, 1996). Whilst undercapitalisation is the main cause of failure in industries such as manufacturing and construction, in the tourism sector operations and management problems are the primary factors. Moreover, tourism small firms may experience different business life-cycles. The standard framework of business life-cycle, from the start up and survival to take-off and maturity is not so frequently valid for tourism businesses. Many of them face lack of demand and/or managerial problems and do not go beyond initial stage of survival. Consequently, even though start-up is not so difficult, appropriate management skills are still required. This is crucial to enable the transition from the initial stage (very often lifestyle-related) towards business growth.

Entrepreneurship, Sustainability and Tourism

Not surprisingly, the rise of the green agenda and sustainability over the last 20 years reflects societal increasing awareness of green issues and holds potential entrepreneurial opportunities in the emerging green consumer market. Thus, on the basis of opportunity in environmentally friendly products/services, we identify: *green entrepreneurship* in the beginning of the 1990s (Blue, 1990, Berle, 1991) and *environmental entrepreneurship* (Keogh and Polonsky, 1998), followed by *ecopreneurship* (Schaper, 2002), and the more recent *sustainable entrepreneurship* (Dean and McMullen 2007, Hall et al., 2010). In this context, of the three types of entrepreneurship identified by Parrish and Tilley (2010) the following are particularly significant:

- Responsible entrepreneurs: conventional, profit-seeking entrepreneurs, but motivated to reduce their negative environmental and social impacts; considered by the EU (EC, 2003) as those that: treat customers, business partners and competitors with fairness and honesty; care about the health, safety and general well-being of employees and customers; offers training and development opportunities; acts as a 'good citizen' in the local community; and is respectful of natural resources and the environment.
- Sustainability-driven entrepreneurs: whose motives to starting a business are strictly related to environmental and social commitments, and '... earn market-based income as a means of achieving these ends' (Parrish and Tilley, 2010: 35).

To this typology we can add "sustainability entrepreneurs" derived from the Schumpeterian approach of the entrepreneur, who destroy existent modes of doing business by creating a new paradigm. Sustainable entrepreneurship is defined by Gerlach, in a broad sense, as '... innovative behaviour of actors in the context of sustainability, including actors from governmental and non-governmental, profit and non-profit organisations', and in a narrow sense, as '... innovative behaviour of single actors or organisations operating in the private business sector who are seeing environmental or social issues as a core objective and competitive advantage' (2003: 3). Thus our "sustainability entrepreneurs" are motivated primarily not by profit-seeking reasons but by the desire to provide sustainable services, to contribute to ecological and social wellbeing. Their values and motives are based on the '... equanimity between self, other people, and nature", and the "responsibility for environmental and social outcomes is not simply a cost of doing business, but a central purpose for being in business' (Parrish, 2010: 521). This new entrepreneur, also synonymously referred to as *environmental entrepreneur, green entrepreneur* or *ecopreneur* (*eco-entrepreneur*) aims to contribute through his or her business to reducing environmental degradation (Dean and McMullen, 2007); basing his or her business on the provision products or services catalysed through identifying environmental-related innovation and market opportunities (Lober, 1998; Pastakia, 1998; Gerlach, 2003). Sustainable entrepreneurship opportunities, as per Pacheco et al.(2010: 470), can be classified as:

- "sustainable entrepreneurship discovery opportunities" – opportunities that are "exogenously created" and available for exploitation on existing economic incentives and reward system, or
- "sustainable entrepreneurship creation opportunities" – opportunities requiring "the alteration or creation of economic incentives and reward systems", and allowing entrepreneurs to create sustainable opportunities.

The role of entrepreneurship in tourism can be better understood if we refer to changes in tourism demand and the need to adjust products and destinations to meet these changes over the last two decades. Demand has increased for small scale tourism and different tourist experiences, more activity based. This is well illustrated in the development of nature-based tourism in more sustainable oriented forms, more environmentally friendly, more responsible and more entrepreneurial. This "new" form of nature-based entrepreneurship is: '… nature-centred, domestic, local, handcrafted, individual …' [and includes]:

- Responsible tourism and other experience services based on opportunities offered by nature.
- Sustainable exploitation of wild berries, mushrooms, herbs and other products gathered from nature and utilisation of wild plants in landscaping;
- Small-scale and sustainable processing of woods and products obtained from wood, exploitation of peat, stone and other minerals.
- Sustainable exploitation of water resources (for example, spring waters), snow and ice.
- Other services based on nature (for example, photography of nature, implementation of recreation services, also renewable energy services such as solar energy, tidal energy, EMS services, green purchase, education etc. (Lordkipanidze et al., 2005: 791).

Sustainability Entrepreneurship and Tourism: Case Examples

There are potentially many opportunities for the sustainability entrepreneur in tourism. Here we present diverse examples of such entrepreneurial activity, commencing with a more detailed discussion of "wine tourism". This is particularly apposite example given that wine is considered a 'territorial intensive product' (TIP), since it contains a strong reference to the territory in which it is produced …' (and) 'The typical products and the territory perform reciprocally, in continuum that sees the one tied to the other and vice versa' (Asero and Patti, 2009: 2). It is both local and community based. Secondly, wine tourism is one of the fastest growing tourist activities not only in the traditional destination areas of France, Italy and Spain but also in emerging wine tourism locations in Bulgaria, Romania, Moldavia and Hungary. Hall describes it as '… visitation to vineyards, wineries, wine festivals, and wine shows for which grape wine tasting and/or experiencing the attributes of a grape wine region are the prime motivating factors for visitors' (1996: 109). Other pull factors include purchase, hospitality, entertainment and the rural setting whilst push factors include socialising, relaxing, meeting the winemaker, and acquiring specialised knowledge (Yuan et al., 2005). In the same line but referring to wine festivals, Taylor (2007) identifies motivations such as: socialising with family and friends, special visits and routes, participation in wine festivals, traditional products tastings, interest in music/entertainment, arts/craft value. According to Hall and Macionis (1998), there are three different kind of wine tourists: wine lovers, "dedicated wine tourists" ; these are wine lovers who frequently visit wine regions and have a well developed knowledge and interest in wine. Secondly, there are those persons interested in wine; they see a cellar door visit as an enhancement to their trip, but not the prime motivation for visiting the region, and they show moderate to high interest in wine. Thirdly, we have the curious visitor (or accidental tourist): they consider wineries as a tourist attraction of the region and a cellar door visit as an opportunity for a social occasion with friends or family. They share moderate/below-average knowledge of wines and interest in wine.

The Benefits of Wine Tourism or Why to Start-up a Wine Tourism Business?

The development of wine tourism reflects increasing demand and diversification and presents opportunities for entrepreneurs as well as the oft-cited benefits for local and regional communities attributed to tourism development. In the search for innovation, the opportunity for diversifying the offer, revitalising traditional destinations or new destination development is evident. A key advantage is the potential it holds for sustainable tourism development in rural communities and the opportunity for preservation of cultural values and traditions: the revenues coming from tourists willing to pay for it are financial sources to be invested in activities related to cultural heritage preservation and restoration. Rural communities can develop wine tourism as an alternative, for example, to contrived cultural events in rural communities (Mitchell and Hall, 2002). Wine tourism development fosters further development in the local/regional economy, for example, agri-tourism and transportation, and contributes to raise awareness and pride for local and regional traditions and values; and to promote entrepreneurial business in the field. Thus, the benefits and success of wine tourism activities can spread in the entire region, This is why the support of local and regional authorities for wine tourism is an important aspect of sustainable development policies. However, success relies not only on the quality of wine products, but also on the services accompanying the tourist activity itself. Getz and Brown (2006) suggest that successful wine tourism is based on three critical factors: the core wine product, the destination and the cultural product. The wine, as the core product, should be the focus of the winery and wine festival or tour, while the destination should include cultural and natural attractions of the locality; named by Hall and Mitchell (2002) as "touristic terroir", and supported by hospitality and accommodation facilities at moderate prices.

Moreover, as with other tourism activities, the consumers' perception of service quality is critical and highly influenced by its particular features and differences from other services. As O'Neil et al. (2002) emphasised, wine tourism involves tourists seeing the wine making process and tasting a tangible product, which fosters the tourist experience. High service quality at the cellar door leads to many benefits, such as product distribution at lower costs, development of brand equity and the ability to add value (O'Mahony et al., 2008). Moreover, image and destination brand, and creating a brand loyalty among tourists are very important in a competitive market. Dodd and Bigotte (1997: 51) state that '..in addition to sales revenue, wine tourism offers benefits such as opportunities for market intelligence, increased margins above other retail outlets, and the chance to encourage brand loyalty toward a winery.' The entrepreneurial opportunity and challenge are precisely the innovation and product differentiation able to create added value and attract tourists. This is well illustrated in the case of Iasi in Romania. Seven dedicated wineries and a Wine Museum in Iasi county (Romania) organise wine tastings, traditional foods and cultural sites, particularly for foreign tourist groups. The "liturgical" wines from the Bucium and Cetatuia monasteries are of special interst to tourists; tastings take place in a sacred atmosphere wherein visitors, in parties of 12, sit at a round, red velvet covered table. There are also the most important cellars of the area – *Cotnari*, which has a central corridor of 100 meters and 15 cellar caves of 80 sqm each. Visits are often included in wider tourism programmes (with brass concerts, bird watching or fishing, for large groups of visitors), and the wide range of Romanian wine products can be bought at promotional prices.

As noted earlier, we present the following selection of 'mini-cases' to illustrate further both sustainable entrepreneurialship in the use of local resources and the diversity of opportunity.

A Danish Caravan Site (Blichfeldt, 2009)

This case concerns an alternative use of farm land, converted into a caravan site. The site consists of more than 100,000 square meters of land assigned both for accommodation areas (caravans, tents, cabins etc.), simple restoration, bathroom and kitchen facilities, and recreational areas: pool, mini golf, pony rides, tennis, wellness etc. The operation is distinguished by the continuous search for innovation and market opportunities ("We listen and when we've heard it enough times, then there must be something to it ..."), product differentiation and hospitality, achieving in 2008, 10,000 tourists and 60,000 person nights. In 2008, the site was sold when the entrepreneurs who started up the business, decided to move on and start up a new business elsewhere.

Björn Kristjánsson: A Tourist Entrepreneur in Iceland (Jóhannesson, 2002)

Björn Kristjánsson and his wife have been involved, since the early 1990s, in tourism-related entrepreneurial initiatives. First, they bought a state owned farm and renovated the buildings; the natural and historical attractions of the region and its popularity for sightseeing trips contributed to the next step. They renovated an old barn and converted it into two small apartments for rent. Another entrepreneurial opportunity originated from the existing local ferry operating cruises across the Lögurinn, one of the biggest lakes in Iceland. Björn, also folk-poet and storyteller, has built a small cabin in a small inlet of the lake and he barbecues and entertains the passengers with his stories and poems. Björn's entrepreneurship rests on his personal characteristics and skills, on his training and experience as poet and storyteller, his life experience, network and connections, and certainly his continuous search of innovative approaches.

Alternative Tourism in Inner Istria, Croatia (Tomljenoviœ, 2006)

In a region well known for its seaside tourism – Istria, Croatia, local entrepreneurs seek to promote the hinterland area through tourism, and the provision of traditional food and wine. There are about 64 tourism entrepreneurs, with excellent facilities, owning old houses renovated into luxury villas or boutique hotels. They have organised bike trails along scenic routes and quiet country roads. There are also about 1,000 selected restaurants (*konobas*) with ambience and traditional dishes prepared with local ingredients, including the area's renowned truffles, which are at the heart of the Truffle Festival. Similarly, the wine-sector was revived through the establishment in 1995 of the Association of winegrowers and winemakers of Istria, in order to provide technical assistance for members, creating a strong brand and promoting wines from Istria (*Malvasia* wine brand), to facilitate distribution of wine and preserving heritage and traditions related to viticulture and winemaking. Entrepreneurs also organise various events for visitors, such as the "Open Winery" (some 90 winemakers and wineries are involved), commercial events (VINISTA) or food and wine festivals (for example, "Apples and wine") and participating in projects such as the "Istria Wine Road", a unique combination of agricultural routes and coastal landscape and promoted as a wine trail.

Collaborative Destination Marketing: The Case of Three Entrepreneurs in Northern Sweden (Axelsson, 2009)

An example of entrepreneurs seeking to develop and promote their businesses in co-operation with local or regional authorities can be found in three locations situated in the Northern Swedish Region of Norrboten. Each of the organisers (local authorities and small entrepreneurs in Gamelstadt Churchtown, tours and events entrepreneurs at Rodbergsfortret or at the Ice Hotel Kiruna) tries to work at local, municipal and regional level to take advantage of promoting the area as a single destination – "Lapland Sweden". According to Axelsson (2009), although each activity is well designed and based on individual attractions, they suffer from certain limitations regarding the number and variety of attractions, target segments (for example, children can find the Ice Hotel or Rödbergsfortret relatively boring, also the Ice Hotel is not recommended for small children), and limited financial resources. Each destination has an individual set of attractions, objectives, target groups and strategies. The three are as follows:

- Churchtown Gamelstadt (registered on the UNESCO World Heritage List, where visitors can stay in the town, in traditional cottages dating from 15th century) offers guided tours all year round, with a focus on local handcrafts. There is also a lantern night tour. In this area, local entrepreneurial enterprises include lodging, restaurants, craft and/or souvenirs shops. The competitive advantage is seen as their status as a world heritage listed site.

- Rödbergsfortret, the largest fortress in a system built in the early 20th century, as a defence line against invaders, offers guided tours to private visitors over seven weeks during the summer, and also offers spaces for groups wishing to hold conferences or events, weddings and parties. The visitors can sleep in the authentic environments of the soldiers who were stationed there and, to a certain degree, the activities organised can be adjusted for groups – for example, participants can wear authentic uniforms, themed menus, for example "spartan soldiers dinner", or, the more luxurious, "fortress chef dinner";
- Ice Hotel Kiruna – the main offer of the Ice Hotel is the hotel itself, where people can stay in the rooms designed by ice artists, or take a drink in the bar, also made out of ice. The entrepreneurs offer other activities for visitors such as a trip to a Sami village (the native inhabitants of Lapland), reindeer sled rides, snowmobile safaris, dog sledding, or car riding on the iced lake. Because of the highly seasonable activities ("the melting of the hotel" in spring) the entrepreneurs offer alternative summer attraction and activities, for example, wild river paddling, hiking and paddling, many of which can be tailored to meet the specific desire of groups.

Conclusion

Entrepreneurship is one of the most important engines of economic growth and local development. Given its contributions to fostering innovation, enhancing productivity and job creation, policies promoting and supporting entrepreneurship are conducted at EU and national level. But, entrepreneurship and small business ownership are not the same – the essence of entrepreneurship is not creating a venture per se, but creating the framework within which to apply an innovative idea for a product, a market or a process. The entrepreneurs are not only – and not even in the first place – the owners of that firm. On a small scale, they are the persons who, having an idea and following it, identify an opportunity and take the associated risks. Innovation, creativity, inventiveness and opportunity are the key words in entrepreneurial ventures. On a large scale, the entrepreneurs overturn the *status quo*, generate disequilibrium situations and "creative destruction" and resource re-allocations. They are the dynamic spirit of modern capitalism enterprise. The entrepreneurial process starts with the idea and concludes with the opportunity of exploitation and implementation of the business idea. This final stage, however, is only the beginning of the difficulties facing the entrepreneur.

Tourism is a sector full of entrepreneurial opportunities and relatively easy access to the market given the low entry barriers. Moreover, the "raw materials" are invariably the local resources, offering the opportunity of exploiting various and diverse resources. However, today there is an increasing awareness concerning the necessity for the sustainable use of resources. This imperative has consequences for demand and supply. On the demand side, tourists are becoming more diverse in their interests and activities. On the supply side, tourism holds entrepreneurial opportunities to exploit local resources that could not have been exploited by other sectors. The business model emerged from these new trends has integrated the use of local resources to the benefit of local communities.

Many of the opportunities are strictly related to sustainability issues, and the "sustainability-driven" entrepreneurs are searching (or even creating!) them. Nevertheless, many more entrepreneurs are profit seeking, though are becoming aware of their responsibility for the environmental impact of their activities, for the social outcomes and for community wellbeing. Sustainable entrepreneurship in tourism covers both the discovery and exploitation of sustainable opportunities, and especially *creation* of sustainable opportunities, as the entrepreneur is the *adventurer* always alert to opportunities which others miss. As we have emphasised in the cases presented, innovation, imagination, creativity, but also entrepreneurial skills are the decisive factors of business success.

References

Asero, V. and Patti, S. (2009) *From Wine Production to Wine Tourism Experience: The Case of Italy*, AAWE Working Paper No. 52 *Business* [Online]. Available at: http://www.wine-economics.org/workingpapers/AAWE_WP52.pdf [Accessed: 29 March 2011].

Axelsson, F. (2009) *Destination Marketing as a Team Effort: The Practices and Experiences of Three Tourism Entrepreneurs in Northern Sweden.* Bachelor Thesis, Lulea University of Technology. Available at: https://pure.ltu.se/ws/files/31129675/LTU-CUPP-09126-SE.pdf [Accessed: 20 May 2011].

Baumol, W. (1993) *Entrepreneurship, Management, and the Structure of Payoffs.* Cambridge, MA: MIT Press.

Berle, G. (1991) *The Green Entrepreneur: Business Opportunities that can Save the Earth and Make you Money.* Blue Ridge Summit: Liberty Hall Press,.

Blichfeldt, B.S. (2009) Innovation and Entrepreneurship in Tourism: The Case of a Danish Caravan Site. *PASOS. Revista de Turismo y Patrimonio Cultural*, 7(3), 415-31.

Blue J. (1990) *Ecopreneuring: Managing the Results.* London: Scott Foresman.

Casson, M. (2003) *The Entrepreneur: An Economic Theory*, 2nd edition. Cheltenham: Edward Elgar.

Chell, E. (2008) *The Entrepreneurial Personality: A Social Construction, 2nd edition.* London: The Psychology Press.

Chell, E. (2009) Introduction and Overview to the Entrepreneur and Entrepreneurial Process, in J. Ateljevic and S. Page (eds) 2009. *Tourism and Entrepreneurship: International Perspectives*. Oxford: Elsevier.

De Clerq, D., Crijns, H. and Ooghe, H. (1997) *How a Management School Deals with Innovation in Entrepreneurship Education*. International Entrepreneurship conference. Monterey Bay, California, USA, 25-27 June.

Deakins, D. and Freel, M. (2006) *Entrepreneurship and Small Firms*. 4th edition. London: McGraw-Hill Companies.

Dean, T.J. and McMullen, J.S. (2007) Toward a theory of sustainable entrepreneurship: Reducing environmental degradation through entrepreneurial action. *Journal of Business Venturing*, 22(1), 50-76.

Dodd, T. and Bigotte, V. (1997) Perceptual Differences among Visitor Groups to Wineries. *Journal of Travel Research*, Winter, 46-51.

European Commission (2003) *Responsible Entrepreneurship: A Collection of Good Practice Cases among Small and Medium-sized Enterprises across Europe*. Luxembourg: Office for Official Publications of the European Communities.

European Commission (2010a) *European SMEs under Pressure: Annual Report on EU Small and Medium-sized Enterprises 2009*. EIM Business & Policy Research.

European Commission (2010b) *Europe, The World's No. 1 Tourist Destination – A New Political Framework for Tourism in Europe*. European Commission Communication COM (2010) 352/3.

European Commission (2011) Eurostat database on Structural Business Statistics. Available at: http://epp.eurostat.ec.europa.eu/portal/page/portal/statistics/search_database [Accessed: 14 March 2011].

Gerlach, A. (2003) *Sustainable Entrepreneurship and Innovation*. Centre for Sustainability Management, University of Lueneburg [Online]. Available at: http://andersabrahamsson.typepad.com/sustainable%20entrepreneurship%20and%20innovation.pdf [Accessed: 12 March 2011].

Getz, D. and Carlsen. J. (2000) Characteristics and goals of family and owner-operated business in the rural tourism and hospitality sector. *Tourism Management*, 2, 547-60.

Getz, D. and Carlsen, J. (2005) A Framework for Family Business Theory and Research in Tourism and Hospitality. *Annals of Tourism Research*, 32(1), 237-58.

Getz, D. and Petersen, T. (2005) Growth and profit-oriented entrepreneurship among family business owners in the tourism and hospitality industry. *International Journal of Hospitality Management*, 24, 219-42.

Getz, D. and Brown, G. (2006) Critical success factors for wine tourism destinations. *Tourism Management*, 27(1), 146-58.

Hall, C.M. (1996) *Wine Tourism in New Zealand*. Proceedings of the Tourism Down Under II: A Research Conference, edited by J. Higham. University of Otago, 109-19.

Hall, C. and Macionis, N. (1998) Wine Tourism in Australia and New Zealand, in R.W. Butler, C.M. Hall and J. Jenkins (eds) *Tourism and Recreation in Rural Areas*. London: John Wiley.

Hall, C.M. and Mitchell, R. (2002) The Touristic *Terroir* of New Zealand Wine: The Importance of Region in the Wine Tourism Experience, in A. Montanari (ed.) *Food and Environment: Geographies of Taste*. Rome: Societa Geografica Italiana, 69-91.

Hall, J.K., Daneke, G.A. and Lenox, M.J. (2010) Sustainable development and entrepreneurship: Past contributions and future directions. *Journal of Business Venturing*, 25, 439-48.

Hirshleifer, J. (1976) *Price Theory and Applications*. Englewood Cliffs: Prentice Hall.

Ioannides, D. and Petersen, T. (2003) Tourism 'Non-Entrepreneurship' in Peripheral Destinations: A Case Study of Small and Medium Tourism Enterprises on Bornholm, Denmark. *Tourism Geographies*, 5(4), 408-43.

Iversen, J., Jorgensen, R. and Malchow-Moller, N. (2008) Defining and Measuring Entrepreneurship. *Foundations and Trends in Entrepreneurship* [Online]. Available at: http://www.entrepreneur.com/tradejournals/article/171539783_1. html [Accessed: 26 February 2011].

Keogh, P.D. and Polonsky, M.J. (1998) Environmental commitment: A basis for environmental entrepreneurship? *Journal of Organizational Change Management*, 11(1), 38-49.

Kirzner, I. (1973) *Competition and Entrepreneurship*. Chicago, IL: University of Chicago Press.

Knight, F. (1942) Profit and entrepreneurial functions. *The Journal of Economic History 2 (supplement)*, 126-32.

Kruger, M.E. (2004) *Creativity in the Entrepreneurship Domain*, Ph.D. thesis [Online]. Available at: http://upetd.up.ac.za/thesis/available/etd-08242004-145802 [Accessed: 2 March 2011].

Leach, P. (1996) *The BDO Stoy Howard Guide to the Family Business*. London: Kogan Page.

Lee-Ross, D. and Lashly, C. (2008) Hospitality, Commercial Homes and Entrepreneurship, in D. Lee-Ross and C. Lashley (eds) *Entrepreneurship and Small Business Management in the Hospitality Industry*. Oxford: Butterworth-Heinemann, 169-90.

Lober, D.J. (1998) Pollution prevention as corporate entrepreneurship. *Journal of Organizational Change Management*, 11(1), 26-37.

Lordkipanidze, M., Brezet, H. and Backman, M. (2005) The entrepreneurship factor in sustainable tourism development. *Journal of Cleaner Production*, 13, 791.

Lumpkin, G.T. and Dess, G.G. (1996) Clarifying the entrepreneurial orientation construct and linking it to performance. *Academy of Management Review*, 21, 135-72.

Mitchell, R. and Hall, M.C. (2002) WWW (World Wide Web): Wine Tourism and the Internet, in C. Hall, L. Sharples, B. Cambourne and N. Macionic (eds) *Wine Tourism around the World: Development, Management and Markets*. Oxford: Butterworth-Heinemann, 212-16.

Nickerson, N.P., Black, R.J. and McCool, S.F. (2001) Agritourism: Motivations behind farm/ranch business diversification. *Journal of Travel Research*, 40(1), 19-26.

Nieman, G. (2001) Training entrepreneurs and small business enterprises in South Africa: a situational analysis. *Education and Training*, 43, 445-50.

Pacheco, D.F., Dean, T.J. and Payne, D.S. (2010) Escaping the green prison: Entrepreneurship and the creation of opportunities for sustainable development. *Journal of Business Venturing*, 25, 464-80.

Parrish, B. (2010) Sustainability-driven entrepreneurship: Principles of organization design. *Journal of Business Venturing*, 25.

Parrish, B. and Tilley, F. (2010) Sustainability Entrepreneurship: Charting a Field in Emergence, in M. Sharper (ed.) *Making Ecopreneurs: Developing Sustainable Entrepreneurship*, 2nd edition. Farnham: Gower Publishing.

Pastakia, A. (1998) Grassroots ecopreneurs: Change agents for a sustainable society. *Journal of Organizational Change Management*, 11(2), 157-73.

Saayman, M. and Slabbert, E. (2001) *Tourism Entrepreneurs: Opportunities and Threats*. SAESBA Conference Paper, quoted in Maia Lordkipanidze, 2002. *Enhancing Entrepreneurship in Rural Tourism for Sustainable Regional Development: The Case of Söderslätt Region, Sweden*, The International Institute for Industrial Environmental Economics, Lund University.

Salerno, J.T. (2007) *The Entrepreneur: Real and Imagined* [Online]. Available at: http://mises.org/journals/scholar/salerno4.pdf [Accessed: 28 February 2011].

Schaper, M. (2002) The essence of ecopreneurship. *Greener Management International*, 38, 26-31.

Shane, S. (2000) Prior knowledge and the discovery of entrepreneurial opportunities. *Organization Science*, 11, 448-69.

Shaw, G. and Williams, A.M. (1998) Entrepreneurship, small business culture and tourism development, in D. Ioannides and K.G. Debbage (eds) *The Economic Geography of the Tourist Industry*. London: Routledge, 235-55.

Shaw, G. (2003) Entrepreneurial cultures and small business enterprises in tourism, in M.C. Hall, A. Lew and A. Williams (eds) *A Companion to Tourism Geography*. Oxford: Blackwell.

Smith, A. (1776) *An Inquiry into the Nature and Causes of the Wealth of Nations* [Online]. Available at: http://www2.hn.psu.edu/faculty/jmanis/adam-smith/ Wealth-Nations.pdf [Accessed: 16 February 2011].

Stoy Hayward (1996) *A Study to Determine the Reasons for Failure of Small Businesses in the UK*. London: Stoy Hayward.

Taylor, R. (2007) Wine Festivals and Tourism: Developing a Longitudinal Approach to Festival Evaluation, in J. Carlsen and S. Charters (eds) *Global*

Wine Tourism: Research, Management and Marketing. Wallingford: CABI International, 179-95.

Timmons, J.A. and Spinelli, S. (2003) *New Venture Creation*, Sixth Edition. Irwin: McGraw Hill.

Timmons, J.A., Smollen, L.E. and Dingee, A.L.M. (1985) *New Venture Creation* (2nd ed.), Irwin: Homewood.

Welford, R. and Gouldson, A. (1993) *Environmental Management and Business Strategy*. London: Pitman Publishing.

Williams, A.M., Shaw, G. and Greenwood, J. (1989) From tourist to tourist entrepreneur, from consumption to production: Evidence from Cornwall, England. *Environment and Planning A*, 21, 1639-53.

Yuan, J.J., Cai, L.A., Morrison, A.M. and Linton, S. (2005) An analysis of wine festival attendees' motivations: A synergy of wine, travel and special events? *Journal of Vacation Marketing*, 11(1), 41-58.

Chapter 9

Sustainable Tourism Development: A Viable Development Option for Polish Rural Areas?

Piotr Zientara

Introduction

Across Eastern Europe, rural and remote communities have borne the brunt of communist mismanagement and post-communist neglect. This holds particularly true of Poland – a new European Union (EU) Member State that aims to catch up with its western counterparts and, at the same time, is marked by growing rural-urban, core-periphery divides (Gorzelak and Tucholska, 2007; Zientara, 2008). Thus, whilst large cities and core regions are thriving, peripheral areas – with fragmented agriculture and low-end services constituting the backbone of local economies – are lagging behind in terms of GDP per capita and employment rates (Bąk et al., 2007; Kalinowski, 2006; Central Statistical Office, 2009). This is because, among other things, Poland's agriculture, while employing considerable resources (capital and labour), makes a negligible contribution to the country's GDP and is heavily subsidised by the (Polish and European) taxpayer (Central Statistical Office, 2009; KRUS, 2009; Zientara, 2009). The implication is that, notwithstanding the existence of several successful and well-managed farms, the primary sector is generally inefficient and uneconomical (KRUS, 2009; Zientara, 2009).

The unfavourable situation is further exacerbated by the fact that the urban-rural divide manifests itself in the form of the civilisation gap (Sztompka, 2002). Accordingly, many rural communities – in sharp contrast to metropolitan areas – still lack sewage systems, water-treatment plants, sanitation facilities, good roads and access to the internet (Zientara, 2009). It follows that, in order to improve things, it would be necessary to carry out large-scale investment outlays (in infrastructure), to reform the entire agricultural sector and, crucially, to diversify local economic activity (Chaplin et al., 2007). In this sense, it is often argued that tourism – which today is seen as one of the major drivers of economic growth and societal advancement (Wahab and Pigram, 1997; Bosselman et al., 1999; Butler, 1999; World Travel and Tourism Council, 2009) – might help achieve this objective. The implication is that tourism could potentially constitute an effective vehicle for regional development. This assumption is based on the premise that the country – albeit doing badly in the tourism and travel competitiveness ranking (World Economic Forum, 2008) – has an untapped tourist potential.

From one point of view, Poland can indeed be perceived as an attractive tourist destination (Zientara, 2007). It is endowed with various attractions that could act as a draw for foreign and national tourists alike (Institute of Tourism, 2005); encompassing a rich cultural heritage (usually, in major cities), unspoiled environments (pristine forests and lakes, mainly in the east and south) as well as renowned regional food and folkloristic traditions (in rural communities all over the country). All this means that there is scope for using tourism – or rather different forms of tourism (ranging from cultural and culinary tourism to agri-tourism and nature-based tourism) – as a tool for the transformation of the fortunes of Polish poorer regions (Cynarski et al., 2007; Ministry of Agriculture and Rural Development, 2007; Obodyński et al., 2007).

Yet, given that tourism-based development strategies frequently make negative impacts on a location's culture and environment, the notion of sustainable tourism development needs to be brought to the fore. However, there has recently been debate over what actually is sustainable tourism and what is the relationship between it and sustainable development (Stabler, 1997, Mowforth and Munt, 1998; Sharpley, 2000; Moscardo, 2008). What it comes down to is confusion between sustainable tourism (in its own right) and tourism as part of sustainable development. Moscardo (2008) proposes to see tourism as a potential resource for communities seeking sustainable development options in lieu of seeing communities' attractions as a resource for tourism. To push the argument even further, it is possible to assume that sustainable tourism could be conceived as just *one* development option amongst many other (possible) regional strategies.

The present chapter is based on this reasoning and attempts to answer the question of whether sustainable tourism indeed offers – as is increasingly suggested (Ministry of Agriculture and Rural Development, 2007) – a feasible development option for Poland's rural and remote areas. The study, adopting a critical-interpretivist approach (Neuman, 2003), argues that – for a variety of reasons – serious doubts can be cast over the viability of such a strategy. The structure of the chapter is as follows. The first section focuses on the concepts of sustainable tourism and sustainable development. We then focus on the socio-economic situation in disadvantaged regions of Poland as well as briefly examine the country's tourist attractiveness. This provides the necessary background for further analysis and subsequent discussion of the issues under consideration. In concluding, we summarise the argument and suggest directions for future research. It is hoped that the study will deepen our understanding of the problems related to sustainability and regional development.

Sustainable Tourism and Sustainable Development

Even though many central- and local-level decision-makers increasingly regard tourism as an important tool for regional development (Forstner, 2004; Moscardo, 2008; Zientara, 2009b), there has been much debate on the putative merits – and the actual effectiveness – of tourism-based developmental strategies (Moscardo, 2008). To reiterate, it is hardly in dispute that tourism-driven development, however promising *per se* and successful in some cases, produces various negative outcomes (Wagner, 1997; Archer and Cooper, 1998; Bosselman et al., 1999; Butler, 1999). In fact, it can potentially bring about large-scale environmental damage (Cooper and Wanhill, 1998), translate into inadequate economic returns for local inhabitants (Kiss, 2004), affect local culture and social fabric in an undesirable way (Ratz, 2000; Forstner, 2004; Bohdanowicz and Zientara, 2009) and, last but not least, pose a threat to cultural-heritage sites (Briassoulis, 2002). In the era of climate change and fast-rising ecological awareness, the environmental impacts of tourism-based development are the subject of special consideration (Hall and Higham, 2005; World Travel and Tourism Council, 2009; Zientara and Bohdanowicz, 2010). This is also because an unspoilt environment is one of the principal factors determining the attractiveness of most tourist destinations.

All this has led many theoreticians and policy-makers to make a case for drawing on alternative forms of tourism. For instance, much attention has been paid to community-based tourism, which stresses the involvement of local stakeholders in the decision-making processes concerning the types (and locations) of proposed tourism developments (Richards and Derek, 2000; Hall, 2005) and is thought to cause lesser environmental damage (Kirsten and Rogerson, 2002). However, doubts have recently been cast over the very *raison d'être* of this approach. Relevantly, it is argued that the rationale for the engagement of local residents in decision-making is problematic as they often lack the necessary knowledge of their rights and the understanding of the nitty-gritty of the processes in which they are supposed to participate. This implies that there is a risk that either they will take (potentially) mistaken developmental decisions or that the very decision-making will be dominated – if not taken over – by external agents such as government-appointed consultants and NGOs.

Hence much hope has been pinned on sustainable tourism and sustainable development. While the former aims to minimise the impact of tourist activity on a given location's environment and culture (Stabler, 1997, Sharpley, 2000), the latter is about ensuring that humanity 'meets the needs of the present without compromising the ability of future generations to meet their own needs' (Kates et al. 2005: 10). With the notion of sustainability being publicised in the official discourse and making inroads into managerial thinking (Dow Jones Sustainability Index, 2009), both notions have become the focus of growing public and policy interest. Accordingly, extensive research has been undertaken into the conceptualisations and practical implications of sustainability-driven tourism and development (see, *inter alia*, Coccossis, 1996; Joppe, 1996; Priestley et al., 1996; Stabler, 1997; Wall, 1997; Bramwell, 1998; Middleton and Hawkins, 1998; Mowforth and Munt, 1998; Devuyst and Hens, 2000; Hall and Richards, 2000; Richards and Derek, 2000; Sharpley, 2000; Moscardo, 2008).

Yet, as Moscardo (2008) points out, there has been some confusion over what actually is sustainable tourism and, even more importantly, over what is the relationship between sustainable tourism and sustainable development. This – to follow Moscardo's line of thought – bears upon two interrelated queries: *Is tourism sustainable in its own right?* or *Is tourism part of sustainable development?* (6). In other words, the question is whether the focus is on sustainable tourism *per se* or on tourism understood as a sort of contributor to sustainable development (Stabler, 1997; Mowforth and Munt, 1998; Sharpley, 2000). Wall (1997) pertinently argues that, while analysing the relationship between tourism and sustainability, one should in fact ask 'whether and in what form might tourism contribute to sustainable development?' (34). Moscardo (2008) pushes the argument even further by proposing to challenge the assumption that tourism 'can be sustainable in its own right' and, consequently, to label it more explicitly as 'a potential resource for communities seeking sustainable development options' (7). It follows that 're-conceptualising tourism as just one among many possible development options is likely to result in a more direct comparison of tourism to other development options' (Moscardo, 2008: 7).[1]

As mentioned in the introduction, this study, following the above line of argument, aims to answer the question of whether sustainable tourism is really a developmental option for rural areas. Yet, before we move on, let us first focus on the socio-economic situation in Poland's rural and peripheral regions.

Poland's Rural Areas and the Regional Agenda

Poland is thought to be marked by rural-urban, core-periphery divides (Gorzelak and Tucholska, 2007; Zientara, 2008). Thus, whilst large cities and core regions are thriving (and *de facto* function as regional engines or poles of growth), rural areas – whose local economies are dominated by fragmented agriculture and low-end services – are lagging behind, being plagued by very high unemployment and poverty rates (Bąk et al., 2007; Central Statistical Office, 2009).[2] Indeed, prior to the accession to the EU of Romania and Bulgaria in 2007, the Lubelskie region (or *voivodship*) (Figure 9.1) – a rural area *par excellence* – was the poorest region

---

1   In this context, one should recognise the existence of synergies between tourism and other activities that can be exploited by rural and remote communities. According to Holmefjord (2000), one can distinguish three distinct categories of such synergies, namely, product, market and marketing synergies. Specifically, product synergies have to do with the shared use of facilities – such as transport infrastructure and communication systems – by tourism and other activities. Market synergies see tourists as extra customers for other (regional) products and services, while marketing synergies result from using tourism to promote and publicise other (attractive) characteristics of a given region.

2   For instance, in January 2011, unemployment in some areas (such as Szydłowiecki sub-region in Mazowieckie *voivodship*) exceeded 30 per cent, against the national average of 12 per cent.

Figure 9.1   Map of Polish regions (*voivodships*)

on a GDP *per capita* basis in the entire Community (Eurostat, 2006).[3] However, region-level aggregate statistics do not reveal the whole truth. In fact, the worst situation is in certain rural sub-regions and communities within less affluent, underdeveloped regions themselves (Bąk et al., 2007; Zientara, 2009; Central Statistical Office, 2009).

Furthermore, the rural-urban divide, to reiterate, manifests itself not only in terms of income or unemployment disparities, but also in the form of the civilisation gap (Sztompka, 2002; Hryniewicz, 2007; Zientara, 2008). It follows that the generally-understood quality of life in rural communities is far lower than

---

3   It is essential to note that Poland is a country with the largest number of regions (13 out of 16) in which disposable income (after state intervention) exceeds the primary income, which suggests a high degree of income redistribution. As Poland is characterised by high GDP per capita disparity, this may imply that wealth is generated mainly in a few economically strong regions that end up subsidising the underdeveloped rural periphery. Note that GDP per head disparity is measured in PPS and compared to other EU countries. For instance, Ireland, in contrast to Poland, has the lowest GDP per capita disparity (a factor of 1.6) in the entire Community.

in metropolitan areas. This is due, among other things, to inadequate infrastructure (roads in bad repair, lack of water-treatment plants and sewerage systems, housing without sanitation facilities), insufficient ICT deployment and substandard schooling (Zientara, 2009).

All this needs to be seen in a broader context: Poland – being the largest beneficiary of European aid within the framework of EU cohesion policy and the Common Agricultural Policy (CAP) – fares badly in competitiveness and business-friendliness rankings (World Economic Forum, 2010; World Bank, 2011). Equally importantly, in Poland, approximately 30 per cent of the population live in rural areas and 18 per cent is engaged in agricultural activity (Central Statistical Office, 2009). In neighbouring Slovakia, by contrast, the respective figures are 70 per cent and five per cent. In modern developed economies it is the service sector that generates jobs and income. Indeed, in Anglo-Saxon countries – where between three and five per cent of the population live off agriculture – services account for three-quarters of income and four-fifths of jobs. Hence Poland, with such a disproportionate reliance on agriculture, compares unfavourably with most western economies.

The predominance of farming is deeply rooted in Poland's complicated history (Hryniewicz, 2007). On the one hand, only a few Polish regions had experienced industrial revolution (in the 19th century) and, on the other, the communist authorities (in the 20th century) imposed collective ownership of land only in some areas, mainly in the regions which, prior to 1945, belonged to Germany. In most areas, private ownership of land (that is, of relatively small plots) survived. As the plot – frequently, the only asset of any value in many a rural household – had been passed from father to son, it acquired almost a totemic meaning in some strata of Polish society (Sztompka, 2002). The communists, fully aware of this, were reluctant to do away with this attribute of capitalism. Since 1989, farmers, constituting an important electorate, have opposed reform.

All of which goes some way towards explaining why the primary sector is still fragmented (Chaplin et al., 2007)[4] and, on the whole, inefficient (see also Zięba and Kowalski, 2007). Indeed, Polish agriculture's contribution to the country's GDP growth and value added is very low (Central Statistical Office, 2009). In 2005, its share in employment was almost four times higher than its contribution to value added. From one perspective, this is testament to the structural backwardness of the Polish economy (World Bank, 2011; World Economic Forum, 2011) and can shed light on the socio-economic situation in the areas in which agricultural activity plays an important role. Thus it is in Lubelskie (34.8 per cent), Podlaskie (35.9 per cent) and Świętokrzyskie (33.6 per cent) where agriculture's share in total employment is highest (Central Statistical Office, 2007). In another region, Podkarpackie, those employed in agriculture (25 per cent of the total) generated only 3.3 per cent of its value added in 2005 (Central Statistical Office, 2007).

---

4   It is estimated that in 2008 there were 1.9 million small (one- or two-hectare) farms (Central Statistical Office, 2009).

Podkarpackie is actually marked by the lowest effectiveness of agriculture (as measured by the ratio of agriculture's share in regional employment to its contribution to regional value added).[5]

In addition, poorer rural areas are often regarded as being characterised by low-quality social capital (Grabowska and Szawiel, 2001). The problem takes on a particular acuteness in those sub-regions (chiefly in Zachodniopomorskie and Warmińsko-mazurskie *voivodships*), where, under communism state-owned collectivism, farms were mostly ineffective and mismanaged, but still formed the backbone of local economies. In such communities social bonds were conspicuously weak and everyday life was dominated by over-reliance on the state as a provider of rudimentary welfare, grass-roots passivity, overall indifference and mutual mistrust (Sztompka, 2002). The collapse of communism laid bare the economic unsoundness of the collectives. Most of them, therefore, were shut down, which triggered large-scale redundancies. As a result, thousands of farm employees, who for years had become accustomed to a socialist work ethos (characterised by little effort and insufficient work commitment coupled with very low labour productivity and aversion to change), found themselves simultaneously unemployed and unemployable (Zientara, 2009). This bred frustration, which, in turn, even further aggravated the quality of social capital.

All this inevitably raises the question of whether sustainable tourism indeed constitutes a vehicle for addressing the deep-rooted problems affecting Polish rural areas. But, before attempting to explore the issue further, let us first examine briefly Poland's potential as a tourist destination.

Poland's Attractiveness as a Tourist Destination

There is little doubt that it is the attractiveness of a destination that encourages people to spend time there. Destination attractiveness is usually understood as the extent to which a given place lives up to the expectations and needs of its visitors. This attractiveness manifests itself in the form of recreational amenities, natural beauty (wildlife reserves or scenic landscapes), cultural richness and historic heritage, food and accommodation. Of course, there are many other factors that condition, to varying degrees, the attractiveness of a destination. These include,

---

5   What is more, as transpires from our calculations based on data from Central Statistical Office (2007), in 1995-2005, Lubelskie experienced the largest decrease in agriculture's contribution to regional value added (a fall of 8.4 percentage points). It was followed by Podkarpackie (-6.5 percentage points), Opolskie (-6.3 percentage points) and Świętokrzyskie (-6.2 percentage points). By contrast, Śląskie (-1.1 percentage points), Pomorskie (-2.9 percentage points) and Małopolskie (-2.9 percentage points) experienced the smallest fall in the value added generated by agriculture. Note also that Lubuskie is the only voivodship in which services' contribution to value added decreased in 1995-2005 (a fall of 2.4 percentage points).

inter alia, security, currency exchange rate and infrastructure. Critically, as MacKay and Fesenmaier (1997) point out, attractiveness is the function of perceptions, beliefs and impressions about a destination that are formed over time through processing information from various sources. The implication is that, for a place to have a tourist potential, it is not enough to be endowed with particular resources or standard tourist assets. What counts is their identification and utilisation as such (Formica and Uysal, 2006). Thus smart marketing – in particular, by means of social network sites – can ascribe tourism-related connotations to a destination's assets. Yet subjectivity plays a part, too: a destination comes across as attractive only if those who visit it consider it attractive.

That said, there is another increasingly important determinant of the attractiveness of a given destination, namely, its broadly-understood commitment to environmental protection. Due to a growing environmental awareness (Bohdanowicz, 2006), a destination's 'green credentials' or 'eco-friendliness' are taken into account while assessing its tourist attractiveness. In practice, at issue is, for instance, whether electricity is generated from coal or renewables and whether hotels, which consume significant amounts of energy and produce large quantities of waste (Bohdanowicz and Zientara, 2009), introduce initiatives aimed at reducing their negative environmental impact. In this sense, the need to respond effectively to ecological concerns is no longer viewed as a threat, but as an opportunity to enhance a destination's competitiveness (World Economic Forum, 2008). A growing number of policy-makers (and managers) realise that the effectiveness of their environmental policies are likely to condition the long-term economic sustainability and growth of tourist activity at local and national levels.

With all this in mind, it is legitimate to claim that there is a great deal of ambiguity to Poland's tourist attractiveness. For one, the country has a lot to offer: rich cultural heritage (mainly – but not only – in big cities and smaller provincial towns), natural beauty and pristine environment (mostly in peripheral areas in the east and south) as well as increasingly famous regional food and actively-cultivated folkloristic traditions (in rural and remote communities). Indeed, special emphasis should be placed on the country's nature: forests, which cover nine million hectares and constitute 28.3 per cent of the national territory, and still-uncontaminated lakes and rivers. What is more, Polish National Parks – which protect areas distinctive for their unique scientific, natural, cultural and educational values – are exceptional in Europe for their range of wildlife, their size and varying geographical interest. All of this means that, at least theoretically, there is much scope for the development of assorted forms of tourism: cultural tourism, culinary tourism, agri-tourism and nature-based tourism.

For another, Poland does too little to protect its environment and, in this respect, lags behind its western (and, especially, Scandinavian) counterparts. To start with, coal-fired power generation accounts for 94.8 per cent of total electricity consumption, which, obviously, has a negative impact on the environment (World Coal Institute, 2005). Burning coal in obsolete power plants contributes to high levels of greenhouse gas emissions. It is true that these are lower than in Britain

(659 million tonnes), but the fact remains that – as far as only CO_2 is concerned – Poland, alongside China and the USA, is one of the world's major CO_2 producers (on a per-capita basis). Yet, in contrast to America and China, in Poland not a single coal-fired power plant based upon one of the modern coal burning technologies (fluidised bed combustion, integrated gasification combined cycle or pressurised pulverised coal combustion) is currently under construction (Zientara, 2007). Accordingly, electricity sent over the grid to any commercial end-user – such as, for instance, a small hotel – is ecologically-unfriendly (only two to three per cent of electricity is generated from renewables). This has also other implications as Poland, because of its reliance on coal, will have to purchase additional rights to CO_2 emissions (which, of course, will translate into higher electricity prices in the near future).

Besides, the quality of air in most metropolitan areas is very low due to the presence of heavy industry and, critically, to traffic congestion (itself the result of the underdeveloped network of motorways and lack of ring roads). Also, ineffective environmental law enforcement (coupled with insignificant penalties for, say, dumping rubbish and industrial waste in forests) as well as non-existent waste segregation and inefficient recycling all speak volumes of the country's lacklustre commitment to environmental protection. In sum, Poland can hardly be held up as a paragon of modern environmentalism and needs to do much more – simultaneously in different areas – to burnish its green credentials. In this context, the fundamental question arises of what all that means for the view that sees sustainable tourism as a development option for Polish rural and remote regions.

Sustainable Tourism and Polish Regions: Is it Really a Viable Option?

Above all, there needs to be a recognition that the problems affecting Polish disadvantaged areas are so complex and deep-seated that addressing them effectively calls for a holistic approach. This means, in practice, that action needs to be taken, at the same time, at different levels of governance and in different domains (discussion of which is beyond the scope of this chapter). Granted, tourism *per se* can – and should – be part of strategies aimed at transforming the fortunes of Poland's rural and remote areas. But that is not to say that it can be sustainable or that it can lead to sustainable outcomes. First, were tourism to make any considerable impact in terms of employment generation, it would have to assume a large scale (in other words, only a *massive* influx of tourists can guarantee the viability of tourism-related businesses and thus the diversification of local economic activity). However, this – in line with what has been indicated in the theoretical section – would not only produce, but also magnify all sorts of undesirable environmental and societal effects, which sits uneasily with the principal tenet of sustainable tourism.

Logically, all those tourists would have to stay in hotels and guest houses endowed with green modes of operation (which contributes to minimising negative environmental impacts). This is unrealistic in the Polish circumstances. As is well known, in rural and peripheral areas, it is independent, usually family-run, hotels and guest houses that form the backbone of the hospitality industry. And Polish small business has particular difficulties coping with the country's hostile business climate (World Bank, 2011). Whereas for international hotel chains – such as Hilton or Marriott (whose facilities are located mainly in big cities) – red tape and high non-wage labour costs are a nuisance, for independent hotels and guest houses they often constitute a serious hindrance. The same applies for other small tourism-related businesses such as restaurants and agro-tourist farms.

The implication is that excessive regulation and high taxation not only prevent tourism-related businesses from creating (more) much-needed jobs, but also, fundamentally, from investing in more ecologically-friendly, energy-efficient technologies (since higher costs of operation translate into scarcer financial resources that can potentially be earmarked for investment in ecological solutions). Indeed, there is evidence that Polish hoteliers and hotel managers, while indeed recognising the need to take action to protect the environment, are not particularly willing to do so, due, among much else, to the fiscal and bureaucratic burden resulting from the country's unfavourable business climate (Bohdanowicz, 2006). Admittedly, the very fact that almost 95 per cent of electricity is produced from coal does not conduce towards sustainability, too.

What about transport? After all, tourists would have to reach somehow Polish remote localities. Without a well-developed road and railway infrastructure, this would mean even more congestion (leading to an increase in carbon dioxide emissions) and more road accidents (exacerbating an already-high death toll). It follows that, at least for the time being, travelling by car or train in Poland is neither safe nor environmentally friendly, which again sits awkwardly with the ideals of sustainable tourism. Related to this is the question of moving around *within* concrete localities. Ideally, tourists should use ecological means of transport to reduce their impact on the environment. That would mean, for instance, using bicycles (instead of cars). However, in the vast majority of rural communities – again, in contrast to most big cities – cycle tracks are few and far between. Arguably, this makes it harder to ensure the sustainability of tourist activity in those areas.

Another problem relates to waste disposal. Tourists, like ordinary citizens for that matter, produce tonnes of rubbish, which needs to be disposed of with as little damage to the environment as possible. It is true that in big cities more and more residents do segregate waste, but the fact remains that in rural communities it is either not practised at all or simply unheard of (what is more, there is evidence that in urban areas already segregated rubbish ends up being mixed up again and is transported in one container to a waste disposal site, which simply makes a mockery of environmental efforts on the part of city residents). Hence, a failure to introduce effective schemes facilitating waste segregation (and recycling) does not auger well for development of sustainable tourism in smaller rural communities and large metropolitan areas alike.

It has also been suggested that propagation of smaller-scale higher-margin organic (ecological) farming – which forms part of sustainable development thinking – might act as a draw for some green-minded tourists (especially from the Scandinavia). Ecological farming is based on the assumption that the farmer produces food without destroying land and feed the consumer without doing harm (see also *Economist*, 2006: 71). Moreover, the farmer not only produces food, but also protects the environment. It follows that the eco-farmer should make use of renewable sources of energy, manage the farm in a holistic, sustainable manner, protect the landscape, maintain the high quality of produce, avoid using chemical additives and fertilisers (as well as genetically modified organisms), protect water and soil from contamination.

For these reasons, organic farming poses a variety of challenges. Above all, compliance with the above requirements – at least in the short term – exponentially raises operating costs. The very process of getting an eco-certificate, which formally attests the status of an ecological farm and grants the owner the right to use the organic-food label, takes two years. Under the current circumstances, it is almost impossible to meet the renewable-energy requirement since, as already noted, almost all electricity is produced from coal. Protection of water and soil from contamination might be equally problematic given that many Polish rural communities – as we have already mentioned on several occasions – still lack sewage systems and water-treatment facilities. Refraining from using chemicals also increases the risk that the crop will fall prey to disease and insects. Furthermore, many Polish farmers are sceptical about the effectiveness of natural fertilisers. All this might therefore act as a deterrent to those who consider starting up an organic-farming business.[6]

On the other hand, the question of community involvement – albeit less manifest than in community-based tourism – also occupies an important place in the sustainable-tourism discourse (this is even more so, given that the EU also emphasises this aspect). However, as already noted, it is increasingly suggested that the rationale for engaging local residents in decision-making is open to doubt as they could have insufficient understanding of the processes at hand. Thus there are reasons to believe that, in practice, local development and planning decisions

---

6   There is disagreement about the actual merits of organic farming. Borlaug (2007), the father of the green revolution, points out that *globally* organic farming can be more harmful to the environment than traditional agriculture since it produces lower yields and hence necessitates more land under cultivation (to turn out the same quantity of food). Furthermore, it is suggested that organic farming may actually require 'more energy per tonne of food produced, because yields are lower' and weeds are kept at bay by natural means (*Economist*, 2006: 72). So its environmental impact (in terms of carbon emissions) might well be bigger than that of traditional farming. Nevertheless, others contest this line of reasoning, pointing out that the artificial fertiliser used in conventional farming is made using natural gas, which is ecologically unsustainable. Moreover, the case is made for organic *local* food – produced as close as possible to the consumer – so as to reduce distance and hence, by extension, to minimise carbon emissions due to transportation.

might be taken over by external agents (such as EU or government-appointed bureaucrats). There is another serious obstacle to progress in this respect. It is hardly in dispute that working out a local-level development strategy calls for efficient co-operation between various local actors (including *ordinary* citizens), which, in turn, highlights the significance of social capital. As we remember, the quality of social capital – underpinned by general indifference and passivity – in rural and remote localities leaves much to be desired.

This indirectly bears upon the issue of tolerance and openness (which, after all, are a prerequisite for any tourist activity). Indeed, Polish rural communities are still thought to be marked by insularity and hostility to strangers (Sztompka, 2002). Many Poles living in the rural periphery tend to be suspicious of foreigners and any external influence (see also Jasińska-Kania and Marody, 2002). In western and north-eastern parts of the country, many worry – not least thanks to populist politicians who try to drum up support by demonising Poland's western neighbour – that Germans will come and buy out Polish land. In Pomeranian villages farms that belonged to Dutch emigrants (who, unable to buy costly land in The Netherlands, had decided to settle in Poland) were burnt down. This was commonly regarded as an act of provincial xenophobia. Yet there needs to be a recognition that, with EU subsidies for farmers flowing in, this inward-looking mentality is slowly changing (Ministry of Agriculture and Rural Development, 2007). Still, this is just the beginning of a long process.

Conclusion

This chapter follows Moscardo's (2008) proposition to 're-conceptualise tourism as just one among many possible development options'. In doing so, it has set out to answer the question of whether sustainable tourism can constitute a development option for Polish rural and remote areas. In the light of the above discussion, it is fair to say that – as things stand now – it might be very hard to put the 'ideals' of sustainable tourism into practice. It follows that sustainable tourism can hardly be regarded as a panacea. Granted, tourism *per se* could – and should – indeed become an integral constituent of any development strategy aimed at transforming the fortunes of these communities (but this would still leave the question of considerable negative impacts unanswered!). Yet, to really help them overcome their deep-seated socio-economic problems, change must happen simultaneously in different areas. This would involve, to simplify, introducing free-market reform (cutting red tape and high taxes) and, for another, capitalising on EU funds, which – in line with the experience of old Member States – are best used to improve transport, ICT, power and water infrastructure. This is exactly what Polish rural areas need to reduce the civilisation gap.

Given rural communities' reliance on inefficient agriculture (and, generally, the entire structure of the Polish economy), decision-makers need to restructure the agricultural sector so as to render it capable of both contributing far more to the country's GDP and – in the longer run – of functioning without explicit and implicit subsidies (financed by the Polish and European taxpayer). This would mean consolidation of land and the creation of larger, specialised farms that – professionally managed like other businesses – would both invest state-of-the-art technologies and use economies of scale with the aim of improving efficiency and, by implication, enhancing competitiveness. Also, the framers' pension and tax system should be profoundly reformed (this has not only to do with economics, but also with ethics and equality before the law). The existence of small one-hectare plots, whose owners cling to subsistence farming, has simply no *raison d'être*. Yet many Polish farmers, receiving considerable subsidies from the EU, paying no income tax and low social-security contributions, see no point in change.

Instead of seeing sustainable tourism as a tool for regional development, it might be more sensible to ask – following Wall's (1997) reasoning – whether and in what form might tourism contribute to sustainable development. Indeed, potential growth of tourist activity theoretically offers numerous incentives to deal with obstacles that obstruct progress towards sustainable outcomes. The fact that, say, small hotels and independent guest houses have difficulty investing in eco-friendly solutions should help convince policy-makers to ease the fiscal and bureaucratic burden (by making Poland's investment climate more business-friendly) or to introduce measures facilitating adoption of energy-efficient, renewables-based technologies (tax breaks, etc.). Of course, this would also require modification of national energy policy that is still reliant on coal burning. The same goes for waste segregation and construction of new roads (and cycle tracks) all over the country. It is hoped that the present chapter, while deepening our understanding of the interrelated phenomena of regional economic development and sustainability, will provoke further discussion and multidisciplinary research.

References

Archer, B. and Cooper, C. (1998) The Positive and Negative Impacts of Tourism, in W.F. Theobald (ed.) *Global Tourism*. Oxford: Butterworth-Heinemann, 63-81.

Bąk, A., Chmielewski, R., Krasowska, M., Piotrowska, M. and Szymborska, A. (2007) *Report on Development and Regional Policy*. Warsaw: Ministry of Regional Development.

Bohdanowicz, P. (2006) Environmental Awareness and Initiatives in the Polish and Swedish Hotel Industries – Survey Results. *International Journal of Hospitality Management*, 25(4), 662-82.

Bohdanowicz, P. and Zientara, P. (2009) Hotel Companies' Contribution to Improving the Quality of Life of Local Communities and the Well-Being of their Employees. *Tourism and Hospitality Research*, 9(2), 147-58.

Borlaug, N.E. (2007) Sixty-two Years of Fighting Hunger: Personal Recollections. *Euphytica*, 157(3), 287-97.

Bosselman, F.P., Peterson, C.A. and McCarthy, C. (1999) *Managing Tourism Growth: Issues and Applications*. Washington, DC: Island Press.

Bramwell, B. (1998) Selecting Policy Instruments for Sustainable Tourism, in W.F. Theobald (ed.) *Global Tourism*. Oxford: Butterworth-Heinemann, 361-79.

Briassoulis, H. (2002) Sustainable Tourism and the Question of the Commons. *Annals of Tourism Research*, 29(4), 1065-85.

Butler, R.W. (1999) Problems and Issues of Integrating Tourism Development, in D.G. Pearce and R.W. Butler (eds) *Contemporary Issues in Tourism Development*. London: Routledge, 65-80.

Central Statistical Office (2007) *Voivodships*. Warsaw: Central Statistical Office.

Central Statistical Office (2008) *Regions of Poland*. Warsaw: Central Statistical Office.

Central Statistical Office (2009) *Statistical Yearbook of Agriculture and Rural Areas 2008*. Warsaw: Central Statistical Office.

Chaplin, H., Gorton, M. and Davidova, S. (2007) Impediments to the Diversifications of Rural Economies in Central and Eastern Europe: Evidence from Small-scale Farms in Poland. *Regional Studies*, 41(3), 361-76.

Coccossis, H. (1996) Tourism and Sustainability: Perspective and Implications, in G.K. Priestley, J.A Edwards and H. Coccossis (eds) *Sustainable Tourism? European Experiences*. Wallingford: CAB International, 1-21.

Collins, A. (1999) Tourism Development and Natural Capital. *Annals of Tourism Research*, 26(1), 98-109.

Cooper, C.P. and Wanhill, S. (eds) (1998) *Tourism and Development: Environmental and Community Issues*. Chichester: Wiley & Sons.

Cynarski, W.J., Obodyński, K. and Niziot, A. (eds) (2007) *Borderland and Trans-Border Tourism for European Integration*. Rzeszów: Podkarpackie Towarzystwo Naukowe Kultury Fizycznej.

Devuyst, D. and Hens, L. (2000) Introducing and Measuring Sustainable Development Initiatives by Local Authorities in Canada and Flanders (Belgium): A Comparative Study. *Environment, Development and Sustainability*, 2(2), 81-105.

Dow Jones Sustainability Index (2009) [Online]. Available at: http://www.sustainability-index.com/ [Accessed: 21 May 2010].

Economist (2006), 'Food Politics', 8507, 71-3.

Eurostat (2006) *Regions: Statistical Yearbook 2006*. Available at: http://epp.eurostat.ec.europa.eu/ [Accessed: 2 February 2007].

Formica, S. and Uysal, M. (2006) Destination Attractiveness Based on Supply and Demand Evaluations: An Analytical Framework. *Journal of Travel Research*, 44(4), 418-30.

Forstner, K. (2004) Community Ventures and Access to Markets: The Role of Intermediaries in Marketing Rural Tourism Products. *Development Policy Review*, 22(5), 497-514.

Gorzelak, G. and Tucholska, A. (eds) (2007) *Development, Region, Space.* Warsaw: Ministry of Regional Development & European Centre of Regional and Local Studies at the University of Warsaw.

Grabowska, M. and Szawiel, T. (2001) *Building Democracy. Social Divisions, Political Parties and Civil Society in Post-Communist Poland.* Warsaw: PWN.

Hall, C.M. (2000) *Tourism Planning: Policies, Processes and Relationships.* Harlow: Prentice Hall.

Hall, C.M. (2005) *Tourism: Rethinking the Social Science of Mobility.* Harlow: Prentice Hall.

Hall, D. and Richards, G. (eds) (2000) *Tourism and Sustainable Community Development.* New York: Routledge.

Hall, M. and Higham, J. (eds) (2005) *Tourism, Recreation and Climate Change.* Clevedon: Channel View Publications.

Holmefjord, K. (2000) Synergies in Linking Product, Industries and Place? Is Co-operation Between Tourism and Food Industries a Local Coping Strategy in Lofoten and Hardanger?, Paper presented at the MOST CCPP Workshop: *Whether, How and Why Regional Policies are Working in Concert with Coping Strategies Locally.* Joensuu, Finland.

Hryniewicz, J. (2007) Economic, Political and Cultural Factors of Space Differentiation. *Przegląd Zachodni*, 2, 21-46.

Institute of Tourism (2005) *Survey of the Social Profile of Tourists Visiting Poland.* Warsaw: IOT. Available at: http://www.pot.gov.pl [Accessed: 20 July 2008].

Jasińska-Kania, A. and Marody, M. (eds) *Poles amongst Europeans.* Warsaw: Wydawnictwo Naukowe SCHOLAR.

Kalinowski, T. (ed.) (2006) *Investment Attractiveness of Poland's Voivodships and Subregions*, Gdańsk: Ministry of Regional Development.

Kates, R.W., Parris, T.M. and Leiserowitz, A.A. (2005) What is Sustainable Development? Goals, Indicators, Values, and Practices. *Environment: Science and Policy for Sustainable Development*, 47(3), 8-21.

Kirsten, M. and Rogerson, C. (2002) Tourism, Business Linkages and Small Enterprise Development in South Africa, *Development South Africa*, 19(1), 29-59.

Kiss, A. (2004) Is Community-based Ecotourism a Good Use of Biodiversity Conservation Funds? *Trends in Ecology and Evolution*, 19(5), 232-7.

Joppe, M. (1996) Sustainable Community Tourism Development Revisited. *Tourism Management*, 17(7), 475-9.

KRUS (2009) *KRUS in Numbers.* Available at: http://www.krus.gov.pl/krus/krus-w-liczbach/ [Accessed: 11 January 2010].

MacKay, K.J. and Fesenmaier, D.R. (1997) Pictorial Element of Destination in Image Formation. *Annals of Tourism Research*, 24(3), 537-65.

Middleton, V.T.C. and Hawkins, R. (1998) *Sustainable Tourism: A Marketing Perspective.* Oxford: Butterworth-Heinemann.

Ministry of Agriculture and Rural Development (2007) *Sectoral Operation Programme. Restructuring and Modernisation of the Alimentary Sector and*

Development of Rural Areas, 2004-2006, Warsaw. Available at: http://www. minrol.gov.pl/ [Accessed: 1 May 2008].

Moscardo, G. (2008) Sustainable Tourism Innovation: Challenging Basic Assumptions. *Tourism and Hospitality Research*, 8(1), 4-13.

Mowforth, M. and Munt, I. (1998) *Tourism and Sustainability: New Tourism in the Third World*. London: Routledge.

Neuman, W.L. (2003) *Social Research Methods: Qualitative and Quantitative Approaches*. Boston: Allyn and Bacon.

Obodyński, K., Kosiewicz, J. and Cynarski, W.J. (eds) (2007) *Tourism in Borderlands – Multi-Aspect Study of Development*. Rzeszów: Podkarpackie Towarzystwo Naukowe Kultury Fizycznej.

Priestley, G.K., Edwards, J.A. and Coccossis, H. (eds) (1996) *Sustainable Tourism? European Experiences*. Wallingford: CAB International.

Ratz, T. (2000) Residents' Perceptions of the Socio-Cultural Impacts of Tourism at Lake Balaton, Hungary, in G. Richards and H. Derek (eds) *Tourism and Sustainable Community Development*, London: Routledge, 36-47.

Richards, G. and Derek, H. (eds) (2000) *Tourism and Sustainable Community Development*. London: Routledge.

Roberts, L. and Hall, D. (2001) *Rural Tourism and Recreation: Principles to Practice*. Cambridge, MA: CABI.

Sharpley, R. (2000) Tourism and Sustainable Development: Exploring the Theoretical Divide. *Journal of Sustainable Tourism*, 8(1), 1-19.

Stabler, M.J. (1997) An Overview of the Sustainable Tourism Debate and the Scope and Content of the Book, in M.J. Stabler (ed.) *Tourism and Sustainability: Principles to Practice*. Wallingford: CAB International, 1-21.

Sztompka, P. (2002) *Sociology*. Kraków: Znak.

Wagner, J.E. (1997) Estimating the Economic Impacts of Tourism. *Annals of Tourism Research*, 24(3), 592-608.

Wahab, S. and Pigram, J.J. (1997) (eds) *Tourism Development and Growth*, London: Routledge.

Wall, G. (1997) Sustainable Tourism – Unsustainable Development, in S. Wahab and J.J. Pigram (eds) *Tourism Development and Growth*. London: Routledge, 33-49.

Weaver, D.B. (ed.) (2001) *The Encyclopaedia of Ecotourism*. Wallingford: CABI.

Vail, D. and Hultkrantz, L. (2000) Property Rights and Sustainable Nature Tourism: Adaptation and Mal-adaptation in Dalarna (Sweden) and Maine (USA), *Ecological Economics*, 35, 223-42.

World Bank (2011) Doing Business 2011. Available at: http://doingbusiness.org/ rankings/ [Accessed: 27 January 2011].

World Coal Institute (2005) *The Coal Resource: A Comprehensive Overview of Coal*. London: World Coal Institute.

World Travel and Tourism Council (2009) *Leading the Challenge on Climate Change*. London: WTTC.

World Economic Forum (2011) Global Competitiveness Index 2010/2011. Available at: http://gcr.weforum.org/gcr2010/ [Accessed: 28 January 2011].

World Economic Forum (2008) Travel and Tourism Competitiveness Report 2008. Available at: http://www.weforum.org/en/initiatives/gcp/TravelandTourismReport/index.htm/ [Accessed: 20 May 2009].

Zientara, P. (2007) Coal Mining, Economic Development and Environmental Sustainability: A Case of Poland. *Journal of Energy and Development*, 32(2), 189-206.

Zientara, P. (2008) Polish Regions in the Age of a Knowledge-Based Economy. *International Journal of Urban and Regional Research*, 32(1), 65-80.

Zientara, P. (2009a) Development of Tourism in Poland: Policy Implications. *International Journal of Tourism Policy*, 2(3), 159-66.

Zientara, P. (2009b) *New Europe's Old Regions*. London: The Institute of Economic Affairs.

Zientara, P. and Bohdanowicz, P. (2010) The Hospitality Sector (Chapter 5), in J. Jafari, and L.A. Cai (eds) *Tourism and the Implications of Climate Change: Issues and Actions* (*Bridging Tourism Theory and Practice, vol. 3*), 91-111.

Zięba, S. and Kowalski, A. (eds) (2007) *Development of Agriculture, Food Production and Polish Rural Areas in the EU*. Warsaw: Almamer i Instytut Ekonomiki Rolnictwa i Gospodarki Żywnościowej – Państwowy Instytut Badawczy.

Chapter 10

Tourism Workers and the Equity Dimension of Sustainability

Dimitri Ioannides and Evangelia Petridou

Introduction

Despite the stress social security systems in Europe have been under since the 1990s, Europeans have come to expect high levels of comprehensive social protection in the form of liberal health benefits, child allowances, parental leave, free education, subsidised child care and other benefits forming '... an elaborate and expensive network of publicly funded ... programs designed to protect everyone in Europe against the vicissitudes of contemporary life' (Ostergren and Rice, 2004, Reid, 2004: 146).

This comprehensive social safety net is part of the "European model of society" – '... a normative concept standing for moderating the pursuit of economic growth and competitiveness with concerns about social welfare and equity; sustainability and governance also are factored in for good measure' (Faludi, 2007: 1). The European model of society articulates the Community's shared values, which include adequate health and safety in the workplace, quality of life and quality in work, cohesion, solidarity and sustainable development (Faludi, 2007). It also conveys the shared concerns of sustainability, equity and competitiveness and the idea that '... the market is not everything and that there are values beyond growth giving legitimacy to intervention by a strong but unobtrusive state'. (Faludi, 2007: 20) Despite the fact that this model is not monolithic and there are variations among European countries, it refers to the European way of dealing with relations among the state, the market and civic society, between efficiency and equity, as well as the individual and the collective. This makes the European model distinct from its American and Anglo-Saxon counterparts (Davoudi, 2007). It also conveys the shared concerns of sustainability, equity and competitiveness and the idea that '... the market is not everything and that there are values beyond growth giving legitimacy to intervention by a strong but unobtrusive state' (Faludi, 2007: 20).

In this chapter we argue that despite the mainstreaming of cohesion but also sustainability in European policy making resulting from the European model of society, the reality is that intrinsic attributes of too many tourism-related jobs hinder the well-being of the workers who are employed in them. Indeed, despite tourism's phenomenal ascendancy as a key component of employment-creation strategies in numerous localities throughout the EU, work in the sector often suffers the image of low skills and poor pay as well as being seasonal and/or part time and highly feminised with few chances for promotions and wage raises (Riley et al., 2002; Zampoukos and Ioannides, 2011).

The chapter is divided into four parts. First, we review the literature demonstrating that despite the ample rhetoric that has appeared over the last two decades or so regarding sustainable development and tourism, the issue of equity and social justice as a key component of this concept has largely been underplayed (Chok and Macbeth, 2009). In fact, most commentators ignore aspects relating to tourism workers, their working conditions and their overall quality of life preferring, instead, to focus on the need to balance a community's economic growth objectives with environmental conservation. Our attention then shifts toward an overview of salient policy-making events and initiatives relating to sustainability in tourism labour specifically within Europe. This is followed by a discussion examining the status of tourism jobs, paying particular attention to the inequities arising from the noticeable division of labour that characterises this sector. The chapter ends with concluding remarks.

Sustainable Development, Tourism, Equity and Labour

In his seminal piece, Campbell (1996) likened sustainable development in any given community to reconciling economic growth goals (targeting economic growth and efficiency), with those of environmental protection, and the pursuit of social equity (aimed at social justice, economic opportunity, and income equality). Essentially, Campbell portrayed these three goals in constant conflict with each other; each of these respective tensions is described as follows:

Firstly, there exists a 'resource conflict' (298) when the regulations protecting the natural resources are overly strict and perceived as anti-development; this situation can curtail a community's ambition of achieving economic growth. However, Campbell admits that the goal of economic growth requires a modicum of regulation "… to conserve those resources for present and future demands" (299).

Secondly, the need to protect the natural environment is likely to inhibit the objective of achieving social equity for the community's residents. How can the local inhabitants benefit if the environmental regulations are so strict they end up leading to the prohibition of specific vital activities and the exclusion of certain population groups? For example, what gain do the residents of a community receive when forced to abandon their traditional hunting grounds as authorities convert these to a national park? Campbell, labels this situation the "development conflict" (299).

Finally, there exists according to Campbell a "property conflict" (298) namely the one between the respective goal for economic growth and that of achieving greater equity. This conflict is represented through the tensions between landlords and tenants, managers and workers or new residents. In the case of tourism one

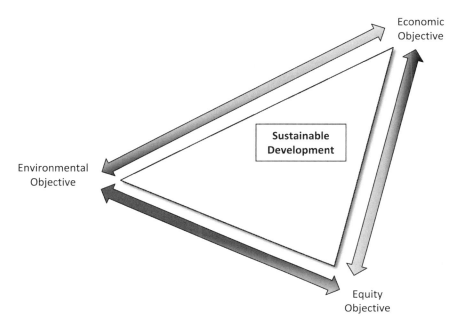

Figure 10.1   Balance of forces affect in sustainable development

of the conflicts can be between visitors and long-term inhabitants or between the sector itself and the residents.

Only by balancing these competing goals, each of which is represented as a corner of a hypothetical triangle, does a community hope to get closer to the utopian dream of sustainable development. Campbell likens this objective to pinpointing the centre of this triangle (Figure 10.1). To be sure, he accepts this centre is elusive and can never be precisely located. Rather, in reference to the actions of planners, he maintains that for them to pretend '… at all times to be at the center of the … triangle will only make sustainability a hollow term' (1996: 309). A far more useful approach for planners and policymakers, he argues, is to actually "orient themselves in the triangle" by consciously choosing which of the three conflicts they will concentrate on. For instance, if they are committed to improving the social equity of their community they would be best placed to serve this commitment by immersing themselves within the property conflict. Whereas such an approach to sustainable development surely generates ambiguities, McCool has argued that this is not altogether a bad thing. Rather, he maintains that sustainability is useful as a "guiding fiction" since because of its vagueness '… everyone can agree that it is a goal and discussion can proceed' (1996: 2). In a nutshell, whereas sustainable development in which there is perfect harmony between all of the aforementioned goals is not likely to be reached, this does not mean we should not use it as a beacon towards improving circumstances for people and the overall environment in any given community.

Within the field of tourism studies sustainable development has truly emerged as a leading mantra of the last two decades. The quantity of literature generated on the topic during this timeframe has been staggering (McCool, 1995; Wall, 1997; Hall and Lew, 1998; Bosselman et al., 1999; Ioannides and Holcomb, 2001; Weaver, 2006; Ioannides, 2009). Yet, much of this work favours overwhelmingly the environmental aspect of sustainable development (Neto, 2003), concentrating specifically on the resource conflict between the overriding need for economic growth and the goal of environmental protection (Leslie, 2009). This is not altogether surprising given the realisation that the longevity of any destination is highly dependent on the protection of the very natural and built resources, which made this a visitor attraction in the first place. Unfortunately, this obvious bias reflects the dominance of the weak or treadmill approach to sustainable development prevailing at most destinations whereby the protection of the environment is promoted only in recognition that failure to do so jeopardises long-term economic growth concerns (Kousis, 2001).

The definite predisposition most researchers demonstrate towards environmental issues and their conflict with economic growth concerns within the sustainability debate, especially as it relates to tourism, has not gone unnoticed. Chok and Macbeth (2009) lament the fact that indicators relating to sustainable tourism focus almost exclusively on environmental measures. Similarly, Neto (2003) acknowledges that the rhetoric relating to sustainable tourism development must surely extend beyond the pursuit of minimising negative environmental impacts to take into account the participation of local communities and, most importantly, cause the reduction of poverty. Importantly, he spells out that while the concept of sustainable development implicitly calls for a greater degree of community participation, by explicitly adopting a pro-poor approach there is a much greater opportunity for increasing "… the participation of and opportunities for the poorest segments of society" (2003: 220).

Overall, the pro-poor approach in tourism consists of three parts (Neto, 2003). First, it can be a means for generating both business and job opportunities for the poorest segments of any society while concurrently ensuring these people are trained to a level that allows them to truly benefit from these situations. Second, the pro-poor approach calls for reducing both the environmental but also the social effects resulting from tourism growth. Finally, it requires a degree of policy reform, enabling the involvement of the poorest people in a community in '… planning, development and management of tourism activities pertinent to them, removing some of the barriers for greater participation by the poor, and encouraging partnerships between government agencies or the private sector and poor people in developing new tourism goods and services' (Neto, 2003: 220).

Chok et al. (2007) and Chok and Macbeth (2009) acknowledge the pro-poor strategy's importance as a central approach for reducing the costs and maximising the benefits of tourism development in local communities. Maintaining that the discussion on poverty alleviation focuses almost exclusively on the developing world they point out that '… the tourism industry's 'job creation' rate is often cited as a primary reason to adopt it as a pro-poor strategy' (Chok and Macbeth, 2009: 2). However, they warn that this discussion does not go far enough since it largely ignores '… redistributive justice as an explicit goal [while] considerations of structural injustice as contributing to and/or exacerbating poverty are rare, particularly within policy circles' (ibid.). In other words, they believe that one of the pivotal points of sustainable development, namely social equity, which effectively recognises that in addition to gains, gross inequities arise from development, is all too often circumvented. In their eyes a central question that must come to the forefront is how to ensure all inhabitants can end up with a significant improvement in their quality and standard of living following an initiative aimed at economic growth, even if this initiative is constrained by the necessity to protect, as far as possible, precious environmental resources.

Referring specifically to tourism, Chok and Macbeth (2009) acknowledge that environmental sustainability must receive special attention given the sector's resource-intensive nature. However, they express dismay that social justice issues remain marginalised, especially given tourism's labour-intensive nature. After all, if one of the objectives put forth so often by policymakers in support of tourism's development is that it will generate jobs directly and indirectly, then why is the emphasis on the number of positions created whereas a discussion concerning the types of jobs (specifically the lower end jobs), not to mention the poor remuneration and benefits' packages associated with these, avoided?

Related questions that could be put forth are: What is the point of promoting the development of a major hotel resort in a country like Portugal or Greece, which meets all the latest requirements of eco-friendly design and construction if concurrently this development results in displacement of local residents and/or the creation of many sub-standard and poorly paid jobs? What benefits will derive for the immigrants inhabiting a run-down part of a major city if a tourism-driven redevelopment project in the name of job-creation and economic growth ends in these individuals' displacement and further marginalisation? Or, what value do the many lower paying tourism-related jobs deriving from a major initiative like hosting the World Cup or the Olympic Games have for a particular locality's inhabitants if in the long term they lead to a significant rise in the cost of living and, by association, the exclusion of these individuals from the housing market?

When examining the case of the "instant city" of Dubai one is justified in expressing concern that despite the frenzy of construction over the last decade minimal attention has been paid to the fact that much of this development, which aims heavily at the reimaging of the city into a major tourism destination, depends on the exploitation of guest workers from countries like India, Sri Lanka and the Philippines. In an article focusing on Dubai, the *National Geographic* described the following situation prevailing in the areas where thousands of these guest workers live:

> 'The laborers' barracks stood among many battered, squat buildings along a dirt
> and gravel road littered with garbage. Hundreds of men with sun-soaked brown

faces scuttled past in tank tops, baggy slacks, and torn flip flops. Some of these workers joined in recent strikes, fed up with being treated as 'less than human' in the words of Human Rights Watch. The average worker makes about five dollars a day, working 12 hour-shifts in scorching heat. (Molavi, 2007: 106)

The fate of Dubai's workers is far from unique. In Singapore, tourism employees regularly work in excess of 80 hours per week or 350 hours per month and it is not unusual for some of these poorly paid individuals to work 24-hour shifts without compensation for overtime (Chok and Macbeth, 2009). Moreover, as Seifert and Messing (2006) have reported, much of the work done by tourism workers on the lower rungs of the employment spectrum (e.g., hotel room cleaners) is dirty, exposing these individuals to the risk of injury. A cleaner in a luxury-level hotel, for instance, is expected to single-handedly flip a heavy king-size mattress, risking serious back injury, all in the name of ensuring the next guest will receive the highest level of quality money can buy. Because of inadequate training, it is possible for these workers to be injured from the harmful cleaning substances they are exposed to on a daily basis (OnsØyen et al., 2009).

The marginal status of many workers in the tourism and hospitality sector is not a phenomenon unique to places like Singapore, Dubai, or indeed the developing world. Rather, it is a problem observed and commented on from time to time throughout the world, including many parts of Europe and North America (ILO, 2002). Zampoukos and Ioannides (2011) have discussed the division of labour which dominates the tourism and hospitality sector. Their review acknowledged this sector generates a variety of high-end jobs requiring individuals with a modicum of training and skills (for example, managerial positions or ones where knowledge of information technologies is a must). However, they also highlight the existence of a multitude of lower-end positions, many of which focus on reproductive tasks commonly associated with the housewife's unpaid chores within the home (e.g., room cleaning, food preparation, and dish washing) (see also McDowell, 2009). These peripheral jobs are often part-time and/or seasonal, offering few opportunities for career advancement. Importantly, many of these positions, especially in more economically advanced societies (including Western Europe) are occupied by women and/or immigrants, many of whom are younger persons with little formal education and limited language skills.

In reference specifically to a major city hotel in Stockholm, Zampoukos and Ioannides highlighted the existence of front-of-the-house positions (e.g., receptionists and head waiters), requiring a high degree of interaction with the clientele. These are commonly occupied by native (light-skinned) speakers who are fluent in one or more additional languages and have probably had at least some education and training in hospitality management. Meantime, many workers occupy various back-of-the house positions. These include the dishwashers and the room cleaners. Many of these people are immigrants (most likely darker skinned) and they perform their tasks outside the visitor's gaze (Ainsworth and Purss, 2009). The only evidence of their "invisible" work comes '... in the guise of a perfectly made bed, an empty paper basket, a clean bathroom and perhaps new towels' (Zampoukos and Ioannides, 2011: 38).

The lowly status of the myriad bottom-end tourism-related jobs, specifically within Europe, despite the sector's prominence as a driver of employment creation, is a point agreed on by various observers (Head and Lucas, 2004; Shaw and Williams, 2004; Devine et al., 2007; Baum, 2007; Lai et al., 2008). A decade ago the International Labour Office (ILO, 2001) discusses how the sector is notorious for the low paying jobs it generates, specifically singling out the EU, where wages in such jobs were below 20 per cent of the average. At the time, in the United Kingdom weekly wages for men and women in the tourism sector were £225.80 and £170.80 respectively compared with average wages for manual workers, which were £328 for men and £211 for women. The ILO also highlighted the problems of poor working conditions and inconvenient employment schedules, not to mention the absence of bonus pay, and that of a significant number of illegal jobs. Indeed, the organisation stressed the point that in some European countries there are substantial numbers of people working in the tourism sector without pay; in all likelihood these are relatives helping out during periods of high demand, especially within smaller family owned and operated establishments. It was estimated, for example, that in Greece as many as 48 per cent of hospitality workers were employed without pay. Given the European Union's significant emphasis over the last few years on developing concepts such as the enhancement of economic, social, and territorial cohesion coupled with rhetoric relating to sustainable development the question is to what extent are measures such as these effective in terms of raising the status of jobs in tourism? Enough anecdotal evidence exists suggesting that the labels, which give rise to the notoriously poor image of many tourism-related jobs, have not disappeared, and are unlikely to do so any time soon.

The next section proceeds to examine the key rhetoric that have been put forth within the European Union over the last few years aimed at the improvement in the quality of life of all its citizens but also at enhancing the Union's competitive position in the global arena. Whereas some of the measures advocated are general and not sector-specific others have not only direct or indirect significance for the concepts of sustainable development but also tourism.

The European Policy Framework in Reference to Tourism

The EU consistently ranks as the number one tourism destination internationally (ECORYS, 2009). In 2007, 380 million people visited the Union, making up 42 per cent of the total international arrivals worldwide. A highly fragmented and complex sector, tourism accounted for 5.2 per cent of total employment in the EU, or 9.7 million people in 2006. The accommodation and travel organisation sectors alone comprised approximately 340,000 companies, 90 per cent of which employed fewer than 10 people. These sectors provide jobs for about 2.8 million people, about 1.2 per cent of total employment in the 27 EU countries (ECORYS, 2009). Within specific European countries tourism demonstrates its apparent economic clout when considering the sector's contribution to GDP. Between 1995 and 2005 the approximate average contribution of tourism to GDP in Norway, Sweden and France was respectively 4.7 per cent, 2.7 per cent, and 6.4 per cent (NUTEK, 2008). In Sweden alone the travel and tourism sector generated 151,000 full time equivalents in 2006, which is '... more than agriculture, forestry, and fishing combined' (NUTEK, 2008: 5). Notably, while the country's entire work force had grown by 7.4 per cent between 1995 and 2005, in the case of travel and tourism it grew by a staggering 45 per cent.

The importance of tourism within the EU was heralded with the creation of the Tourism Advisory Committee in 1986 and the subsequent designation of 1990 as European Year of Tourism. In 1992, the Council of Europe implemented a three-year Action Plan for assisting tourism as part of the 'Tourism and Employment' process. Then, in 1997, a joint Presidency/Commission conference on Tourism and Employment was held in Luxemburg, leading to the establishment of a High Level Group on Tourism and Employment. As a result of the group's 1998 report (*European Tourism: New Partnerships for Jobs: Conclusions and Recommendations of the High Level Group on Tourism and Employment*), the Commission and Member States agreed to set up four working groups, each of which aimed at training in order to improve the skills of tourism workers. By 2003 sustainability within the context of competitiveness plus the concept of cooperation for promoting Europe as a single destination entered the official discourse through the Communication *Basic Orientations for the Sustainability of European Tourism*. These terms were first consolidated in the language of the Lisbon Strategy and renewed in later Communications. Finally, in 2004 the Commission set up the Tourism Sustainability Group (TSG), composed of experts from industry associations, civil society, trade unions and representatives from destinations (Notarstefano, 2007).

The Lisbon Strategy itself was drawn up in 2000 in response to the challenges of an ever-changing, increasingly globalised world. This document, which was revisited in 2005 and 2010 and monitored by the European Lisbon Strategy Observatory, steered the European discourse relating to the Union role as a global player as well as providing a comprehensive vision for the future. Even though the Lisbon Strategy did not refer specifically to tourism, the essence of any post-2000 document discussed in this section is in line with the strategic goal put forth in its context, namely '... to become the most competitive and dynamic knowledge-based economy in the world, capable of sustainable economic growth with more and better jobs and greater social cohesion' (European Parliament, 2000: 2, emphasis original).

This mission statement, though ambitious, was crystal clear. First, the EU gave full recognition to the prevalence of the knowledge-based economy. Thus emphasis was placed on the dynamic creation and dissemination of knowledge. Importantly, the ambition to become the most competitive economy was qualified by a call for sustainable economic growth. Notably, the text within the Lisbon Strategy addressed not only the number of jobs ("more jobs") but also their quality ("better jobs"), the latter being crucial for engendering greater social cohesion and equity. The absence of the environmental tenet of sustainability should not be construed as lack of interest within this document in the natural environment. Rather, the Lisbon Strategy specifically targeted job creation and the economy. Indeed environmental protection has generally been built in EU regulatory policy and has a prominent place in various documents and policies regarding sustainable tourism to a point where it overshadows the social equity aspect of sustainability (see Leslie, 2010).

A report by the Employment Task Force chaired by Wim Kok, warned that Europe was in danger of falling short of the Lisbon Strategy goals. Adopting a fiscally liberal tone echoing American rhetoric, this report called for '… reducing administrative and regulatory obstacles to the setting up and management of businesses' (CEC, 2003: 8.8) because business expansion is often stifled by '… recruitment formalities, administrative procedures and conditions for dismissals' (ibid.: 20). Its focus was on more people (especially the young, women and the ageing population) working, and working more productively. Two paragraphs of the report were specifically dedicated to addressing job quality, admitting that an alarming number of people perceive themselves to be in a low quality job. The Employment Task Force report addressed job quality from an economic standpoint, focusing on the angle that low-end jobs do not contribute as much to growth and high productivity. The social cohesion aspect – the prosperity of the workers – is only obliquely present within the text.

By contrast, the quality of job opportunities in tourism as well as the prosperity and quality of life of the local communities feature prominently in the Tourism Sustainability Group's report, (TSG, 2007). Building on the World Tourism Organisation's 12 aims for sustainable tourism from 2006, the group identifies three objectives for the EU Sustainable Development Strategy (SDS) that are in tandem with the three aspects of sustainability. The provision of quality employment with fair pay and without discrimination is embedded in the economic prosperity objective. The report makes repeated calls for increased '… social dialogue between employers, employees and their representatives' (TSG, 2007: 11), better human resources practices as well as lifelong learning for the tourism industry employees. This is a normative document. It acknowledges the issues that plague tourism employment and proposes better cooperation between the business and the public sectors, as well as compliance with labour laws as solutions leading to a better workplace.

Two years later the *Study on the Competitiveness of the EU Tourism Industry* was published. The mission statement articulated in this report begins by mirroring the first part of the Lisbon Strategy but its focus soon shifts onto the customers: '… *to strengthen the tourism industry to become a dynamic and sustainable growth sector that aims to provide all its customers with a high quality travel experience at a balanced price/quality ratio*' (ECORYS,

2009, original emphasis). Perhaps this does not come as a surprise as the goal articulated in the language above is not only more attainable, but also easier to quantify than one focusing on the quality of employment in the tourism industry. Consequently, this is language suitable to a document with clear, measurable objectives. The report further identifies 'megatrends' and 'challenges' faced by the European tourism industry. Sustainability, in terms of '… ecologically, socially and economically responsible consumerism …' (p.III) is listed as a megatrend. Again, the point of departure here is the consumer, not the employer or the tourism worker.

The quality of jobs in the tourism industry is discussed as part of the challenges faced by the industry, permeating three of these: the challenge to '… reinforce the EU tourism industry as a high quality service sector … make the tourism industry part of the knowledge economy' and '… develop EU tourism in a sustainable manner' (p.IV, V). The authors of the report acknowledge that many tourism jobs have unfavourable working conditions and low remuneration, resulting in high turnover and an increasingly widening gap between the knowledge-rich and the knowledge-poor workers. What is more, innovation levels are low in a sector dominated by SMEs that perhaps are not familiar with the concept and its practical applications in tourism. Finally, the report directly addresses the fact that the questionable quality of tourism jobs, the recipient of which tend to be women, the young and the less skilled, is a threat to the sustainable development of the industry as a whole (ECORYS, 2009).

Aspects from the various documents discussed above inform the 2010 Communication of the European Commission (CEC), which sets a new political framework for European tourism (CEC, 2010). In line with the Lisbon Strategy this document addresses increased competitiveness and sustainable growth concomitantly. The quality and sustainability of tourism jobs are recognised as an integral part of the development of responsible high-quality tourism. Notably, this document goes one step further by proposing actions for ensuring increased quality in employment. These include an awareness-raising campaign as a means of combating the exploitation of women and children, a charter and a '*Qualité Tourisme*' brand to acknowledge responsible businesses as well as establishing a European prize for businesses and destinations, which respect the values of this chapter. What is more, the document acknowledges migration and calls for the reduction of the negative effects of globalisation on workers and their families as well as adapting social protection measures to account for increased migration.

To what extent does all this EU rhetoric, which deals either directly or indirectly with tourism, have an effect specifically on the social equity side of sustainable development? How, if at all, can workers occupying the lower ranking positions in tourism within the Union's member states benefit from these measures? One could also seek to examine the barriers which prohibit this rhetoric from actually benefiting tourism workers? We turn to examine these issues in the next section.

Do European Tourism Workers Benefit?

Detailed studies relating to the status of tourism workers, specifically within the context of the European Union, are rare and many of these dated (Ball, 1988; Bull and Church, 1994; Church and Frost, 2004; Baum, 2007; Devine et al., 2007). Much of the research that has appeared has focused heavily on the British Isles while only a few English language writings exist concerning the situation in other European countries (e.g., Lazaridis and Wickens, 1999; Hjalager, 2008). Regardless, as we have already mentioned, the gist of this extant work is that there is an obvious division of labour within the tourism sector (along the lines of gender, age, income and ethnic background) and that the vast majority of positions are found at the lower rungs of the employment ladder.

An interesting aspect of tourism-related jobs is that, irrespective of the employment level we are talking about (higher-end versus lower-end) the motivations of the workers performing these tasks vary, sometimes significantly (see, for example, Adler and Adler, 1999). For instance, whereas it is true that recent immigrants in a place like Copenhagen or Paris often gravitate toward lower-end jobs in the tourism sector, this does not mean all of these individuals have identical reasons for choosing this type of work in the first place. A female political refugee from Afghanistan or Somalia arriving in Malmö with limited language and formal education skills is unlikely, at least initially, to have much say in choosing a job. She is not unlikely to end up doing a menial task including working as a room cleaner in a hotel or a dishwasher in a restaurant. She is also more likely to be locked into such a low-level type of employment (where any movement from one position to the next is likely to be lateral) especially if she is unable to gain the qualifications necessary for higher end positions in tourism or, for that matter, any other sector.

Meanwhile, a second person, a young temporary migrant from Poland to London, may well make the conscious decision to work as a cleaner in a mid-size hotel in Bayswater or Earl's Court precisely because the hours of employment at this establishment, not to mention the remuneration, jive with this individual's primary purpose for coming to the city, namely to better learn the language and perhaps, experience an exciting new lifestyle for a relatively short period of time (Church and Frost, 2004; see also Devine et al., 2007). Indeed, as Devine et al. have noted, it is not unusual for workers such as this one to arrive from another country to work in the hospitality sector realising that the wages paid may in fact be lower than in their homeland. Such a person then, is well aware the job in tourism is only for a short while and is not likely to make a career in the sector.

We can add to these type of workers a third group, namely locally-born younger persons who perhaps are students choosing to work in the lower rungs of the tourism sector (e.g., as waiters or servers at a fast-food restaurant). Church and Frost (2004) argue that at least in the case of the United Kingdom the introduction of university fees combined with the setting of a minimum wage has led to an explosion of younger persons looking for work over the last few years. However, while financial remuneration obviously becomes an incentive to find employment there exist several non-pay-related reasons explaining why these individuals choose this line of work over something else. These include the flexible hours that tourism-related work offers compared to most other jobs especially since periods of peak demand (e.g., summers, weekends, and evenings) do not normally clash with study schedules. Lucas and Ralston (1997) have also argued that student workers enjoy working in tourism jobs since these often allow them the opportunity for social interaction.

Thus, the situation throughout many parts of Europe, especially within the lower-end of the tourism labour market, is that whereas there exists a substantial number of workers with few opportunities and negligible say in the type of work they end up doing, there are substantially more individuals choosing to work in the sector only as a means to an end (Devine et al., 2007). The latter group treats their work within tourism with an eye to sooner or later moving on to something considerably better and more permanent. This predominantly negative attitude towards tourism work, arising from the fact that so many employees regard the sector as a stepping stone and not a long-term career path, serves as a major '… downward pressure on tourism wages' (Shaw and Williams, 2004: 66). In other words, given that a substantial number of low-ranked workers in tourism apparently take their poor status largely for granted, this situation leads to few calls for higher levels of organised labour and, consequently, lower levels of worker protection. This problem is accentuated by the existence within the EU of a sizeable and highly mobile labour market that is enticed into the tourism sector precisely because the skills necessary for performing much of the work are low and often acquired on the job.

An additional force, which suppresses pay and benefits in the tourism sector is the tendency of employers themselves to have an exceptionally myopic perspective of the work since they treat employees as substitutable. Moreover, in many destinations salaries and wages in much of the sector are dampened because of the uneven patterns of demand arising from seasonality. This situation forces many companies, particularly the numerous small and medium tourism enterprises (SMTEs) that dominate the European tourism landscape, to hire workers on a seasonal/temporary basis, in turn leading to few opportunities for promotion and benefits or, for that matter, pay increases or bonuses (Zampoukos and Ioannides, 2011). The ILO (2001) has pointed out that because a significant number of these SMTEs are owned and operated by older individuals, who in all likelihood come into the tourism sector from somewhere else lacking formal tourism and/ or hospitality education, signifies they have little interest in improving their employees' skills and positions by providing them the opportunities to receive training. Consequently, this tendency to avoid treating their employees as assets (Devine et al., 2007) further discourages the latter in terms of their desire to remain within the industry and turnover is high.

Such barriers to improving overall conditions, including pay and benefits, for the numerous low-end workers in Europe's tourism industry are a good reason as to why the current documents coming out of the EU, which were discussed in the previous section, appear to have negligible effect, especially in terms of the social equity dimension of sustainable development within the context of tourism. Putting it mildly, regardless of how many policy directives and other official briefs the EU produces in order to steer tourism development within the confines of sustainable development, the present environment as far as low level jobs is concerned is such that this rhetoric has little bite.

The situation is made worse through the existence of a not insignificant number of illegal workers in various sectors of the tourism industry, a situation which has proven almost impossible to combat. In many cases, especially within SMTEs, family members (e.g., children) work with little or no pay, especially during periods of high demand. This is certainly the case in places like the Greek islands or Cyprus. However, even in major metropolitan areas the problem of a "shadow" economy within the tourism sector is quite common. Hjalager (2008) has pointed out that the excessive costs in the restaurant business regularly cause owners in many countries to seek to improve their profits by avoiding payment of taxes and employing undeclared workers. Writing specifically about the situation in Denmark she discusses how between eight and ten thousand jobs in hotels and restaurants are undeclared with places like pubs and pizzerias being the main culprits. Another reason for hiring illegal workers is that this practice affords the business owners the ability to circumvent Denmark's employment laws that provide protection even to flexible (part-time) workers (e.g., they have the right to paid holidays and sick leave). What is also interesting is that many employers choose to hire clandestine workers rather than make use of Denmark's training schemes, which provide subsidies to businesses to take on employees with reduced wages. The reason is that the employers pay wages to illegal workers that are even lower than those they would be obliged to pay legally if they received the subsidies in the first place.

The existence of illegal workers within many European environments suggests the likelihood that these individuals lack protection from any local, national, or EU-level directives. Ironically, as Schierup (2006) has noted, the situation in certain countries when it comes to illegal employees within tourism has inadvertently become worse given the promotion of measures such as the EU's Services Directive. This document was meant to enable companies, especially small and medium enterprises to avoid the red-tape (e.g., legal and administrative hurdles to trade). However, as Schierup describes, business owners, especially in new member countries (i.e., Eastern European countries) have liberally interpreted this directive to mean they are permitted to operate in places like Sweden while paying the (sometimes substantially) lower wages expected in their own countries. In the case of Sweden what often happens is that these businesses register as sub-contractors, providing services to companies like cleaning agencies and ones involved in the hotel and restaurant business. Effectively, they tend to hire immigrants, many of whom are illegally in the country due to increasingly stricter immigration policies, paying wages substantially below those that have been agreed on by collective agreements. Further, the work on offer is regularly in violation of rules regarding overtime and common safety standards. Consequently, workers are more likely to be injured on the job than ones that are hired directly by the companies.

Conclusions

While undoubtedly the EU places enormous emphasis on promoting economic growth and competitiveness within a framework meant to meet all the tenets of sustainable development, including environmental protection and social equity, it is apparent that much of the rhetoric that has been produced to this aim has been and continues to be largely ineffective. To be sure there have been considerable attempts to combat tourism's negative environmental effects, albeit to various levels of success in different destinations. There is also recognition in some of the documents specifically aimed at the tourism sector (for example TSG, 2007), that the quality of many jobs in the sector is in serious need of improvement. However, so far there is little to suggest that anything effective has been accomplished in this domain, especially in regard to the multitude of lower-end positions that appear to dominate within the sector.

A major blame for this status quo is the inertia emanating from the sector itself in terms of its unwillingness to tackle the downward pressures on salaries, benefits and consequently, quality of such jobs within the industry. The simple reality is that within the EU territory there is a readily available and highly mobile labour force that is drawn to the various destinations depending on demand. These workers are either willing to accept the poor employment circumstances they encounter or, in many instances, they may simply not be in a position to express dissatisfaction (e.g., in the cases where they are illegally employed or they do not have any other options). Indeed, the situation is such that the ability of this class of workers to organise collectively remains at minimal levels. The sector itself is cognisant of this situation and in the absence of any well-defined legal instruments aimed at protecting this army of workers is unlikely to be willing to do anything about improving their situations. Rather, exploitation seems to be the order of the day.

This situation signifies that it will be very hard to implement measures to improve the equity dimension for the numerous workers who happen to be employed at the lower echelons of the tourism business any time soon. Ending on this pessimistic note we would like to ask the readers to spare a thought for those who made their beds, cleaned their bathrooms, and laid a piece of wrapped chocolate on their pillows the next time they stay at a downtown hotel.

References

Adler, P.A. and Adler, P. (1999) Resort Workers: Adaptation in the Leisure-Work Nexus. *Sociological Perspectives*, 42(3), 369-402.

Ainsworth, S. and Purss, A. (2009) Same Time, Next Year? Human Resource Management and Seasonal Workers. *Personnel Review*, 38(3), 217-35.

Ball, R.M. (1988) Seasonality: A Problem for Workers in the Tourism Labour Market? *The Service Industries Journal*, 8(4), 501-13.

Baum, T. (2007) Human Resources in Tourism: Still Waiting for Change. *Progress in Tourism Management*, 28(6), 1383-99.

Bosselman, F.B., Peterson, C.A., and McCarthy, C. (1999) *Managing Tourism Growth: Issues and Applications*. Washington, DC: Island Press.

Bull, P.J. and Church, A.P. (1994) The Geography of Employment Change in the Hotel and Catering Industry of Great Britain in the 1980s: A Subregional Perspective. *Regional Studies*, 28(1), 13-25.

Campbell, S. (1996) Green Cities, Growing Cities, Just Cities: Urban Planning and the Contradictions of Sustainable Development. *Journal of the American Planning Association*, 62(3), 296-312.

CEC (Commission of the European Communities) (2003) *Jobs, Jobs, Jobs: Creating More Employment in Europe*. Luxembourg: Office for Official Publications of the European Communities.

CEC (Commission of the European Communities) (2010) *Europe, the World's No 1 Tourist Destination—a New Political Framework for Tourism in Europe*. Luxembourg: Office for Official Publications of the European Communities.

Chok, S., Macbeth, J., and Warren, C. (2007) Tourism as a Tool of Poverty Alleviation: A Critical Analysis of "Pro-Poor Tourism" and Implications for Sustainability. *Current Issues in Tourism*, 10(2, 3), 144-65.

Chok, S. and MacBeth, J. (2009) 'Labour Justice and Sustainable Tourism: The Centrality of Equity as a Sustainability Principle', BEST Education Network Think Tank IX. Singapore. June 15-18.

Church, A. and Frost, M. (2004) Tourism, the Global City and the Labour Market in London. *Tourism Geographies*, 6(2), 208-28.

Davoudi, S. (2007) 'Territorial Cohesion, the European Social Model and Spatial Policy Research', in A. Faloudi (ed.) *Territorial Cohesion and the European Model of Society*. Cambridge, MA: Lincoln Institute of Land Policy, 81-103.

Devine, F., Baum, T., Hearns, N. and Devine, A. (2007). 'Cultural Diversity in Hospitality Work: The Northern Ireland Experience', *International Journal of Human Resource Management*, 18(2), 333-49.

ECORYS (2009) *Study on the Competitiveness of the EU Tourism Industry*. Available at: http://ec.europa.eu/enterprise/newsroom/cf/itemlongdetail. cfm?item_id=3702 [Accessed: 10 January 2011].

European Parliament (2000) *Lisbon European Council 23 and 24 March 2000: Presidency Conclusions*. Available at: http://www.europarl.europa.eu/summits/ lis1_en.htm [10 January 2011].

Faludi, A. (2007) 'The European Model of Society', in A. Faludi (ed.) *Territorial Cohesion and the European Model of Society*. Cambridge, MA: Lincoln Institute of Land Policy, 1-22.

Ioannides, D. and Holcomb, B. (2001) Raising the stakes: implications of upmarket tourism policies in Cyprus and Malta, in D. Ioannides, Y. Apostolopoulos and S. Sonmez (eds) *Mediterranean Islands and Sustainable Tourism Development*. London: Cassell, 234-58.

Ioannides, D. (2009) Hypothesizing the Shifting Mosaic of Attitude Change Through Time: A Dynamic Framework for Sustainable Tourism Development on a "Mediterranean Isle", in S. McCool and N. Moisey (eds) *Tourism, Recreation and Sustainability* (2nd Edition). Wallingford: CABI, 51-75.

Hall, C.M. and Lew, A.A. (1998) *Sustainable Tourism: A Geographical Perspective*. Harlow: Longman.

Head, J. and Lucas, R. (2004a) Does Individual Employment Legislation Constrain the Ability of Hospitality Employers to "Hire and Fire"? *Hospitality Management*, 23, 239-54.

Hjalager, A.M. (2008) The Illegal Economy in the Restaurant Sector in Denmark. *Tourism and Hospitality Research*, 8, 239-51.

International Labour Office (2001) *Human Resources Development, Employment and Globalization in the Hotel, Catering and Tourism Sector*. Geneva: International Labour Office.

Kousis, M. (2001) Tourism and the Environment in Corsica, Sardinia, Sicily, and Crete, in D. Ioannides, Y. Apostolopoulos and S. Sonmez (eds) *Mediterranean Islands and Sustainable Tourism Development*. London: Cassell, 214-33.

Lai, P.C., Soltani, E. and Baum, T. (2008) Distancing Flexibility in the Hotel Industry: The Role of Employment Agencies as Labour Suppliers, *The International Journal of Human Resource Management*, 19(1), 132-52.

Lazaridis, G. and Wickens, E. (1999) "Us" and the "others": Ethnic Minorities in Greece. *Annals of Tourism Research*, 26(3), 632-55.

Leslie, D. (ed.) (2009) *Tourism Enterprises and Sustainable Development: International Perspectives on Responses to the Sustainability Agenda*. London. Routledge.

Leslie, D. (2010) The European Union, sustainable tourism policy and rural Europe, in D.V.L. Macleod and S.A. Gillespie (eds) *Sustainable Tourism in Rural Europe*. London, Routledge, 43-60.

Lucas, R. and Ralston, L. (1997) Youth, Gender and Part-Time Employment: A Preliminary Appraisal of Student Employment. *Employee Relations*, 19(1), 51-66.

McCool, S. (1995) Linking tourism, the environment, and concepts of sustainability: Setting the stage, in S. McCool and A. Watson (eds) *Linking Tourism, the Environment, and Sustainability*. Ogden, UT: U.S. Department of Agriculture, Intermountain Research Station, 3-7.

McCool, S. (1996) Searching for sustainability: A difficult course; an uncertain outcome. Presented at the Global Congress on Coastal and Marine Tourism, June 1996, Waikiki, Hawaii.

McDowell, Linda (2009) *Working Bodies: Interactive Service Employment and Workplace Identities*. Oxford: Wiley-Blackwell.

Molavi, A. (2007) Dubai: Sudden City. *National Geographic* (January 2007), 94-113.

Neto, F. (2003) A new approach to sustainable tourism development: Moving beyond environmental protection. *Natural Resources Forum*, 27, 212-22.

Notarstefano, C. (2007) *European Sustainable Tourism: Context, Concepts and Guidelines.* Paper presented at the European Union and World Sustainable Conference, Brussels (November).

NUTEK (2008). *Tourism and the Travel and Tourism Industry in Sweden.* Stockholm: NUTEK.

OnsØyen, L.E., Mykletun, R.J. and Steiro, T.J. (2009) Silenced and Invisible: The Work-Experience of Room-Attendants in Norwegian Hotels. *Scandinavian Journal of Hospitality and Tourism*, 9(1), 81-102.

Ostergren, R.C. and Rice, J.G. (2004) *The Europeans: A Geography of People, Culture and the Environment.* New York: Guilford Press.

Reid, T.R. (2004) *The United States of Europe.* New York: Penguin Press.

Riley, M., Ladkin, A. and Szivas, E. (2002) *Tourism Employment: Analysis and Planning.* Clevedon: Channel View Press.

Seifert, A.M. and Messing, K. (2006) Cleaning Up After Globalization: An Ergonomic Analysis of Work Activity of Hotel Cleaners, in L.L.M. Aguiar and A. Herod (eds) *The Dirty Work of Neoliberalism: Cleaners in the Global Economy.* Oxford: Blackwell, 129-49.

Shaw, G. and Williams, A.M. (2004) *Tourism and Tourism Spaces.* London: Sage.

Schierup, C. (2006) The Swedish "Vertical Mosaic", in J. Olofsson and M. Zavisic (eds) *Routes to a More Open Labour Market.* Stockholm: National Institute for Working Life, 63-76.

TSG (Tourism Sustainability Group) (2007). *Action for More Sustainable European Tourism.* Available at: http://ec.europa.eu/enterprise/newsroom/cf/_getdocument.cfm?doc_id=237 [Retrieved: 15 January 2011].

Wall, G. (1997) 'Sustainable Development- Unsustainable Development', in S. Wahab and J.J. Pigram (eds) *Tourism Development and Growth: The Challenge of Sustainability.* London: Routledge, 33-49.

Weaver, D. (2006)) *Sustainable Tourism: Theory and Practice.* Burlington, MA: Butterworth-Heinemann.

Zampoukos, K. and Ioannides, D. (2011) The Tourism Labour Conundrum: Agenda for New Research in the Geography of Hospitality Workers. *Hospitality and Society*, 1(1), 25-45.

Conclusion

David Leslie

The opening discussion brought into contention that economic development, as we know it in the "western world", could not continue unabated without generating irreversible damage to the biosphere. Whilst this may be so, actually seeking to address this prognosis and re-dress it effectively is in itself another problem. Essentially it comes down to the "haves" consuming less whilst helping the "have nots" to develop – to gain equitable access to resources and a comparable quality of life. Basically this is the overall objective of sustainable development; to reduce unsustainable patterns of non-renewable resource consumption whilst allowing for economic development.

Ironically, perhaps, it is the "have nots", be it a lesser developed country or people within society in comparative terms, who are by default making a greater contribution to addressing issues of consumption of non-renewable resources. Tourism is one such "pattern of westernised consumption" and significantly a by-product of affluent societies. It is therefore all the more appropriate that tourism should be a focus of sustainability. After all it is not a need but a want on the part of the consumer. In many societies today it is considered a necessity as opposed to a luxury – rather akin, for example, to a second television or car. Hence we should be addressing its environmental performance whilst also acknowledging that in the short term at least demand will not decline and neither will the competition in supply. Ergo all the more reason why tourism enterprises should seek to adopt those measures which will reduce their consumption of resources and generation of waste and the ways in which provision of their offering may impact more widely on the environment. Such notions are no flight of fancy, being equally applicable to industry per se, the basic premise being that as it is difficult (understatement) to change demand, then at least production processes and products can be addressed and measures taken to encourage these to be more sustainable through polluting less, using less energy and then retrieving and recycling as much as possible. Thus we come to our focus and what progress is being made by tourism enterprises across Europe towards sustainability. As each chapter in some way evidences there are signs of progress – steps are being taken. In the first instance, as many chapters attest, the greening of supply is taking place in many areas but the extent of this either within a specific category of enterprise or geographically is unclear. Furthermore the pace of such progress as suggested within these pages is slow when we take into account the outcomes of earlier research. Even so, progressive steps have been achieved which to some degree may be due to the EU who, as identified in the introduction, have been notably supportive in progressing sustainability.

Consumers – tourists – overall show little substantive evidence of demand for tourism enterprises to address and improve their environmental performance; particularly if such steps involve higher prices. This is not unexpected given consumer behaviour for consumer goods in general. Opposition to price increases is all the more manifest in recessionary periods. But here we may find that tourists trade down and also that business demand for air travel falls. In small degree this has happened as a consequence of the wide economic recession over the last few years and therefore this is not surprising. Even so, it does indicate how a recession can actually encourage businesses to take actions that serendipitously are a positive for sustainability. But this also holds problems for other aspects of sustainability such as social and community well-being. A sustained decline in demand for air travel, for example, holds implications for the financial health of the airline sector which, as Button notes, is recognised by the EU as an important sector of the European economy. The low margins gained by airlines throughout Europe suggests that the introduction of green taxes, for example, carbon tax, may have more of an impact on the finances of the companies involved and thus be potentially counterproductive in some ways. Airlines have made progress – cleaner, quieter planes which are more fuel efficient but these gains are counterbalanced by increased demand. Whilst encouraging further measures other options include reducing demand elsewhere to compensate, for example, as would arise if everyone had their own "carbon allowance". Secondly, there is the potential to encourage the use of alternative modes of transportation and non-air flight based holidays.

This is encompassed in the concept of slow travel, which is well illustrated by Holland and Holland who discussed a range of examples of how travel and transport organisations are responding to the challenge of sustainability and adapt and create travel alternatives and holidays that reduce the reliance on the traditional aviation and car based holidays. But how many of such packages commence with an air flight on the part of the tourist – to get to the start of the holiday as quickly as possible! The air component of package holidays is still crucial and unlikely, in the short term at least, to be replaced by land based alternatives. The greatest contribution to promoting alternatives to air travel for tourism probably lies in changing the expectations of the consumer. In furtherance of which a range of principles are presented. The reference to package holidays brings into focus tour operators, who have and continue to play a major role in the development and promotion of popular resorts across Europe and particularly around the Mediterranean.

There is an expectation, on the part of the advocates of sustainability, that in terms of business generally they should be addressing sustainability issues and also, to some extent, on the part of tourists. In other words they are seen as the ones with responsibility. That this is the case, certainly on the part of some tour operators was well illustrated in the Dutch case study on outbound tour operations (Chapter 4). For some time efforts have been made to endorse social and environmental responsibility in the sector and evidently progress has been made. As van der Duim et al. argue, the merits of *people* and *planet* have thus become part of the commercial business agenda. As in most sectors, there are leaders that serve to exemplify best practice. But how representative are they? Certainly they demonstrate progress but what of the sector as a whole and will the laggards follow? In respect of this point, further research is advocated and the undertaking of a comparative case study of the driving forces behind CSR in the tour operations industry across different EU countries could enhance our understanding of external and internal drivers of CSR. But, once again, we can identify the importance of the need for clear leadership that is committed to addressing environmental issues and the presence of clear support from the appropriate agencies. Furthermore, and notably in this case, there was evident commitment from the professional associations involved in this category of tourism supply.

Attention to CSR was continued in the context of international hotel operations, which as Bohdanowicz and Zientara argue, is largely due to increased expectations that business operates responsibly. Indeed, as they eloquently point out, dissatisfied consumers can rapidly communicate such dissatisfaction throughout the globe through today's diverse internet based, social networking sites. Their study into the practical dimensions of greening hotel operations and best practice makes an important contribution to the ongoing debate on corporate environmentalism. They also point out that CSR inspired initiatives can contribute to employee motivation and satisfaction, factors which are particularly significant in operations dependent on the quality of service. Further, these are aspects also gaining comment in the promotion of the introduction of an EMS. The realisation of such outcomes is all the more significant given the realities of working in the tourism sector (see Chapter 10). However, their study shows what can be done though much of this is driven by business, which international companies increasingly demonstrate can be rapidly enacted throughout their operations.

In comparison with such companies, CSR gains limited attention in studies into the small and micro enterprises wherein the focus is far more on businesses to actively implement eco-management measures, as well illustrated in the subsequent chapters (Chapter 6 and 7). Lebe and Zupan demonstrate just what may be achieved through a comprehensive, government initiated, programme designed to promote adoption of an accredited EMS, such as the Eco-Flower scheme, by all hotels. However, it should be recognised that this is within the context of a comparatively very small country in the terms of the other member states of the EU. The "norm", which is not to gainsay the achievements in Slovenia, was well illustrated by Kučerová's research in Slovakia. Overall, and bringing into consideration similar studies, the evidence is that whilst there are signs of progress in the implementation of EMSs on the part of tourism enterprises (predominantly hotels), there is still a long way to go before we could say that these enterprises in general or in a specific category or country are addressing their environmental performance and sustainability.

Tourism holds opportunity for the entrepreneur responding not only to initiatives promoting greener products and services but also sustainable entrepreneurship based on local resources, small in scale and not exclusive. As discussed by Badulescu and

Badulesco sustainable entrepreneurship in tourism involves the identification and then exploitation of sustainable opportunities arising because of sustainability issues and the quest for greater sustainability, more responsible products – in terms of the consumption of resources. The cases presented demonstrate entrepreneurial skills such as innovation and creativity. But as the authors note, such innovation is not always evidence of attention to issues of sustainability; many more entrepreneurs are profit-seeking albeit they may show some awareness of sustainability. However, questions arise as to whether such opportunist developments contribute more widely in terms of the local/regional economy and, more pertinently perhaps, the community? To take this theme a broad step further leads to questioning the promotion of tourism development as if it is some kind of panacea; as one might come to believe given the EU's proactive stance.

This theme was taken up by Zientara (Chapter 9) who challenged prevailing assumptions about tourism and regional development. In the context of the rural economy of Poland, he reminded us that tourism is not *the* answer to addressing more substantive economic issues than "just" a decline in a major sector of a region's economy. It may be a part of the solution but not THE solution. The case presented serves well to deepen our understanding of the interrelated phenomena of regional economic development and sustainability and in the process should provoke further discussion and multidisciplinary research. As is so often the case in such matters, there is a need for much more of a holistic approach. For example, as Zientara argued, rather than regarding sustainable tourism as a tool with which to help rural communities transform their fortunes, it is more appropriate to ask the question of how it can contribute to sustainable outcomes (all over the country). It is thus not just a matter of the economy nor greening but also jobs. Employment arising through tourism development is almost as often cited as its perceived contribution to the economy. Thus the concluding chapter, by Ioannides and Petridou, brought into contention employment and employees in the tourism sector. This area has gained all too little attention in the context of sustainable development despite the issue of equity and social justice being key dimensions of sustainability. They raise a range of substantive issues including poor employment circumstances, lack of representation and exploitation. A situation they do not see changing in the foreseeable future.

Our tour thus comes to an end. Along the way we have found evidence of progress towards sustainability, a substantial research agenda and a raft of recommendations. But this has also raised more questions than answers, not least of which is why progress is so slow – small but not insignificant steps; especially given the advocacy of the EU. Promotion of the sustainability agenda has been evident since the early 1990s, apparent also in national policies and manifest in tourism policies. Perhaps such limited progress is due to these policies being strong on rhetoric but weak on detail such as clearly defined "SMART" objectives and guidelines as to how and the ways of implementation. In contrast to tourism, the EU has been particularly effective in the environment policy arena which is one of the leading sectors in the introduction of EU standards and in regard to pollution and energy saving measures, for example, CFCs, household appliances, waste management practices. This is apparent in the environment measures introduced by States seeking to join the EU and the subsequent harmonisation with EU policy and regulation. But this enlargement has increased diversity across and between countries and the "one size fits all" approach is now even less suitable. This has lead to the need for some flexibility; hence the EU now presents proposals more often as a framework with broader policies allowing Member States some leeway in their interpretation. However, this leads to a dilution of the primary objective(s). It may also be argued that much of what emanates from Brussels on tourism is more rhetoric based on good intentions and to an extent unintended conflicts or contradictions arising through different initiatives, for example promoting tourism development whilst at the same time seeking progress towards sustainability.

Is there a need for Directives, for example, the adoption of EMSs by all enterprises, to stimulate substantial progress? But this will raise argument over disadvantaging enterprises, unfair competition and so forth. Such a step could also be counterproductive in that it may only achieve minimum compliance in many cases – including those owners/managers who would otherwise have done more. There is no doubt that this is a complex situation – there are no quick fixes. Address one issue here and there are potential domino effects elsewhere that may have a negative influence on other areas. Even so, regulation/legislation alone will not work. All stakeholders in the tourism system will need to play an active role. Management and education also have a part to play which may have greater effect in the long term. Though information in itself is not sufficient, it needs to be well targeted and often face to face to achieve better results. Even then much of this activity is aimed at developing "end of pipe" solutions when steps towards sustainability are more than just a matter of addressing environmental performance and more broadly perhaps CSR. They require change. Tourism is complex, not simply a consumer good that could be removed from the marketplace. Thus, our focus should be on addressing the causes generating such consumption and the related consumer attitudes, thus the wider context within which the tourism system operates. Essentially there is a need for fundamental change in consumerism – in habits and lifestyles as currently exemplified in post-industrial countries. In this context the most influential factor is the recognition of responsibility, that is, taking on personal responsibility for the environmental consequences of one's own actions.

In the final analysis, tourism is a part of an unsustainable system and thus if tourism in general is to be sustainable then so must the processes which underpin it. If this is to be achieved then the norms, values and attitudes of societies (predominantly 'westernised') also need to change.

References

Leslie, D. (1994) Sustainable Tourism or developing sustainable approaches to lifestyle? *World Leisure and Recreation Association*, 36(3), 30-36.

Index